KU-532-766

The
Woman
at the
Keyhole

UMETLO

THEORIES OF REPRESENTATION AND DIFFERENCE

General Editor, Teresa de Lauretis

The
Woman
at the
Keyhole

Feminism and Women's Cinema

JUDITH MAYNE

INDIANA UNIVERSITY PRESS

Bloomington and Indianapolis

©1990 by Judith Mayne

All rights reserved

No part of this book may be reproduced or utilized in any form or by any means, electronic or mechanical, including photocopying and recording, or by any information storage and retrieval system, without permission in writing from the publisher. The Association of American University Presses' Resolution on Permissions constitutes the only exception to this prohibition.

The paper used in this publication meets the minimum requirements of American National Standard for Information Sciences—Permanence of Paper for Printed Library Materials, ANSI Z39.48-1984.

Manufactured in the United States of America

Library of Congress Cataloging-in-Publication Data

Mayne, Judith.
    The woman at the keyhole : feminism and women's cinema
/ Judith Mayne.
        p.   cm.
    Includes bibliographical references.
    ISBN 0-253-33719-4 (alk. paper).
— ISBN 0-253-20606-5 (pbk. : alk. paper)
    1. Feminism and motion pictures. 2. Feminist motion pictures.
3. Women in motion pictures. 4. Motion pictures—Philosophy.
I. Title.
PN1995.9.W6M36   1990
791.43'082—dc20   90-34125
                                                          CIP

1 2 3 4 5   94 93 92 91 90

LEEDS METROPOLITAN
UNIVERSITY LIBRARY
1700729146
A v
5021892   14.6.93
29·11·93
791·439

For **Terry**

Contents

ACKNOWLEDGMENTS

Several agencies and film distributors were enormously helpful in facilitating my access to films discussed in the book. I am therefore grateful to World Artists, distributors of *Je tu il elle;* First Run Features *(The Man Who Envied Women);* and especially Women Make Movies *(Illusions, Reassemblage,* and *Ten Cents a Dance [Parallax]).* The Australian Film Commission obtained a copy of *A Song of Ceylon* (now distributed by Women Make Movies) for my use. Thanks to Tom Gunning and Charles Musser for help in finding some of the early films discussed in chapter five; and to Andy Spencer for translation of a German text.

For help in locating stills for illustrations, thanks to Terry Geesken of the Museum of Modern Art Film Stills Archive, to Women Make Movies, to Yvonne Rainer, and to Sam McElfresh of the American Federation of Arts. The illustrations in the book are reproduced courtesy of the Museum of Modern Art, Women Make Movies, Yvonne Rainer, the American Federation of Arts Film/Video Program (from the "Before Hollywood" exhibition; Patrick G. Loughney, photographer), World Artists, The British Film Institute, Corinth Films, and New Yorker Films. Thanks to Lucretia Knapp for technical assistance.

Early versions of portions of some chapters have appeared elsewhere. Portions of the introduction and chapter three appeared in *New German Critique,* no. 23 (1981); an early version of part of chapter one in *Wide Angle* 6, no. 3 (1984). A previous version of the discussion of *Redupers* (chapter two) appeared in *New German Critique,* no. 24–25 (1981–82). Earlier versions of parts of chapter five appeared in *frauen und film,* no. 41 (1986), and in *Before Hollywood: Turn-of-the-Century Film from American Archives* (New York: American

Federation of Arts, 1986); © American Federation of Arts, reprinted with permission.

I am grateful to the students who have taken my course on "Women and Film" at Ohio State University over the years; many of the ideas developed in this book began, one way or another, in the classroom. For conversation and encouragement at crucial moments, thanks to Lucy Fischer, Anne Friedberg, Mitchell Greenberg, Dana Polan, Leslie Mitchener, B. Ruby Rich, and Marie-Claire Vallois. I have received grant support from the Ohio Arts Council, as well as the College of Humanities and the Center for Women's Studies at Ohio State, and released time from the Department of French and Italian—all of which made the completion of the book possible. For friendship and more, special thanks to Teresa de Lauretis. Most of all, thanks to Terry Moore for being such a good sport.

Introduction

This book examines how contemporary women filmmakers working in North America, Europe, and Australia have attempted to reinvent cinema as a narrative and visual form. The films and filmmakers to be discussed in subsequent chapters cover a fairly wide range, but share nonetheless a preoccupation with the devices of cinematic narration as central to a reinvention of film and to the representation of female desire and female points of view. Most of the films have had limited audiences, and so raise that nagging question of feminist "accessibility." While I do not presume to make difficult films easy, I do attempt to situate films in contexts that engage with different aspects of feminism and feminist theory, contexts therefore which seem to me considerably more open to discussion than some of the theoretical agendas that have defined feminist film studies. Although for some feminist literary critics, women's writing is anything written by a woman, women's writing cannot be so easily or so readily defined. Given the extent to which cinematic representation is defined by a wide range of practices, and by the input of a number of "writers," it is even more difficult to make the assertion that women's cinema is any and all films made by a woman.

From the outset, there is an ambiguity in the phrase "women's cinema." The term has acquired two different meanings which to some minds are diametrically opposed. The examples of "women's cinema" to be discussed in this book have redefined or challenged some of the most basic and fundamental links between

1

cinema and patriarchy. To use Adrienne Rich's phrase, which has been cited so often in the context of women's cinema, these films are all engaged in a "re-vision" of the institutions of the cinema.[1] I assume from the outset that the exploration of the kind I want to undertake here must engage with the complex and often contradictory connotations that have arisen from the juxtaposition of "women" and "cinema." First, women's cinema refers to films made by women, and by women *directors* for the most part (as opposed, say, to screenwriters or actresses). These directors range from classical Hollywood directors such as Dorothy Arzner and Ida Lupino to their more recent heirs, including Claudia Weill *(Girlfriends)* and Amy Heckerling *(Fast Times at Ridgemont High)*; and from directors whom many feminists would just as soon forget, such as Leni Riefenstahl or Lina Wertmüller, to other contemporary directors concerned directly and consciously with female modes of expression, such as Chantal Akerman and Helke Sander. They range as well from such independent documentary filmmakers as Connie Fields *(Rosie the Riveter)* and Michelle Parkerson *(Stormé),* to more experimental independents attempting to reconcile feminist politics and avant-garde form, including Michelle Citron and Sally Potter. To attempt to account for the wide diversity of films represented in even this simple definition of "women's cinema" is a gigantic task in and of itself.

The term *women's cinema,* or more precisely, the *woman's film,* has acquired another meaning, referring to a Hollywood product designed to appeal to a specifically female audience. Such films, popular throughout the 1930s, '40s, and '50s, were usually melodramatic in tone and full of high-pitched emotion, from which came the pejorative title "the weepies." Indeed, Molly Haskell characterizes the "woman's film" as the "most untouchable of film genres." Here is how Haskell defines the genre:

> At the lowest level, as soap opera, the "woman's film" fills a masturbatory need, it is soft-core emotional porn for the frustrated housewife. The weepies are founded on a mock-Aristotelian and politically conservative aesthetic whereby women spectators are moved, not by pity and fear but by self-pity and tears, to accept, rather than reject, their lot. That there should be a need and an audience for such an opiate suggests an unholy amount of real misery.[2]

As Mary Ann Doane has argued, the "woman's film" identifies female pleasure in the cinema as complicit with masochistic constructions of femininity. Hence, a typical theme of the woman's film, in Doane's category of the maternal melodrama, is obsessive sacrifice for one's children at the expense of self.[3] At the conclusion of *Stella Dallas* (1937), for instance, Barbara Stanwyck is a pathetic spectator who peeks longingly through the window of an elegant mansion where her daughter's wedding is taking place.[4] Yet another typical theme of the woman's film—in the category of what Doane calls "medical discourse"—is affliction.[5] In *Magnificent Obsession* (1954), for example, Jane Wyman is stricken blind and is nursed back to emotional and physical health by her doctor, Rock Hudson.

Doane's analysis assumes that if the woman's film is indeed an exemplary form insofar as female subjectivity and female spectatorship are concerned, it is because the woman's film demonstrates, again and again, the impossible position of female desire vis-à-vis the cinema—impossible, that is, in the terms of voyeurism and fetishism so central to cinematic pleasure in the first place. That the strategies of the woman's film should be so evocative of psychoanalytic readings of femininity is no more of a surprising coincidence than the historical overlap so often claimed as the privileged bond between cinema and psychoanalysis. For Doane, much of the interest of the woman's film has to do with its contradictory explorations of female desire:

> because the woman's film insistently and sometimes obsessively attempts to trace the contours of female subjectivity and desire within the traditional forms and conventions of Hollywood narrative—forms which cannot sustain such an exploration—certain contradictions within patriarchal ideology become apparent. . . . The formal resistances to the elaboration of female subjectivity produce perturbations and contradictions within the narrative economy.[6]

The contradictions which engage Doane's attention are not contradictions *within* the classical Hollywood cinema, but rather contradictions that erupt when a form made to the measure of male desire and male subjectivity attempts to engage with other desires and other subjectivities. The process is not unlike the attempt, within psychoanalytic discourse, to account for female identity in the form of an analogy to male identity, in what Luce Irigaray would describe as the "old dream of symmetry."[7] The attempt usually fails but—more interesting for feminist analysis—reveals many of the large gaps between male and female subjectivity otherwise obscured. Doane's account of the classical Hollywood cinema as the regime of the male psyche stands in sharp contrast to the views of other feminist critics, for whom the classical Hollywood cinema does not necessarily stand in rigid resistance to female subjectivity. Consider, in this regard, Tania Modleski's argument that the films of Alfred Hitchcock, who has served as a key protagonist (or villain, if you will) in the evolution of feminist film theory, are contradictory texts in which woman's desire figures centrally; or Lucy Fischer's reading of the relationship between women filmmakers and film tradition as a productive intertextual dialogue.[8]

Doane does, however, identify a hypothetical relationship between the woman's film and what I presume she would identify as women's films: "These stress points and perturbations can then, hopefully, be activated as a kind of lever to facilitate the production of a desiring subjectivity for the woman—in another cinematic practice."[9] I read Doane's statement as an indication that the only necessary relationship between the woman's film and women's films will be a purely theoretical one; that is, that the strategies of those women's films which articulate other forms of cinematic pleasure—nonvoyeuristic and nonfetishistic, one assumes—might take as their point of departure a critical reading of the classical Hollywood cinema, but a reading that is detached, somewhat distant. Put another way, the "other cinematic practice" to which Doane refers suggests that the only connection between it and the classical Hollywood cinema will be one of distanced speculation.

While Doane's exploration of the woman's film is remarkably sophisticated and complex, her designation of the status of the classical Hollywood cinema suggests a rigid opposition between Hollywood films, made by men for female consumption, and films by women. Few contemporary critics would use the language of authenticity to describe this opposition (e.g., the inauthentic portrayals of the classical cinema versus the authentic portrayals by women directors), but there is something of that rigid opposition that lingers on in feminist accounts of the classical cinema.

Even while a critic such as Molly Haskell condemns the facile pathos of the woman's film, she wonders why it is that emotional response should be so devalued as to be relegated to an "inferior" genre.[10] I understand the necessity, or desire, to identify the classical Hollywood cinema in terms of its massive strategies for disavowal of the very fact of female difference, and its perpetuation of patriarchal definitions of masculinity and femininity, but I do not think that feminist discussion of the works of women filmmakers is well served by continued insistence upon an absolute division between the classical Hollywood cinema and its alternatives. To begin with, such a division places a kind of utopian burden upon alternative filmmakers, to such an extent that any traces of dominant cinematic practice—lurking fetishism or shades of voyeurism, to be precise—will be seen as suspect. Given the institutionalized ways in which the cinema functions, and how individuals are acculturated to respond to the cinema, it is difficult to know just to what extent a truly alternative cinematic practice is possible. This raises a larger question, and that is the extent to which voyeurism and fetishism, as they have been defined within psychoanalytically inspired film studies (feminist or otherwise), are synonymous with the cinema. It is not always clear when voyeurism and fetishism define the cinema in an absolute sense, and when they define a specific kind of film viewing, within a specific historical and cultural context.

Given the historical parallels so often commented upon between the advent of the cinema and the advent of psychoanalysis, it would seem as though the cinema had some manifest destiny to embody voyeurism and fetishism—and, needless to say, to embody them for the ideal male subject of culture theorized by psychoanalysis. For instance, noting that "dominant film practice orchestrates the burdensome transfer of male lack to the female subject by projecting the projections upon which our current notions of gender depend," Kaja Silverman says that "the displacement of losses suffered by the male subject onto the female subject is by no means a necessary extension of the screening situation. Rather, it is the effect of a specific scopic and narratological regime."[11] This specific "scopic and narratological regime" notwithstanding, it is not always clear just where the terms used to describe the classical Hollywood cinema shade into a description of the cinema as a whole.

Now one could argue that precisely what separates the "woman's film"— where figures of women serve the "scopic and narratological regime" to which Silverman refers—from "women's cinema"—where that regime is problematized or otherwise put into question—is the attempt to metaphorize the cinema in other ways. That is, women's cinema may well be characterized, not necessarily by an outright rejection of voyeuristic and fetishistic desires but by the recasting of those desires so as to open up other possible pleasures for film viewing. It is somewhat ironic, in this context, that there has been more extensive work in feminist literary criticism and theory on female investment in voyeurism and fetishism—from Joan DeJean's hypotheses on female voyeurism in Madame de Lafayette's *La Princesse de Clèves* and Nancy K. Miller's analysis of the "performances of the gaze" in Madame de Staël's *Corinne, or Italy*, to Naomi Schor's exploration of female fetishism in the writings of George Sand.[12] Of course, in these literary works (all of which predate not only the advent of cinema but the advent of psychoanalysis as well), voyeurism and fetishism are not convergent with the pleasures of the text to the extent that they are in the cinema.

I prefer to retain the term *women's cinema* in an ambiguous sense, to suggest simultaneously the enormous impact of Hollywood's versions of femininity upon our expectations of the cinema, and the representation of other kinds of female desire. The discovery in works by women filmmakers of other ways to define the pleasures of the cinema entails by extension a redefinition of the characteristics of "dominant" film viewing as well. While I have suggested that the very phrase "women's cinema" is expressive of this ambiguity, this is not exactly or altogether the case, for it is the singular—the woman's film—which is used more frequently to refer to the Hollywood product, and the plural—women's films—to refer to works by women directors.

The difference in number is not inconsequential, for the "woman's" film does indeed presume a unified set of traits to be ascribed to appropriately feminine behavior or subjectivity, while "women's" films articulate a wide range of perspectives and points of view. Nonetheless, the phrase "women's films" can also be used to suggest a kind of uniformity which, while obviously different from the femininity legitimated by the classical cinema, is rigid in its own way. I am aware, in other words, that the ambiguous sense that I want to attribute to the term *women's cinema* can backfire in problematic ways; that the plurality of perspectives can be a subterfuge, beneath which there remains the specter of femininity, "woman" with a feminist inflection perhaps, but no less problematic for that. The shift from singular to plural is not necessarily an assurance of an emancipatory diversity.

The concealment of singular and plural forms within the phrase "women's cinema," with their attendant and interwoven implications of singularity as an imposed affinity and plurality as diversity, coincides with what Teresa de Lauretis, in *Alice Doesn't: Feminism, Semiotics, Cinema,* describes as the informing tension of virtually all feminist intervention, the opposition between "woman" and "women":

> Represented as the negative term of sexual differentiation, spectacle-fetish or specular image, in any case ob-scene, woman is constituted as the ground of representation, the looking-glass held up to man. But as historical individual, the female viewer is also positioned in the films of classical cinema as spectator-subject; she is thus doubly bound to that very representation which calls on her directly, engages her desire, elicits her pleasure, frames her identification, and makes her complicit in the production of (her) woman-ness. On this crucial relation of woman as constituted in representation to women as historical subjects depend at once the development of a feminist critique and the possibility of a materialist, semiotic theory of culture. For the feminist critique is a critique of culture at once from within and from without, in the same way in which women are both *in* the cinema as representation and *outside* the cinema as subjects of practices.[13]

De Lauretis's insistence on feminist critique as both "within" and "without" a culture suggests not only the difficulty but also the critical impasse of attempting to establish a rigid opposition between the dominant patriarchal culture (in cinematic terms, the classical Hollywood cinema) and alternatives to it. There is an obvious need for feminism to be able to analyze the distortion and lies of patriarchal culture; as Linda Gordon reminds us, because there are no objective truths, that does not mean there are no objective lies.[14] But the notion of "truth" is decidely more problematic. For as de Lauretis's strategic posing of the tension between "woman" and "women" suggests, the perspectives of women as "real historical subjects" may not be reducible to the images of woman projected within patriarchy (if this were the case, there would be no possibility for feminist intervention), but they are not absolutely separable or distinguishable from them, either.

Much of what is commonly referred to as "antiessentialism" within feminist theory has insisted, precisely, that claims for a unique "women's" perspective are in fact nothing more than recuperations of "woman," the feminine as it is defined by patriarchy. Antiessentialism has not, however, been particularly useful in articulating just what the valid terms for the claims of a women's perspective might be, for the only female position that seems acceptably anti-essentialist is one that punctures the illusions of patriarchal visions from the vantage point, not of "women" but of negativity and refusal to assume a gendered identity, the assumption being of course that any gendered identity within patriarchy accepts the terms of patriarchy. Ironically, the antiessentialist position assumes essentialism—the belief that there is a genuine female identity that has been repressed by patriarchy and which emerges through feminist practice—to be a position of noncontradiction. Yet antiessentialism, particularly in some of its current inevitably popularized and schematic forms, avoids what surely is, following de Lauretis, the contradiction most central to feminist inquiry, by bracketing the category of "women" altogether.

My concern in this book is with those works by women filmmakers in which the tensions between "woman" and "women" are articulated in ways that suggest other definitions of cinematic pleasure and desire. While feminist film theory and criticism are obviously informed and influenced by cinematic practices, I do not wish to conflate the works of women filmmakers with the project of a transhistor-ical and transcultural feminist aesthetics of the cinema. Indeed, one of the problems posed within contemporary feminist work on film is the inability to account for works that do not fit neatly within the parameters of theory. I am claiming, for a diverse group of women filmmakers, an activity that may not be avowedly feminist on their part, but which is part of the feminist rewriting of film history, and of cinematic pleasure and identification.

This book is divided into three parts, each of which focuses on an area that has been, in feminist film theory and criticism, both extremely important and extremely difficult insofar as the analysis of women's films is concerned. Each of the three parts is further divided into two chapters, the first of which explores a particular context for the issue at hand, while the second examines a group of women's films. Each of the three sections of the book brings together a familiar topic in feminist film theory with one that is distinctly less familiar. I begin in chapter one ("Spectacle, Narrative, and Screen") with the relationship between narrative and spectacle as it has been theorized, following Laura Mulvey, as one of the most basic conditions of sexual hierarchy in the classical cinema. But I focus on a frequently ignored element of cinematic representation—the screen—which is interestingly and peculiarly resistant to the hierarchy of male subject and female object. I examine a series of more or less "dominant" films in which the screen surface plays a central figural role, films in which more ambivalence is operative than one would suspect, given the relatively monolithic character ascribed to the classical Hollywood cinema by recent analyses. Chapter two, "Screen Tests," examines a group of films by women directors (Helke Sander's *Redupers,* Julie Dash's *Illusions,* Patricia Rozema's *I've Heard the Mermaids Singing,* and Yvonne Rainer's *The Man Who Envied Women*) in which the screen also emerges as a dominant trope, and around which questions of female desire, community, and alternative institutions crystallize.

In chapter three, "Female Authorship Reconsidered," I move to a reassessment of female authorship in the cinema, focusing in particular on the example of Dorothy Arzner as one of the most important discoveries and case studies for feminist film studies. The "less familiar" topic in this section of the book is lesbianism—a subject of obvious interest for any theory of female agency and desire in the cinema, yet one that has received little sustained critical attention in film studies. I suggest that female authorship in Arzner's work is marked by an ironic lesbian signature, and in chapter four ("Mistresses of Discrepancy") I examine two contemporary films which extend the implications of the relationship between female authorship and an erotics of female desire: Chantal Akerman's *Je tu il elle* and Ulrike Ottinger's *Ticket of No Return.*

Chapter five, " 'Primitive' Narration," examines the emerging codes of the early, or "primitive," cinema, particularly insofar as gender is concerned, both in the films themselves and in critical literature on the era. A fair number of women filmmakers have appropriated modes of representation associated with the early cinema, and in chapter six I examine how this appropriation of "primitive" representation engages with gender, in terms of both the female body and traditional female activities, and with cultural definitions of the "primitive other." Although in chapter five I discuss in detail the connotations of the word *primitive* as they apply to the study of early cinema, let me say a few words about the term here: In the context of film history, the word *primitive* is used interchangeably with *early.* But the women's films I examine in chapter six are concerned with the "primitive" in several senses, including the most offensive colonial meanings of the term. Thus I could not simply substitute *early* for *primitive.* What I do throughout, however, is follow the example of Trinh T. Minh-ha (one of whose films is discussed in chapter six), and use the term *primitive* in as foregrounded a way as possible, with quotation marks or with qualifiers, in order to call attention to its dubious status.[15]

Films discussed in chapter six ("Revising the 'Primitive' ") include Maya Deren's *Meshes of the Afternoon,* Suzan Pitt's *Asparagus,* Germaine Dulac's *The Smiling Madame Beudet,* Agnès Varda's *Cleo from 5 to 7,* Chantal Akerman's *Jeanne Dielman, 23 Quai du Commerce, 1080 Bruxelles,* Trinh T. Minh-ha's *Reassemblage,* and Laleen Jayamanne's *A Song of Ceylon.* While extensive attention has been paid to the representation of the female body in film, considerably less attention has been devoted to how other definitions of "otherness" shape and affect women's cinema, and the exploration of the several meanings of the term *primitive* is extremely provocative in this regard.

The title of my book, *The Woman at the Keyhole,* takes as its most obvious point of reference those early films (several of which are discussed in detail in chapter five) in which mostly men, but occasionally women, peek through keyholes, offering bold demonstrations of the voyeuristic pleasure that has been central to virtually every contemporary theory of the cinema. While I have nothing against women peeking through metaphoric keyholes, I intend the figure of the woman at the keyhole to be as ambiguous—hopefully, productively so—as the phrase "women's cinema." For when we imagine a "woman" and a "keyhole," it is usually a woman on the *other* side of the keyhole, as the proverbial object of the look, that comes to mind. I am not necessarily reversing the conventional image, but rather asking—as do, implicitly or explicitly, all of the women filmmakers whose works I discuss in subsequent chapters—what happens when women are situated on both sides of the keyhole. The question is not only who or what is on either side of the keyhole, but also what lies between them, what constitutes the threshold that makes representation possible. For in all of the films discussed in this book, the threshold between subject and object, between inside and outside, between virtually all opposing pairs, is a central figure for the reinvention of cinematic narrative.

When I first began working on women's cinema some years ago, it seemed to me fairly obvious that the metaphor of the woman at the keyhole was an entirely appropriate way to represent the relationship of the woman director to the cinema. Now, I am not so sure—not on account of any deep suspicion on my part concerning the pleasures of the eye, but rather because, ambiguity notwithstanding, single tropes have a habit of hardening into abstractions. If I retain the image of the woman at the keyhole, then, it is not to argue, in the fashion that has been popular in some feminist writing, that women filmmakers should appropriate a cinematic "gaze" that up until now has belonged to men. There is a considerable and impressive body of women's films that establish frames of vision—with keyholes or otherwise—which depart significantly from both the dominant models of classical cinema and the theoretical clichés of film theory. I make no claims to exhaustiveness in this study, and I certainly do not propose the categories of films examined here as exclusive ones. All of the films discussed in subsequent chapters are works that I have found challenging, moving, beautiful, and even on occasion inspiring. But most important, they are films which stretch the limits of feminist theory and criticism.

I.
Spectacle and Narrative

1. Spectacle, Narrative, and Screen

The term *spectacle* has become a shorthand phrase in film studies to refer to a number of different components of the cinema. Virtually all of these components—from the most general to the most specific, from the cultural status of film in Western society to the editing patterns of scenes in individual films—evoke the status of cinema as an institution, that is, as a form which embodies pervasive cultural myths of narrative, image, and representation. The term *spectacle* is fairly straightforward in its designation of subject/ object relationships, defining the object of the look as possessed and controlled by the subject of the look. But *spectacle* contains a number of competing, and sometimes contradictory meanings.

I begin this chapter by unpacking the various associations that *spectacle* has acquired in film studies, from consumerism and postmodernism to ideology and spectatorship and gender. My primary cinematic example is *The Big Sleep* (1946), a film which contains both obvious and not-so-obvious examples of the function of spectacle in film. I will argue that an exclusive focus on spectacle defined—as has been the case in feminist film studies—as a relation between male subject and female object obscures other functions of cinematic spectacle which do not lend themselves to such easy dichotomies.

I then read *The Big Sleep* in relation to other films with similar pre-occupations, and the film screen emerges as a privileged figure for the cinematic spectacle defined in more complex and contradictory terms. I examine the screen on different textual levels—literally, as film screens which appear within films, and figuratively, as surfaces with screenlike capacities—shadows projected on opaque glass, translucent screenlike material. These representations of the screen suggest in their turn that the screen necessary for cinematic projection has been inadequately addressed in film theory. My aim in this chapter is twofold—to argue against an overly monolithic definition of the cinematic spectacle, particularly in the classical Hollywood cinema, and to establish the context for the women's films to be discussed in chapter two, all of which explore and examine the metaphor of the film screen.

In the most general and obvious way, the definition of film as spectacle suggests that the relationship between viewer and screen is situated within—to use Guy Debord's much-quoted phrase—the "society of the spectacle," the society, that is, of modern capitalism, described from the outset by Debord as "an immense accumulation of *spectacles*. Everything that used to be experienced directly has withdrawn into a representation."[1] While Debord's analysis is not concerned with specific representational forms such as the cinema, there is an irresistible match between cinema and the society of the spectacle he describes, particularly when one notes the many coincidences that mark the birth of motion pictures, such as the emergence of modern advertising. Indeed, Charles Eckert's examination of the practices of tie-ins between the film industry and corporations, and his attendant definition of film as a "living display window" for the products of industrial-capitalist society, suggest in quite specific and literal terms that the classical cinema not only is contained by the society of the spectacle, but contributes actively to its continuation. "Hollywood," Eckert argues, ". . . did as much or more than any other force in capitalist culture to smooth the operation of the production-consumption cycle by fetishizing products and putting the libido in libidinally invested advertising."[2]

Eckert's evocation of the cinema as a "living display window" suggests a positioning of the film spectator which allows for an easy fit between cinema as a narrative and visual institution, on the one hand, and as a consumerist one, on the other. Yet the figure of the display window emerges in the writings of Jean Baudrillard to suggest a fundamental *in*compatibility between the society of the spectacle (implying as it does the delineation between spectator and spectacle, and the possibility of a position—however illusory—of contemplation) and the postmodern culture of flow (implying the erosion of any possible boundary between spectator and spectacle):

> There is no longer mirror or looking-glass in the modern order, where man encounters his image, for better or worse; there is only the *display window*—a geometric site of consumption, where the individual is no longer a reflection of himself, but rather is absorbed in the contemplation of a multiplication of objects/ signs, in the order of signifiers of social status, etc. He no longer sees a reflection of himself there, rather he is absorbed and abolished by it. *The subject of consumption is the order of signs.*[3]

Baudrillard's distinction between a society of the spectacle and a society of the simulacra—between contemplation and consumption of images and texts as discrete activities, versus the endless and continuous production of images so that any delineation of "spectacle" or "spectator" is impossible—argues for a radical break between the two different cultures of the image. In cinematic terms, this break reads as a firm and clear distinction between the classical cinema on the one hand, and the cinema of postmodernism on the other (although the very logic Baudrillard describes would make it impossible to isolate the cinema as a discrete form). Such a rigid distinction obscures the extent to which the classical cinema is never so absolutely or exclusively caught up in the myths of narrative causality, and the postmodern never so completely detached from those myths.

Despite Baudrillard's distinctions between spectacle and simulacra, the term *spectacle* has also become a shorthand term for the particular way in which film embodies the postmodern—the fascination with pure surface, with the mixture of signifiers from radically different contexts, with moments of rupture and disloca- tion of conventional narrative and representational forms. As Dana Polan puts it, "what spectacle particularly aspires to is exactly that post-modern discrediting of significance for the sake of *signifiance,* in Kristéva's sense of the term. Spectacle jettisons a need for narrative myths and opts for an attitude in which the only tenable position seems to be the reveling in the fictiveness of one's own fictive acts."[4] In Eckert's account, there is little to suggest that incorporation of consumerist modes into the cinema violates the narrative conventions of cause and effect, linearity, and binary oppositions that have come to be known as constitutive of the "classical Hollywood cinema." However, the association of cinematic spectacle with the postmodern would appear to suggest just the opposite—that spectacle diminishes the importance of the narrative codes of causality, linearity, and rhyming opposition.

This apparent divergence of meaning in the term *spectacle* is problematic if one assumes that the self-conscious display and parading of artifice typical of the postmodern is necessarily contestatory, radical, or otherwise profoundly critical of so-called dominant forms. Otherwise, the ambivalent associations of the notion of the cinematic spectacle are useful reminders that the "spectacle" of the cinema refers simultaneously to consumerist practices that are naturalized by the conventions of the classical Hollywood cinema, or, conversely, which exercise their own power to denaturalize those very conventions. In either case, the effects of spectacle cannot be measured in terms of pure "form" (if there is any such thing), that is, cannot be adequately understood in the exclusive terms of techniques, be they the apparently seamless narrative devices of classical Hollywood films or the more defamiliarized strategies (direct address to the audience, self-conscious style, etc.) of music video, late-night television, performance art, or other postmodern forms. For whether cinematic spectacle is naturalized or self-proclamatory, whether it is embedded within narrative structures or deliriously detached from them, it assumes the equation between the film spectator and the consumer.

Not all definitions of the spectacle of cinema are so firmly entrenched in the equation with advertising and consumerism, however. The cinema has been described more than once as the realization of an ancient dream, or nightmare, depending upon your point of view. For André Bazin, cinema was the materialization of the idealist fantasy to imitate reality so perfectly that the spectator enjoyed a closer relationship to reality than was possible in everyday experience outside the movie theater. For other contemporary theorists—Jean-Louis Baudry in particular—cinema is better described as the actualization of the metaphor of Plato's cave, with spectators so unquestionably passive that they are incapable of distinguishing between what is on the screen and what lies beyond it, or more precisely, incapable of separating perception from representation.[5]

Put another way, the cinematic spectacle as defined by Baudry may be susceptible to particular historical determinations because of its parallels with advertising and with the structures of consumerism. But in his account, "spectacle" is defined in a far more pervasive and embedded way, crossed by the ideological and psychic determinants of Western subjectivity. If the term *spectacle* lends itself simultaneously to definitions of cinema as part of the culture of consumerism (whether subservient to the codes of narrative, as in Eckert's account, or more associated with the postmodern, as in Polan's), and as shaped by the centuries-old formation of the "Western subject," one might begin to sense that it is a term too general, too lacking in precision, to be of much use. This is not to say, however, that the language of spectacle has outlived its usefulness in describing the cinema, but rather that the term *spectacle* has tended, in film studies, to get lost in a sea of generalities.

Nevertheless the identification of cinema as spectacle evokes at least one common thread: the objectifying qualities of the cinematic institution, whether in

the images offered as products to be consumed or in the positions of identification offered as participation in an imaginary world. Defined within the broad
terms of bourgeois subjectivity as they have emerged since the Renaissance, or in
the narrower historical terms of the culture of consumerism, notions of the
cinematic spectacle assume a spectator who is held, contained, and regulated by
the mechanisms of the cinematic apparatus, a spectator who is passive. While
Eckert discusses the female viewer as the ideal spectator for motion pictures, an
analogue to the female consumer pursued by advertising, the gendered contours
of film spectacle have received more careful attention in the most specific terms,
that is, when the notion of "spectacle" is appropriated to analyze the textual
workings of individual films. Indeed, if there is any single notion which under-
lies virtually all feminist analyses of the dominant cinema, it is that of the film as
spectacle, and more specifically, of the woman as object of spectacle. But in
discussions of individual films, "spectacle" loses something of the equation with
consumerism, particularly insofar as the female subject is concerned. For the
equation between film and spectacle has been used to describe the ideal spectator
of film as male and the typical object of spectacle as female.

In Laura Mulvey's account of visual pleasure in film, the ideal psychic
trajectory of the classical cinema involves the interweaving of spectacle and
narrative. Within individual films there are numerous effects of spectacle, the
most obvious of which occur in the musical, whether in the way in which the
narrative is frequently subservient to performance, or in the overall preoccupation with theatricality and staging.[6] In a more general way, most classical films
create spectacles by defining objects of the look—whether the look of the camera
or of protagonists within the film—so as to stage their quality of what Mulvey
calls, referring specifically to the female object of the look, their "to-be-looked-
at-ness." The staging can occur through the literal representation of performances on stage, to scenes staged against the background of doorways or
windows, with attendant performancelike effects.

The spectacle effect which has received the most critical attention, however,
is the practice of systematized looks and gazes in the cinema that define the
structures of editing and the creation of point of view, particularly insofar as the
spectator is "sutured" into a trajectory of narrative and visual desire.[7] It has
become commonplace to note that however diverse the manifestations of spectacle in the cinema, they are all—sooner or later—about men looking at women. In
Mulvey's words, the classical cinema puts forth man as bearer of the look,
woman as its object.[8] In this way, the cinema is evocative of what John Berger
describes, in his study of the female nude in Western oil painting, as the sexual
dichotomy separating the male spectator from the "surveyed female," that is, the
woman defined as object of the male gaze. According to Berger, "Women are

depicted in a quite different way from men—not because the feminine is different from the masculine—but because the 'ideal' spectator is always assumed to be male and the image of the woman is designed to flatter him."[9]

Yet there remains the nagging question of the fit between the textual structures of individual films and the cinema as cultural institution—between, that is, *spectacle* as a convenient term to describe how the various forms of the mise-en-scène of the look in cinema are shaped by the gap between the male subject and the female object, and *spectacle* as an equally convenient term to suggest how the cinema functions in a historical context shaped by the emergence of the Western subject (Baudry) or the emergence of consumerism (Eckert). The question nags in two ways. First, one might assume that despite the reluctance of theorists such as Baudry to address head-on the gendered component of bourgeois subjectivity (e.g., the fact that the ideal subject he describes is the *male* subject), this is a reluctance easily corrected by feminism.[10] In other words, all one need do is add "male" to the list of attributes that define Baudry's cinematic spectator, and the case is easily made for feminism that one large, continuous, unbroken narrative links the subject of Renaissance painting to the subject of psychoanalysis to the subject of the cinema.

Charlotte Bunch has commented on the limitations of what she calls the "add women and stir" syndrome—that is, the tendency to assume that theories of social formation from which women have been absent will nonetheless continue to be valid once women are fit into existing categories of "worker," and so on.[11] While theories of the cinematic apparatus that exclude questions of gender and sexual difference can obviously be useful for their symptomatic status, it is not altogether clear how successful the strategy of "adding women" (or, more appropriate in this case, adding "the feminine") can be. Second, Eckert's designation of the ideal consumer as a woman would seem to conflict somewhat with those notions of sexual hierarchy in the cinema according to which the subject is always male, the object always female. To be sure, just because the woman is identified as a consumer does not necessarily mean she is any less an object, and according to Berger's vocabulary, the woman who buys always buys a representation of herself as the "surveyed female." So there is yet another easy feminist way out of the apparent paradox of the female consumer, this time by insisting upon yet another continuous seamless narrative, now one in which any appeals to the woman as subject are always false appeals, and in which her status as object is firm and absolute.

Commenting on the paradox between woman as (consuming) subject and woman as (consumed) object, Mary Ann Doane has observed that the tension is "only apparently contradictory." The paradox leads Doane to "rethinking the absoluteness of the dichotomy between subject and object which informs much feminist thinking and analyzing the ways in which the woman is encouraged to actively participate in her own oppression."[12] While Doane's criticism of a feminist tendency to dichotomize subject and object is well taken, an analysis of how "the woman is encouraged to participate in her own oppression" can also affirm the dichotomy. For what is at stake is the inevitable consolidation of female subjectivity with female oppression, with the firm duality of the male subject and the female object. While I do not want to undermine the ways in which female consumerism does affirm the woman-as-object, I want nonetheless to suggest that the challenge to facile dichotomous thinking must also involve an examination of ways in which the language of spectacle—the language, that is, of the firm separation between the male subject of the look and the female object of the look—is not necessarily sufficient to analyze *all* of the spectacular effects of the cinematic apparatus.

Given the extent to which contemporary film theory has defined (implicitly or explicitly) "the subject" as fully consonant with patriarchal male authority, an obvious task for feminist theorists of the cinema has been to rearticulate the absolute division of subject and object to account for how women assume positions of desire and identification with the cinema, whether as spectators or as filmmakers. The focal point of most analyses of the subject in film has been the ubiquitous gaze, and virtually every exploration of women's relationship to the cinema has returned to Laura Mulvey's designation of the cinematic gaze as male by addressing and/or reformulating the question raised by E. Ann Kaplan in the first chapter of her book on women and film: "Is the gaze male?"[13]

Subsequent attempts to retheorize the gaze have covered a wide territory. There has been a "return to Freud" in this context, but one which departs significantly from Lacan's famous return to Freud, in an attempt to rethink Lacanian categories as they have emerged in film studies. While Lacanian critics have debated extensively whether it is possible to read the modalities of desire in the strictly polarized terms of male versus female, in film studies Lacan's analyses of the gaze and the construction of the divided self have been read as necessarily complicitous with the duality of the male gaze and the female object of the gaze. Some critics have thus "returned to Freud" to articulate a pleasure in the gaze that resides in bisexuality rather than rigid sexual difference, and which would then account, not only for how women respond to the cinema but also for how the pleasures of the gaze (male or female) follow an itinerary much more complex than that of the voyeuristic/fetishistic control of the female body.[14]

Mary Ann Doane and Laura Mulvey—two of the theorists whose models of the colonization of the woman by the regime of male scopic authority have been so influential—have also theorized a kind of oscillation whereby the gaze remains "male" but is assumed by the female spectator as a disguise, whether in the form of transvestism (Mulvey) or masquerade (Doane).[15] Noting that "Freud conceived of femininity and masculinity primarily in narrative rather than visual terms," Teresa de Lauretis has reread the intertwining paths of spectacle and narrative in Mulvey's account, noting that narrative offers a "double identification with the figure of narrative movement, the mythical subject, and with the figure of narrative closure, the narrative image. Were it not for the possibility of this second, figural identification, the woman spectator would be stranded between two incommensurable entities, the gaze and the image."[16] The necessary *movement* of narrative complicates, then, the relatively simplistic hierarchy of the gaze that has tended to dominate discussions of the "look" in film.

De Lauretis's insistence that spectacle and narrative do not necessarily make for a seamless fit brings to mind another theorist whose work has also sought to demonstrate that the classical Hollywood cinema is made absolutely and perfectly to the model of male desire. While some feminists have found Raymond Bellour's analyses of the classical Hollywood cinema a kind of ideal companion to Mulvey's critique, others have been less enthusiastic.[17] Indeed, much feminist work of the last decade or so has been a response to the assumptions inherent in both Mulvey's and Bellour's work. Consider, in this context, an essay by Bellour which reiterates the monolithic structures of male oedipal desire in the classical Hollywood cinema. Bellour's analysis of segment of Howard Hawks's *The Big Sleep* might be taken as one relatively straightforward critical statement of the function of woman as the object of spectacle, and of the necessary fit between that objectification and the narrative development of the film.

The scene analyzed in detail by Bellour occurs near the conclusion of the film. Philip Marlowe and Vivian Rutledge (Humphrey Bogart and Lauren Bacall) leave one house to return to another, the scene of the crime. A brief dialogue takes place in a car, and seals the relationship between the man and the woman. Now they are working in unison, on the same side, and they declare their love for each other. Bellour shows how the alternation of two-shots and close-ups, and the differentiation of sound and image match, create a fundamental difference between Philip Marlowe and Vivian Rutledge. Bellour's analysis is surely an important corrective to the reputation Howard Hawks has acquired, particularly because of films such as *Bringing up Baby* (1938), as a portrayer of emancipated women. As Bellour argues,

> The well-known independence and initiative of Hawks' heroines brings to certain of his couples—and to none more than to *The Big Sleep*—the slightly legendary character of a relationship of adult reciprocity. But this is only achieved through the codified marks which, in this instance, make it the woman whose magnified face simultaneously and wholly expresses and receives the admission of love.[18]

The Big Sleep is an interesting film to read in terms of cinema-as-spectacle, particularly insofar as its legendary incomprehensibility of plot is concerned (Hawks claimed he could never figure out the story, and Chandler described his novel as "more interested in people than in plot").[19] Despite that incomprehensibility—or even perhaps because of it—the film is quite readable within the conventions of the classical Hollywood cinema. And the film appears to be situated firmly within the confines of patriarchal ideology, containing many of the elements central to representation governed by sexual hierarchy—a male protagonist hired by a father figure, one mysterious woman and another disturbed one (eventually resolving in the stereotypical good girl/bad girl dichotomy), heterosexual romance.

From the very beginning of *The Big Sleep,* a system of difference is put into place, and it draws, in a dramatic way, upon the tensions between seeing and being seen, subject and object, male and female, that feminist critics have identified as central to the mechanisms of the classical Hollywood cinema. The film opens as Marlowe enters the Sternwood mansion for an appointment with the General, father of Vivian and Carmen. As he is led by the butler toward the adjacent greenhouse where the General awaits him, Marlowe's path is intersected by a woman, the General's daughter Carmen; and when he leaves the greenhouse after his discussion with the General, his departure is delayed, this time by Vivian Rutledge's request (conveyed by the butler) to see him in her room. Thus any direct path leading to and from the father is interrupted by the daughters. The interruption is marked by setting off each of the two sisters as an object of spectacle, in a process very similar to what Bellour describes in the later scene. There are full close-ups of the women, while Marlowe is clearly and obviously designated as the subject, the spectator-within-the-film to whom those close-ups are directed, and who thus functions as a kind of stand-in for the spectator in the movie theater.

Marlowe's discussion with the father, wedged between the two encounters with women, is, in sharp contrast, a paragon of symmetry. The two men are portrayed from similar vantage points, at similar distances, and in an unbroken rhythm. A close-up of one man is always matched by a close-up of the other, an over-the shoulder shot of one by a similar shot of the other, and so on. Marlowe's discussion with the General occupies much more screen time than the two encounters with women that frame that discussion. The General introduces himself to Marlowe as a man who is "crippled, paralyzed in both legs. I can barely eat and my sleep is so near waking that it's hardly worth the name. I seem to exist largely on heat, like a newborn spider." This self-described "survivor of a very gaudy life" seems initially to have little resemblance to Marlowe. However, in the course of their discussion, a sense of identification between the two men emerges. When Marlowe describes how his former career in the district attorney's office ended when he was fired for insubordination ("I seem to rate pretty high on that"), General Sternwood remarks on their similarities ("I always did myself"). Sternwood refers to Shaun Regan—a central figure in Raymond Chandler's novel who becomes but a shadow in the film—as the man who formerly occupied the seat now occupied by Marlowe.[20] Sternwood says that Regan "sat there with me sweating like a pig, drinking the brandy I could no longer drink and telling stories of the Irish revolution." Marlowe may not tell stories of the Irish revolution, but he certainly is sweating, and an affinity between Marlowe and the absent Shaun is affirmed.

While Marlowe slides neatly into the patterns of male bonding and friend-ship, his relations with women, as introduced by the encounters with the two sisters, are marked by confusion and mystery. The ostensible motivation for Marlowe's visit is that Sternwood is being blackmailed by Geiger, for reasons having to do with his daughter Carmen. It is up to Marlowe to get rid of the Geiger problem. Sternwood's older daughter, Vivian, is somewhat more mysterious, since at the time of Marlowe's discussion with the General, she has been spoken about but not yet seen on screen. Marlowe can respond to the General's description of Carmen by recalling her attempt to "sit on my lap while I was standing up." Of Vivian, however, he can only ask a question, one that will be asked again and again throughout the film: "Your other daughter, Mrs. Rutledge. She mixed up in this?"

The beginning of the film functions as a matrix, for over and over again in *The Big Sleep,* Philip Marlowe's access to the father's room, the site of patriar-chal authority, is diverted by a woman. This is a concrete example of Laura Mulvey's description of how "[woman's] visual presence tends to work against the development of a story line, to freeze the flow of action in moments of erotic contemplation." Mulvey goes on to say, "This alien presence then has to be integrated into cohesion with the narrative."[21] This is precisely what occurs in the scene described by Bellour. No longer does the woman occupy an "ante-chamber," that is, a hallway in the case of Carmen Sternwood, a bedroom in the case of Vivian Rutledge, a room adjacent to the space of patriarchal authority, and which threatens to upset its balance. And despite the complex twists and turns of the plot of *The Big Sleep,* the sequence analyzed by Bellour does respond to the question Marlowe asks of the General—"Your other daughter, Mrs. Rutledge. She mixed up in this?"

But it is also worth noting that there is more information provided in the scene analyzed by Bellour than the declaration of love. Something very fun-damental is explained. Vivian was attempting all along to protect her younger sister Carmen from blackmail and from prison. The relationship between the two sisters is spoken and alluded to, but rarely are they seen together in the same frame. In fact, only twice in the film do the sisters appear in frame together, and in both instances Carmen is posed as a threat to the nascent relationship between Marlowe and Vivian Rutledge.

Early in the film, Marlowe discovers Carmen in a drugged state at Geiger's home, and proceeds to bring her home to the Sternwood mansion. When Vivian sees her unconscious sister, she asks Marlowe if he "did this." With Carmen unconscious and quite literally in the background, the scene focuses on the exchange between Marlowe and Vivian, recalling both narratively and structurally the initial encounter between them. Carmen reappears within the frame as Marlowe leaves the room; Carmen lies on Vivian's bed, and she and Vivian are framed by the camera. In the earlier conversation between Marlowe and Vivian, the bed figured almost comically in the background as the return of the repressed. Here, the figure of Carmen prone suggests most obviously the possibility that she may be in competition with her sister for the other half of the love relationship; but it suggests the return of a far deeper repressed as well—a bond between two women from which Marlowe may be excluded.[22]

Later in the film, the only other instance where the two women appear in the same scene, Carmen enters an apartment occupied by Marlowe and Vivian. But it is only when the women exit the apartment that they are seen in the same frame, and Carmen is quite literally concealed from full view, as she wears a hood and exits with her back to the camera. A telling exchange during this scene establishes briefly a shot–reverse shot between Carmen and Vivian, although while Vivian looks at Carmen, Carmen speaks to Marlowe. Read one way, this "false" shot–reverse shot suggests that the relationship between the two women is significant only insofar as the relationship to the signifying authority of the man is concerned, but read another way, the scene suggests a disturbance in the field of male-female relationships. If, as Bellour suggests, *The Big Sleep* moves toward a resolution defined by a rigid sexual hierarchy, there nonetheless seems to be a strain in that resolution from the pressure of a possible revelation of the bond between two women.

For anyone acquainted with the history of contemporary film theory, a phrase such as "a strain from the pressure" is a familiar cliché, for it recalls the ways in which film theory and criticism in the 1970s were shaped by the central notion of symptomatic readings of the classical Hollywood cinema. The editors of *Cahiers du cinéma,* borrowing from Louis Althusser, described such readings as follows:

[There are] films which seem at first sight to belong firmly within the ideology and to be completely under its sway, but which turn out to be so only in an ambiguous manner. . . . If one reads the film obliquely, looking for symptoms; if one looks beyond its apparent formal coherence, one can see that it is riddled with cracks: it is splitting under an internal tension which is simply not there in an ideologically innocuous film. . . .[23]

That such an exposure of the repressed of classical film narrative should be appealing for feminist criticism is obvious, allowing as it does the pleasure of contradiction to substitute for the pleasure of dismissal and disavowal.

Yet however great the appeal of the return of the repressed, those so-called ideologically innocuous films, to which I might oppose a film such as *The Big Sleep,* are curious entities. Does the opposition between "ideologically innocuous" and "riddled with cracks" then suggest that in the majority of films, woman is firmly and simply objectified as spectacle in a straightforward way? Then there are other, exceptional films—usually, one might add cynically, films which the critic likes too much to dump in the trash can of dominant ideology—in which there is a "partial dismantlement of the system from within."[24] A rigid and peculiar opposition is implied here, between those films that are completely contained by ideology and those that are resistant to it. Even "ideologically innocuous" films are often characterized not so much by a regurgitation of patriarchal ideals as by an ambivalence toward them, so that it is difficult to know when a film ceases to be "innocuous."

It is unclear as well just what constitutes the critical potential of other films; often it appears to be ambivalence, but ambivalence is no guarantee of "dismantlement," partial or otherwise.[25] Yet in Bellour's analysis of *The Big Sleep,* there is no room for such ambiguity, but only for the straightforward affirmation of man as center of the cinematic narrative. I do not question that *The Big Sleep* is thoroughly imbued with the ideology of patriarchy and its attendant ramifications for the representation of woman. I do question, however, whether this particular film—and perhaps any example of the classical Hollywood cinema—can be so totally, uniformly, and univocally described as contained by patriarchy. My point is neither to "rescue" the classical Hollywood cinema for feminism, nor to affirm ambiguity as an inherently radical or progressive gesture. If women's cinema entertains an ambivalent relationship to the Hollywood cinema, if women filmmakers engage in what Lucy Fischer describes as an "intertextual dialogue with their male counterparts," then it is crucial to see that relationship in its complexity, and not as a series of variations on the same themes of voyeurism and fetishism, sadism and masochism.[26]

Two different positions vis-à-vis the classical Hollywood cinema emerge in this context, both of which have been claimed by feminists. From one perspective, it is crucial to take into account the capacity of the classical Hollywood cinema to subsume every kind of difference into the hierarchy of sexual polarity—hence, the repressed relation between the two sisters in *The Big Sleep* can never be, within classical narrative cinema, any more than a brief eruption, a momentary disturbance.[27] But from another perspective, the momentary disturbances within a film speak to larger tensions and contradictions within classical film narrative that may well be submerged by patterns of crisis and resolution, but which suggest nonetheless that the ideology of patriarchy contains gaps and tensions which are as significant for feminism as the more explicit effects of patriarchy. This second position seems the more productive one insofar as the rethinking of the "absoluteness of the dichotomy between subject and object" (Doane) is concerned. However, the affirmation of these disruptions and tensions can involve a romanticization of marginality, and the attendant assumption that alternative positions exist, within the classical Hollywood cinema, wherever one wishes them to.

Analyses of the classical Hollywood cinema that refer only to homogeneity and hierarchy, on the one hand, or to heterogeneity and disruption, on the other, lose sight of the complex ways in which cinema functions *both* to legitimatize the patriarchal status quo *and,* if not necessarily to challenge it, then at the very least to suggest its weak links, its own losses of mastery, within which may be found possibilities or hypotheses of alternative positions. There is a great risk in arguing for this "both/and," since the insistence upon competing ideological and representational levels can fall into either a vague pluralism (whereby incompatibility and conflict are transformed into peaceful, boring coexistence) or a naive ambiguity (whereby the competing levels become rallying points for a quivering oscillation that effectively denies the political ramifications of patriarchal hegemony). If it is crucial to maintain a tension between the two functions of hegemony and contradiction, and to examine their interrelationships, it is equally important to examine how that tension is constructed within criticism and theory.

One site at which the monolithic and contradictory effects of the classical cinema intersect in *The Big Sleep* is in the simultaneous evocation of the male-female couple as the resolution toward which classical Hollywood cinema moves, and the sisterly bond as the obstacle, however momentary, to that resolution. Does the brief allusion to, and subsequent repression of, the relationship between the two sisters have enough signifying power in the film to constitute a position from which to read *The Big Sleep* symptomatically? Does the relationship between the two women function as the feared underside of the relationship between two other likes, the father and the surrogate son? In a film in which so many plot strands are left unconnected, is there a compelling reason to isolate this particular bit of undeveloped motivation as more significant than any others?

The special significance of the relationship between the two women could be argued on a variety of levels. In a film which takes as its principal means of rereading the Chandler novel the relationship between its costars Bogart and Bacall, lovers in "real life," as it were, the way in which that relationship is constructed, as well as the gaps in that construction (of which the bond between the two sisters is one example), will have particular signifying weight. But if the relationship between the two women could be the basis for a feminist symptomatic reading of *The Big Sleep,* the very possibility of such a reading needs to be approached critically.

For instance, one could demonstrate how one of the most conventional aspects of the classical cinema, a man and woman in love, is produced against the backdrop of the excessive visibility of the father and the accompanying invisibility of the mother, of the maternal, and of female-to-female connection. But to identify the missing maternal element in the film is, already, to assume an empty space that may be repressed by the film, but is also created by it. Put another way, such a feminist reading falls into the trap of what Luce Irigaray calls the "old dream of symmetry," for it assumes—rather than challenges—the patriarchal logic of the film, whereby if men together replicate father-son relationships, then relationships between women must fall into the symmetrical other half.[28] But then again—the cycle continues—empty spaces may be spaces created by the text, but they are still empty, and an insistence on "filling them up" can have the effect of upsetting the logocentric hierarchy of presence and absence.

I would like to pursue the significance of the relationship between the two women in a slightly different direction. The relationship between Vivian and Carmen suggests a mirroring relationship between two likes, but which never attains any kind of visual authority in the film. The very repression of the relationship between the two sisters invites the hypothesis of similarly forbidden relationships between other, male likes. *The Big Sleep* entertains more than a passing preoccupation with the tensions of sexual identity, particularly insofar as male homosexuality is concerned. Geiger's homosexuality in Raymond Chandler's novel was one of several elements immediately censored when the screenplay for the film was begun. Annette Kuhn has argued that while censorship is usually understood as pure elimination, it is read more compellingly as a productive process, particularly insofar as censored elements do not necessarily disappear, but rather return with the force of the repressed.

Thus, Kuhn notes, Geiger's house acquires some of the same characteristics of degenerate sexuality associated with the hothouse where Marlowe first meets the General. Noting that Geiger's house is "shadowy, closed-in, cluttered and messy," "the site . . . of mystery and enigma," Kuhn writes: "The *mise-en-scène* of Geiger's house figures in the film as a discourse across which may be read a series of displaced and condensed representations of an underlying and un-expressed perversity or menace in the area of sexuality."[29] Kuhn's analysis focuses on Geiger's house as a privileged site in the film, where mise-en-scène articulates implicitly what is repressed on the level of narrative. Kuhn notes that the "menace" in the area of sexuality is read in relationship to women as well as "perversity" ("the disturbance in the area of sexuality . . . involves not only homosexuality and heterosexual promiscuity, but female sexuality as well").[30] I want to suggest that the disturbance of which Kuhn speaks erupts in another context as well, in the formulation of spectacle and the attendant structure of the look—a disturbance which is more appropriately described as "homotextual" than "homosexual."[31]

The repressed (female) homotextuality of *The Big Sleep* finds its echo in another form of homotextuality which creates another "scene," another organiza-tion of visual and narrative desire, in the film. Woman becomes an object of spectacle in *The Big Sleep* to complicate but ultimately to facilitate the private detective's access to the various sites signifying patriarchal authority, first represented by the greenhouse in the opening section of the film. This spatial representation of patriarchal authority takes on various guises in the film, from the back room of Geiger's bookstore to Eddie Mars's office in his club. Yet traces of a resistance to this facilitating role remain in the utterance of the relationship between two women. These narrative gestures of utterance and repression are echoed more emphatically in the traces of another kind of specta-cle—that is, different from how the use of shot–reverse shot and close-ups identifies woman as the object of spectacle—that occupies a curious place in the film, a place that has an affinity with the homotextuality involving the two sisters. Marlowe repeats obsessively the itinerary introduced at the beginning of the film as he moves from one room to another. Woman represents a difficulty of access, a diversion, an obstacle, before she is contained within the conventions of Hollywood romance.

In a striking and somewhat unusual scene in the film, Marlowe's movement from one room to another is obstructed by a *male* presence. Harry Jones (Elisha Cook, Jr.) offers Marlowe information on the whereabouts of Eddie Mars's wife in exchange for a fee. When Marlowe arrives at the office in a deserted building where he has agreed to meet Jones, he overhears voices and sneaks into an adjacent office. Hence the distinctive spatial architecture of the film, where the primary room (like the greenhouse in the opening scene of the film) is connected to an antechamber (like the hall at the beginning of the film), is repeated in this scene. From his vantage point in the "antechamber," Marlowe can hear the voices of Canino, one of Eddie Mars's men, and Jones. The scene of what becomes another crime, the poisoning of Jones, is only partially visible through a door left ajar. Shadows of the men are visible, however, through a frosted window in the wall (Figure 1). The obstruction of vision marks the private detective's inability to act, his impotence.[32] A screen, of sorts, separates Marlowe from a room. This is a threshold which cannot be crossed, but through which light and shadow and voices are distinguishable.

This screen surface recalls the credits sequence prior to the beginning of the film proper, where we see shadow images, silhouettes of Bogart and Bacall smoking (Figure 2). One movement, one itinerary in *The Big Sleep* fleshes out that credits image—that is, endows the star personae of Bogart and Bacall with their fictional roles, and complicates those roles within the context of the developing narrative and visual structures of the film.[33] But first, other possibilities are tested against the first image of the couple—notably, Marlowe and Carmen, particularly in the opening sequence of the film in the Sternwood mansion (Figure 3). The successful resolution of the film is indicated by a two-shot of the couple, Philip Marlowe and Vivian Rutledge, now in a perfect match with the first image (Figure 4).

The credits image initiates another, more subtle movement as well. For this image also contains an opaque screen. The screen may be defined as a surface on which to project skeletal images of the film's stars and the attendant promise that they will be quite literally fleshed out, but it also functions as a barrier, a boundary line to be transgressed. The function of spectacle in *The Big Sleep* has two components, both indicated in this credits image. First, and following the argument of Bellour, the screenlike image can be complemented only by its more realistic, detailed counterpart, the two-shot of Marlowe and Vivian at the film's conclusion, once Marlowe has become "bearer of the look," that is, once the formula of male subject and female object has been articulated. Second, spectacle in *The Big Sleep* suggests every bit as forcefully the threshold that separates two spaces, and the opacity of the screen.

These two components correspond roughly to the two different perspectives on the classical Hollywood cinema to which I have alluded: the one emphasizing cinematic spectacle as the insistence on separation and hierarchy, and the other emphasizing spectacle as the difficulty of that insistence, spectacle as a set of boundaries that are simultaneously omnipresent and permeable. In narrative terms, the former involves the heterosexual romance solidified in the union of Vivian and Marlowe, and the latter the various complications that make that union difficult, "dense"—Vivian's bond with her sister, Marlowe's positions of impotence, the "remnants" of homosexuality in the film. While the relationship between the two women functions primarily as a negative presence, temporarily complicating the emergence of the male-female couple, the impotence of Mar-

Figure 1

Figure 2

Figure 3

Figure 4

lowe not only is visualized but affords the representation of another "scene," the opacity of the threshold that separates him and Jones. These screens in *The Big Sleep* are figures not only of spectacle (there is virtually no such thing as "pure" spectacle in the classical Hollywood cinema, given the mediated quality of the image) but rather of the intersection of spectacle and narrative. For the screen is both surface and passageway, mirror and obstacle. Cinematic spectacle is, certainly, the fixing of the image of woman, with the accompanying narrative movement of penetrating the father's room. But spectacle is also a relation to a screen, fixed as unattainable on the other side of a door, embedded in a narrative movement that is thwarted, stopped at the threshold.

Critics such as Noël Burch have suggested that many films from the "primitive" era function to act out what would become repressed or contained by the devices of the classical cinema, and Marlowe's relationship to the frosted window makes for an interesting fit with another, "primitive" image of a spectator's relationship to a screen, a relationship that plays on the double function of the screen as both surface and threshold.[34] In *Uncle Josh at the Moving Picture Show* (1902), a naive spectator visits the cinema for the first time. A variety of transactions occur between his box and the screen during the screening of the three films-within-the-film. After the last film, entitled *A Country Couple*, begins, Uncle Josh tears down the screen, imagining that he can enter the fictional world on screen; instead, he confronts the rear-projectionist, and the film concludes with a tussle between them.

Uncle Josh transgresses the space separating screen from audience. Transgression may be too strong a word, however, for in a sense Uncle Josh is—despite his naiveté—an ideal film viewer. In other words, what filmgoing promises is, precisely, transgression of the boundary line separating two spheres.[35] The two spaces in *Uncle Josh at the Moving Picture Show* are not identical to the adjoining rooms that shape Philip Marlowe's quest, but they are similar. The first two films that Josh sees are *A Parisian Dancer*, in which a woman dances and flounces her skirt, and along with which Josh dances on stage, and *The Black Diamond Express*, a variation on the famous 1895 Lumière brothers short *L'Arrivée d'un train en gare*, which shows a train arriving at a station, and which elicits a terrified reaction from Josh. These two films set the stage for the reaction that will follow. The third film, *The Country Couple*, shows a man and a woman engaged in what appears to be slapstick. It is only when a man *and* a woman appear on screen that Uncle Josh is ready to get inside of the image. An image of a dancing woman may be seductive, and an image of a train thrilling, but they simply oil the machinery that *A Country Couple* sets into motion.

Over forty years separate *Uncle Josh at the Moving Picture Show* and *The*

Big Sleep. But common to both films is a preoccupation with the relationship between a male protagonist and an ambivalent screen surface, a relationship that is foregrounded in *Uncle Josh at the Moving Picture Show* and submerged by other details of narrative and visual structure in *The Big Sleep*. The value in moving from a classical narrative film such as *The Big Sleep* to an early, "primitive" film such as *Uncle Josh at the Moving Picture Show* lies in untangling further the strands of spectacle within narrative, and in identifying spectacle not just as the imposition of a rigid separation between subject and object, but also as the fantasy of submerged boundaries. Like many other early films, *Uncle Josh at the Moving Picture Show* offers a rudimentary story which functions as a primal scene of the cinema, telling a story based on the cinema's own power to affect and move its spectators.[36]

Uncle Josh at the Moving Picture Show does not conclude, as well it might have, with Uncle Josh overcome and overwhelmed by the crumpled screen. Instead, Uncle Josh confronts the rear-projectionist and his machine. Talk about primal scenes of the cinema! If there is something of lifting a woman's skirts suggested by Uncle Josh's reaction to the screen—as the flouncing dress of the dancer surely suggests—then the projectionist appears precisely in order to block any sight of what might be concealed beneath those skirts. At the same time, the projectionist is defined as a puppeteer, the man behind the illusion. *Uncle Josh at the Moving Picture Show* stresses the importance of the threshold in cinema, the crossing over, the movement from one space to another. The rear-projectionist re-marks the separation which the film had fancifully put into question. Philip Marlowe is a more sophisticated version of Uncle Josh, a spectator who conceals, or represses, his shock and surprise at the screen presence as he moves from one room to another.

In both films, the figures behind the screen, the rear-projectionist and the father and his stand-ins, are narrating authorities. They have a double-edged quality. On one level, they assure and maintain the position of the spectator-within-the-film—in Uncle Josh's case by providing entertaining images, and in Marlowe's by giving him the authority to conduct an investigation. At the same time they threaten to disrupt his authority—in Uncle Josh's case by revealing the machine behind the illusion, and in Marlowe's case by setting into motion a series of spectacles controlled by other figures of male authority. In this most obvious sense, both of these films *do* conform to the logic of oedipal desire and authority. However, the screen surface in both films marks the possibility of a desire where the boundaries between identification and objectification are no longer clear.

The implications of the screen and a narrating presence are further developed in another film which stands in between *Uncle Josh at the Moving*

Picture Show and *The Big Sleep*—that is, as a film which is neither "primitive" nor classical, and which brings another dynamic of otherness to bear on the relationship between spectator and scene, that of race. Cecil B. De Mille's *The Cheat* (1915) tells the story of a wealthy society woman who loses a large sum of money and accepts what appears to be the only solution available to her—a loan from an Asian businessman, the condition of which is that she sleep with him. The film's intrigue is based on two systems that work across the female body. The one, Western, is based on money and located in the "smart set" of Long Island. The other, Asian, is based on an icon of ownership, an Oriental character literally branded onto all the belongings of an Asian ivory merchant, whom the film describes as the "rage" among the "smart set."

Central to this intrigue is a privileged space, a room in the Asian man's house where the branding takes place. It is filled with the accoutrements of exoticism, including burning incense and a Buddha. Two surfaces set off the boundaries of the room: a sliding door on one side, and a sliding translucent screen on the other. A love triangle forms the basis of the plot of the film. The Asian merchant desires the woman, wife of a wealthy businessman. She is inside the room with the Asian man when she discovers the loss of a large sum of money which she had "borrowed" from her club's treasury and invested un-successfully. She collapses. The Asian man takes her outside the room and, while reviving her, makes advances to her (Figure 5). Suddenly the lights go on inside the room, and two shadows appear on the screen (Figure 6). The woman's husband and another man are discussing money. The woman discovers that she will not be able to use her husband's money to replace the club's treasury, for he tells his friend that his funds are completely tied up. Thus this shadow theater confirms the woman's acceptance of an offer made by the Asian man, to exchange money for sexual favors.

The screen marks a curious threshold between interior and exterior space, between sex and money, between East and West. The threshold separates, yet some projection still exists. Later in the film, the woman comes upon a sum of money (her husband's investment has paid off). She returns to the room of the Asian man's house to pay back his money and hopefully to get out of their bargain. He wants nothing of it. She resists his advances, and he brands her with the same iron, the same icon of ownership, that he uses for his other "posses-sions." She shoots him and leaves. The husband, suspicious of his wife's departure, has followed her to the Asian man's house. He stands before the translucent screen, the same threshold on the other side of which he had been seen by his wife in the earlier scene. Now, another shadow, that of the Asian man, is projected on the screen, but with a significant difference—blood seeps through the translucent material. The husband tears down the screen and

Figure 5

Figure 6

bursts into the room to find the wounded Asian man now crumpled on the floor.

The violence of tearing down the screen becomes the mirror image of the violence done to the body of the woman, with its obvious implications of rape. The woman's body becomes, precisely, a screen surface. In tearing down the screen, the husband acts on behalf of Western civilization and white woman-hood. And like Uncle Josh, he too wants to get inside the image. For the Asian man is a puppeteer, a manipulator of light and shadow. He is a narrating presence who, on one side of the screen, disperses his marks of possession, and, on the other side, interprets a shadow theater to his benefit. The projectionist in *Uncle Josh at the Moving Picture Show* now acquires the sign of otherness and exoticism.

When the husband bursts through the screen in *The Cheat,* a chain of events begins which will conclude in a court of law. The Asian man's narrative authority is stripped away as the woman rushes to the front of the courtroom to display her wound to the shocked spectators. His narrative power and authority are thus undermined by her spectacular display. Her husband had claimed responsibility for the shooting. In order to protect his wife's reputation, he offers no reasons as to why he might have committed the act. Her display functions as her gesture of devotion to her husband, who is acquitted, while an angry mob descends upon the Asian man. Thus, order is restored—the guilty punished, the just set free—by designating the woman as object of spectacle. Ambivalence is regulated by defining the female body as a distinctively unambivalent object, that is, as the screen surface which, unlike the translucent screen in the Asian man's house, returns the mark of otherness only as a sign of shame.

The Asian man's position as a narrating authority is replaced by the author-ity of the reconstituted couple of (white) man and wife, and the law. However, a distinct irony persists in the film, for the only way in which the ambivalence can be regulated is by stressing the woman's function as object, whether in an Asian or a Western sense. In other words, *The Cheat* also demonstrates, although in ways quite different from the early cinema, what would become repressed with the advent of the codes of the classical Hollywood cinema. The display of the woman's body in the courtroom is not that unlike the Asian merchant's posses-sion of her. The only difference is that his brand is more literal, more dramatic, more visible than the narrative and visual codes that contain her. While the film wants to separate East and West as informed by two different laws, two radically different orders, it can do so only at the price of an equivalence played out on the woman's body. The translucent screen thus is an embodiment of similarity between the two orders, as the woman's body becomes an object of exchange between men.

A curious history unfolds in the movement from *Uncle Josh at the Moving Picture Show* to *The Cheat* to *The Big Sleep*. As threshold, the screen becomes both more embedded within the details of narrative development, and more endowed with the symbolic baggage of self and other—the West and the East, the son and the father. The functions of the screen, as both a surface on which to project and a veil to be torn down, become more dispersed, defined in relationship to a variety of cinematic elements. Yet something of Uncle Josh and the rear-projectionist lingers on into the classical cinema. The ragged edges of spectacle in a film such as *Uncle Josh at the Moving Picture Show* offer fundamental insights into the appeal and the evolution of film form. While there is certainly a long history of cinematic spectacle defined as the separation between self and other, between the male subject and the female object, spectacle has also meant something quite different—the fantasy of merging, the confused boundaries between self and other, now displaced from male/female to male/male relationships. In her classic essay, Mulvey distinguishes between the male gaze at the female body, which is voyeuristic and fetishistic, and the male gaze at the male body, characterized by identification with an ego ideal. Films such as these, however, trace the difficulty of such neat distinctions insofar as male-to-male identification is concerned.[37] Most significant, the representation of the screen embodies the ambivalence which it is presumably the goal of classical film narrative to regulate.

De Lauretis argues that Mulvey's reading of spectacle and narrative as two dynamics working in tandem to support the centrality of male desire has led to a flattening of the differences between the two, the assumption of an equivalence which, if taken to its logical conclusion, would mean not just that women have no position from which to articulate desire in the classical cinema, but that they have not even the possibility of any identification whatsoever. Along somewhat similar lines, the reading of spectacle in terms purely of "image" and "gaze" is problematic not only for the impossible division of female and male with which it is aligned (as de Lauretis suggests), but also for a component that is frequently left out, ignored, or simply assumed to be the unproblematized "ground" for the gaze and the image. I am referring, as should be obvious by now, to the film screen.

De Lauretis makes a provocative observation vis-à-vis the film screen in her discussion of the myth of Medusa and Perseus. She asks the question "What did Medusa feel seeing herself reflected in Perseus' shield just before being slain . . .?" After noting ironically that her equation between Perseus's shield and the movie screen is "indeed naive," de Lauretis continues: "not only does that shield protect Perseus from Medusa's evil look, but later on, after her death (in his further adventures), it serves as frame and surface on which her head is pinned to petrify his enemies."[38] De Lauretis's "naive" equation plays upon the analogies between the film screen and the mirror, on the one hand, and the breast, on the other, that have been central to contemporary psychoanalytic readings of film, except that her equation foregrounds what is generally repressed or assumed in most accounts of the cinematic screen—the death and absence required of the woman so that the mirror-breast-screen can function "successfully."

While the theories of Christian Metz and Jean-Louis Baudry differ in important respects, they share what has become a commonly held assumption in film theory—that the experience of the cinema is a reactivation of the imaginary, a regression to an infantile state. Unlike the classical, presumably "idealist" film theory of André Bazin, in which the screen and the frame work in tandem to create a window on the world, Metz and Baudry substitute metaphors of regression—the mirror and the breast, respectively. This displacement of metaphors occurs not in the name of a principle of aesthetic or formal adequacy, but rather in the name of the subject positioning which is crucial to any theory of the cinematic apparatus.

While Metz has emphasized a complexity of factors that shape how this regression operates, his conception of the "imaginary signifier" of the cinema relies on the analogy between the cinema and the Lacanian mirror stage, the point at which the child's (mis)conception of itself as a whole, unified self occurs through its mirror reflection—whether that mirror be a literal mirror, the gaze of the (m)other, or both. From that founding moment of cinematic identification emerge a variety of components of the classical cinema, and particularly interesting in the present context is the way in which, according to Metz, the classical cinema reactivates the primal scene. Melanie Klein suggested that "any performance where there is something to be seen or heard, always stand[s] for parental coitus—listening and watching standing for observation in fact or phantasy—while the falling curtain stands for objects which hinder observations, such as bedclothes, the side of a bed., etc."[39] Daniel Dervin—writing in a more traditional psychoanalytic mode than Metz—has suggested that film may have a privileged relationship to the primal scene, noting in particular the power of film "to reproduce the scale of infant observation."[40]

For Metz, however, the imprint of the primal scene on the classical cinema has more to do with the properties of identification in the cinema, particularly insofar as the camera and its relationship to the cinematic screen are concerned. Metz notes that the cinema is unlike the theater, where the stage and the audience, despite the boundaries that exist between them, constitute a single space.

[The] space of the film, represented by the screen, is utterly heterogeneous, it no longer communicates with that of the auditorium. . . . For its spectator the film unfolds in that simultaneously very close and definitively inaccessible "elsewhere" in which the child *sees* the amourous play of the parental couple, who are similarly ignorant of it and leave it alone, a pure onlooker whose participation is inconceivable.

Hence, Metz concludes, "In this respect the cinematic signifier is not only 'psychoanalytic'; it is more precisely Oedipal in type."[41]

Uncle Josh at the Moving Picture Show in particular would seem to confirm, with striking precision, Metz's observation, for Uncle Josh's desire to intervene, to get inside the image, occurs only when the presumably parental couple appears on the screen at the movie theater. When he tears down the screen, the material resembles a crumpled curtain (hence evoking the frame of the child's apprehension of its parents' "amourous play," as well as the obstacle creating a distance) and is also suggestive of the flouncing skirts of the "Parisian Dancer." Once Josh has torn down the screen, the rear-projectionist emerges as a figure of simultaneous oedipal and cinematic authority. To be sure, Metz's comments on the film screen do not refer specifically to the screen in the figurative context that I have been discussing, but rather to the screen as a basic element of cinematic representation and identification. However, even as the figure of the screen in *Uncle Josh at the Moving Picture Show* seems to confirm Metz's observation of the inevitably firm link between the Lacanian mirror and the cinematic screen, it suggests the limitations of a theory of cinema in which identification is equated so thoroughly and so firmly with regression, with a founding moment of (oedipal) identity.[42]

For *Uncle Josh at the Moving Picture Show* achieves most clearly and boldly the equation between spectatorial identification and the mirror, not when Josh is astounded by the screen but rather when he tears it down and confronts the rear-projectionist. To be sure, the screen participates in the oedipal scenario Metz describes, but it is not reducible to that scenario. Indeed, the projector that is revealed by Josh's naive intrusion into the screen would appear to suggest much more decisively the analogy between film and mirror, functioning as it does as a stand-in for the camera which Metz designates as the privileged instrument of cinematic identification. If, for Metz, the cinematic screen leads back to the primal scene as its privileged referent, the deployment of the screen as a figure in *Uncle Josh at the Moving Picture Show, The Cheat,* and *The Big Sleep* not only complicates any such direct link between the film screen and the oedipal scenario, but accentuates the contradictory movement *within* that scenario.

For Jean-Louis Baudry, the particular psychic function of the film screen is best understood in relation to regressive fantasies of fusion. As Baudry writes:

taking into account the darkness of the movie theater, the relative passivity of the situation, the forced immobility of the cine-subject, and the effects which result from the projection of images, moving images, the cinematographic apparatus brings about a state of artificial regression. It artifically leads back to an interior phase of his development—a phase which is barely hidden, as dream and certain pathological forms of our mental life have shown. It is the desire, unrecognized as such by the subject, to return to this phase, an early state of development with its own forms of satisfaction which may play a determining role in his desire for cinema and the pleasure he finds in it. Return to a relative narcissism, and even more towards a mode of relating to reality which could be defined as enveloping and in which the separation between one's own body and the exterior world is not well defined.[43]

Borrowing from Bertram Lewin's observations on the significance of the screen in dreams, where it functions much like the mother's breast in relationship to the child, Baudry suggests then that the power of cinematic representation has to do with the reactivation of the imaginary fusion between baby and breast.[44] As Robert T. Eberwein puts it in his study of film and dreams, the cinematic screen "serves as a surrogate, deriving from infancy, for the physiological and psychic union we enjoyed with the mother: the screen is both breast and infant, the mother and the self."[45]

Metz's inquiries into cinematic identification are indebted to Baudry, and there are obvious connections between the emphases on regression in the two men's work. While the breast/screen analogy may say quite a bit about cinematic identification in general, it shares—insofar as the figure of the screen is concerned—some of the same problems encountered in Metz's model. The most obvious criticism to be made, of course, is that neither Metz nor Baudry takes any account of sexual difference, regression in both cases defined in relationship to a subject which can be read only as male.[46] The failure to address sexual difference relates to another characteristic of these theories of the apparatus: the assumption that in its projection of a regressive unity, in its recapture of the imaginary, the cinema functions successfully to ward off the threat of otherness, the division of the self, the impossibility of fusion.

Central to both Metz's and Baudry's theories is a definition of the cinema screen as a fixed ground, as the unwavering support for the fictions of (male) identity, whether as Metz's mirror or as Baudry's breast/dream screen. True, the screen is one of the most stable elements of the cinematic institution. As Stephen Heath notes, for instance, "it is important that the Lumière brothers should set the screen as they do in the Grand Café and not with the audience on either side of a translucent screen, that cinema architecture should take its forms in consequence, that there should be no feeling of machinery to the side of or beyond the screen, that the screen should be one of the most stable elements in cinema's history . . ."[47] But institutional and psychic stability, however much they are connected, are not identical. If the screen is as stable a component of the classical cinema as Metz's and Baudry's theories claim, then one assumes that its function remains fixed, "invisible" within the institution of cinema, and that the visual and narrative codes of the dominant cinema work to maintain the screen as the unproblematized ground for projection. Following this logic, one would have to conclude that films such as *The Big Sleep* are either aberrations or subversive exceptions to the rule of the classical cinema, neither of which is the case.

Theorists such as Baudry and Metz replicate that stability. Put another way, the stability of the screen is as crucial to their articulations of the cinematic subject as it is to the institutional exhibition of films. Given the indebtedness to Lacanian psychoanalysis that informs their work, it is perhaps surprising, however, that the screen is defined in such absolute, fixed terms. Noting that discussions of the "look" tend toward a not only rigid but also impossible separation of the (male) gaze from the (female) image, de Lauretis observes that film theorists in this confusion have followed Lacan and forgotten Freud.[48] That is to say that the entire arsenal of cinematic desire and identification is ascribed, via Lacan, to the gaze, which is ascribed to lack, which is ascribed to castration; the pleasure of film viewing is thus the desire for the phallus, and no matter how many times feminists are scolded into remembering that the phallus and the penis are not the same, the slippage from biological masculinity to psychic trajectory occurs with remarkable frequency.[49]

While I do not wish in any way to "rescue" Lacan, several comments in *The Four Fundamental Concepts of Psychoanalysis* on the construction of the gaze, specifically in relationship to painting, bear directly on the functioning of the gaze in cinema, particularly in relation to the screen. On the one hand, Lacan identifies the screen as having a kind of regulatory function insofar as the relationship between the gaze and its object is concerned:

> If, by being isolated, an effect of lighting dominates us, if, for example, a beam of light directing our gaze so captivates us that it appears as a milky cone and prevents us from seeing what it illuminates, the mere fact of introducing into this field a small screen, which cuts into that which is illuminated without being seen, makes the milky light retreat, as it were, into the shadow, and allows the object it concealed to emerge.

At the same time, the screen evokes a quite different function: "that which forms the mediation from one [the picture] to the other [the gaze], that which is between the two, is something of another nature than geometral, optical space, something that plays an exactly reverse role, which operates, not because it can be traversed, but on the contrary because it is opaque—I mean the screen."[50]

The screen has an ambivalent status insofar as it both "positions" and obscures simultaneously. Describing the work of the screen and frame in film, Stephen Heath notes how the cinema "holds the subject" between "negativity and coherence, flow and image," and observes that "the 'screen' as it figures in various Lacanian diagrams has a similar kind of ambivalence: locus of a potentially ludic relation between the subject and its imaginary captation, and the sign of the barrier—the slide—across the subject and object of desire . . ."[51] In similar terms, Shoshana Felman has suggested that in *Television,* the written version of Lacan's appearance on French television in a program entitled "Psychoanalysis," "Lacan invites us not to take 'the little screen' for granted, but to rethink through it, provocatively, his complex structure of address."[52] Most psychoanalytic film theory conceptualizes the screen in dominant cinema only in its function as the support for the fictions of transparence. As Felman says, "As spectators, we are literally called into the screen and represented there as caught. The screen screens insofar as it reflects our act of seeing as complete, but does not reflect the screen within our gaze."[53] What would it mean to "reflect the screen within our gaze"? Felman uses the phrase "bear witness," the screen bearing witness simultaneously to the necessity of the fiction of completeness and wholeness and to its impossibility.

To be sure, Felman is addressing the screen not just as a function of the split between the gaze and vision, but as a complex figure of the analytic enterprise. It is easy to argue that in dominant practices, such as the cinema, the screen is quite literally covered over, bound within the conventions of narrative and visual coherence—if not rendered invisible, then at least neutralized. In this respect, the screen would be like virtually every other aspect of the classical Hollywood cinema, bound within that oedipal logic which Raymond Bellour and others have postulated as central to cinematic pleasure: "in the regulated order of the spectacle, the return of an immemorial and everyday state which the subject experiences in his dreams, and for which the cinematic apparatus renews the desire."[54] But in the films examined thus far, the figure of the screen does emerge more on the side of "bearing witness" than on that of containment and regulation, and thus loosens up the tightly woven threads of masculine and oedipal fantasy.[55]

Within the present context, I want to stress that in psychoanalytic theories of the cinematic apparatus, the screen emerges as something of a symptom, precisely because of its totally unproblematized status as ground, a symptom not only of the failure to account for sexual difference, but also of a refusal to engage with ambivalence in any kind of signifying capacity. The stakes of this "blind spot" in psychoanalytic theory are high for feminism, since so much feminist analysis of film turns simultaneously on the impossibility of any productive ruptures in the seams of classical cinema, and the exclusive focus on the gaze as the site of virtually all agency. Quite obviously, no one can ignore the function of the look in film, but the facile division of the (male) gaze from the (female) object of the gaze has led to a kind of simplistic either/or—woman either foregrounds her objectification or "returns" the gaze. Some of the most interesting examples of women's alternative cinema which will be examined in the next chapter take as a central figure the screen—not "rather" than the gaze, but in relationship to it. The complex function of the screen must be taken into account, then, to better theorize some examples of women's cinema, but also, and perhaps most important, to better theorize just what it is women filmmakers have sought alternatives to.

I have read the function of the screen in *The Big Sleep* "backwards," to the foregrounding of the screen in the early film *Uncle Josh at the Moving Picture Show*. Several other practices of "foregrounding" the screen could be traced back to *Uncle Josh at the Moving Picture Show* as well. The rudimentary "film-within-a-film" structure suggests an early version of those films where characters act out their fantasy of entering into the fictional world of the film, for example, Buster Keaton in *Sherlock, Jr.* (1924) or Mia Farrow in Woody Allen's *The Purple Rose of Cairo* (1985). Echoes of *Uncle Josh* can also be seen in those films where scenes "at the movies" are represented to suggest a foregrounding of other visual and narrative components of the film, including the Disney cartoon of "Who Killed Cock Robin?" against which the heroine of Hitchcock's *Sabotage* (1936) erupts in simultaneous laughter and grief over the loss of her young brother.

The function of the screen that I have isolated in *Uncle Josh at the Moving Picture Show, The Cheat,* and *The Big Sleep* as the embodiment of ambivalence is quite different from other representations of screen surfaces which function, rather, as reflections in miniature of the cinema. I am thinking here specifically of two kinds of films in which screen surfaces play a role quite different from the one I have described. Mary Ann Doane, in *The Desire to Desire,* discusses two films which contain scenes of literal film projection, scenes in which the woman is identified with the screen surface, and the entire process of projection is a representation of the power of the man over her. The two films in question, *Caught* (Max Ophuls, 1949) and *Rebecca* (Alfred Hitchcock, 1940), belong to what Doane calls the "paranoid" category of the woman's film, and in each case a scene "at the movies" (a screening of an industrial film in the case of *Caught,* home movies in the case of *Rebecca*) condenses the impossibility of female spectatorship except as affirmation of the power and authority of the male gaze.

Unlike the screen surfaces in the films discussed thus far, the screen in *Caught* and *Rebecca* is but one element in a scenario of spectatorship that is absolutely polarized along gender lines. The difference here concerns not just the

LEEDS METROPOLITAN UNIVERSITY LIBRARY

ways in which screen surfaces are evoked, but also and especially the context in which they occur. The projection scenes discussed by Doane "mobilize the elements of a specular system which has historically served the interests of male spectatorship. . . ."[56] While the projection scenes in the films discussed in this chapter suggest ambivalence rather than polarity, nonetheless they prove Doane's point in a kind of circuitous way, since the ambivalence of the screen as simultaneous threshold and obstacle is evoked in these films uniquely in relationship to *male* ambivalence. In each case, the woman retains her function as image and surface. Yet there is an important distinction to be made between the functions of these projection scenes in relationship to the economies of homosexual and heterosexual desire. Although they do so in radically different ways, each of the films discussed in this chapter manifests a trouble in the realm of heterosexual desire and resolution. The screen surface thus becomes a nodal point in the representation of the difficulty of closure in any simplistic sense.

Another category of films in which screen surfaces play a central role is those whose subject matter is the cinema itself—films, that is, which take as their central premise a demonstration and exploration of the dynamics of cinematic desire and representation. In a famous scene at the beginning of Ingmar Bergman's *Persona* (1966), a young boy glides his hands over a screenlike surface upon which are projected huge close-ups of women's faces that merge into one another. While it is impossible to assign the boy a precise or single narrative function in the film, his infantile apprehension of the projections of female faces does correspond to the fascination demonstrated throughout *Persona* with the female body as both image and screen.

Michael Powell's *Peeping Tom* (1960) is concerned at every level with the manifestations of male spectatorial desire in its most extremely sadistic forms through the character of Mark Lewis, the filmmaker-within-the-film who is compelled to murder women and film them simultaneously. At the beginning of the film, we see Lewis as he executes a film/murder—first, as it ostensibly happens, then as the filmmaker watches the film in his home. The scene in his home alternates between shots where the film-within-the-film coincides with the screen of the film we are watching, and shots of the film-within-the-film as watched by Mark Lewis. As extreme close-ups of the woman's face—with her gaping mouth particularly foregrounded—appear on the screen, Lewis stands up in front of the screen and then collapses in his chair, suggesting the simultaneity of sexual release and identification with the woman as screen.[57]

In the course of the film, a potential relationship develops with the young woman who lives with her blind mother on the floor below Mark. At one point, the mother comes to Mark's apartment and asks that he "show" her his films. Mark projects the film of his latest murder, and he and the mother stand before the screen. She reaches out her hand to touch the image of the woman's face, and Mark throws himself at the screen in despair. The irony of the blind woman who possesses keen insight into Mark's condition is fairly obvious here.[58] More interesting in the context of the present discussion is the crisis provoked when a female figure looms large on both sides of the screen. Indeed, the split between the dominant paternal voice—Mark's scientist/filmmaker father who made of his son an object of study, and whose invading eye is imprinted in his son's desire to film and to annihilate simultaneously—and the unattainable maternal image is conveyed at the film's conclusion. Mark commits suicide by thrusting himself upon the knife that he used to kill his victims, while he looks at the mirror in which he forced his victims to witness their own terror, thus, as Linda Williams puts it, "uniting voyeur and exhibitionist in a one-man movie of which he is both director and star."[59]

After the suicide, we hear the voice of Mark's father booming from one of the ubiquitous tape recorders in Mark's apartment, and Mark as a child saying "Good night, Daddy. Hold me." The camera moves from the tape recorder, to the projector with the film spinning on its take-up reel, to, finally, the screen, half in light, half in darkness. If *Peeping Tom* may be said to delineate the centrality of male voyeurism in the cinema, the screen functions in the film to suggest the different levels on which Mark desires not voyeuristic separation from the woman but rather regressive fusion with the female image—an image, that is, to "hold me." *Peeping Tom* in many ways demonstrates Metz and Baudry's theories of regressive desire and the cinema, and the desire thus delineated in Powell's film foregrounds in its turn the extent to which those theories are, precisely, very particular fantasies of how the cinema functions. Yet for all its closeness to the regressive desire postulated by Metz and Baudry, *Peeping Tom* suggests that the man's presumably heterosexual desire is inevitably complicit with a desire for the father, in which the boundaries between identification and erotic attachment are not clearly delineated.

In the following chapter I will turn to a group of films by women directors in which the figure of the screen is a central device for the representation of a number of difficult and complex issues, which, while raised in relation to women's specific relationship to cinema and culture, touch nonetheless on the issues that emerge in the films discussed in this chapter around the figure of the screen. It is tempting to draw two very different kinds of conclusions from the deployment of the screen in *The Big Sleep, The Cheat,* and *Uncle Josh at the Moving Picture Show;* and to be sure, the fact that this discussion serves in some ways as a prelude to a discussion of women's films tempers how those conclusions will be drawn. Confronted with these two conclusions, however, I find myself in an ambivalent position, since the more clearly feminist one strikes me as too pat, while the one that is more problematic in feminist terms is too aligned with a position of male subjectivity to be of much use in making the transition from the classical Hollywood cinema to women's cinema.

To wit: In each of the "screen" films discussed in this chapter, the ambivalent function of the screen as simultaneous passage and obstacle displaces attention away from the logic of the male look/female object, and engages a relationship between male likes—Uncle Josh and the projectionist, the American businessman and the Asian man, Marlowe and Harry Jones. It is tempting, therefore, to read this construction of screens as a paradoxical laying bare of a structure that Luce Irigaray has designated as central to patriarchal economies: "all economic organization is homosexual. That of desire as well, even the desire for women. Woman exists only as an occasion for mediation, transaction, transition, transference, between man and his fellow man, between man and himself."[60] While there is more than a small degree of truth in the analogy between what Irigaray says and how these films function, it is "truth" that is precisely the problem. For in the name of such a truth, the ambivalent function of the screen surface is lost; the sense of the simultaneity of transparency and translucence, the one always holding the other in check, is sacrificed.

A central object of inquiry in what is commonly referred to as "French theory," and specifically that French theory which articulates what Alice Jardine calls "gynesis," the valorization of the feminine, is those in-between spaces, tentative boundaries that put into question the very possibility of demarcation.[61] One well-known figure of that in-between is the hymen, which in its very etymology articulates contradictory meanings of marriage (archaically) and vaginal membrane—of, that is, both union and separation. In "The Double Session," Jacques Derrida reads the function of the hymen in "Mimique," a text by Mallarmé which contemplates the gestures of a mime replaying the murder of his wife. Mallarmé writes: " 'The scene illustrates but the idea, not any actual action, in a hymen (out of which flows Dream), tainted with vice yet sacred, between desire and fulfillment, perpetration and remembrance. . . .' "[62] Derrida's reading of the hymen is evocative of the screen:

> Among diverse possibilities, let us take this: the Mime does not read his role; he is also read *by* it. Or at least he is both read and reading, written and writing, between the two, in the suspense of the hymen, at once screen and mirror. As soon as a mirror is interposed in some way, the simple opposition between activity and passivity, between production and the product, or between all concepts in -er and all concepts in -ed (signifier/signified, imitator/imitated, structure/structured, etc.), becomes impracticable and too formally weak to encompass the graphics of the hymen, its spider web, and the play of its eyelids.[63]

That it should be the female membrane which embodies and disembodies simultaneously suggests what has become by now a familiar feminist discomfort with the celebration of the feminine in Derrida's writing—the suspicion that the body of the woman supplies the metaphor for the male subject's indecidability, with women's bodies left once again subjected to the cold speculum of the male theorist.[64] But perhaps, insofar as the screen in classical cinema is concerned, there is room for both the female membrane as "read" by a male subject, and the feminist discomfort with the reading. In noting the kinds of feminist questions that might be asked of Derrida's reading of Mallarmé, Alice Jardine includes one with a decidedly Irigarayan tinge: "we could ask why Derrida silences the male homosexual potentialities for this Mallarméan/Derridean 'double play.' . . ."[65] Put another way, Irigaray's reading of heterosexuality as ruse and Derrida's reading of the hymen need not constitute an either/or choice insofar as the figure of the screen is concerned; indeed, the ambivalence of the screen in the films examined in this chapter may perhaps best be assessed, not by the tension between the two presumably stable entities of homosexual and heterosexual desire, but rather by the contradiction between the indecidability of the hymen and the "truth" of male homotextual desire.

In the case of women filmmakers, for whom the hymen can "work" only through a most problematic double displacement, the simultaneous celebration of "woman" and the feminist distrust of such celebrations become decidedly more difficult. Indeed, what happens when the *female* subject—whether as filmmaker, protagonist, or spectator—engages with the ambivalence of the screen? Since the number of classical Hollywood films shaped by the itinerary of female agency is limited, it comes as no big surprise that there are even fewer still in which the screen enters into play in complex ways in relation to female desire. In a recent commercial film, however, there is a kind of screen play comparable to what we have seen in *The Big Sleep,* in relation not just to a female protagonist but to her complicated relationship with another woman, a relationship that is decidedly homotextual.

In *Black Widow* (dir. Bob Rafelson, 1987), Debra Winger plays the part of Alex, a Justice Department investigator who becomes intrigued, and gradually obsessed, by a woman who assumes an identity in order to attract a wealthy husband, and then kills him before moving onto yet another disguise and another husband. At two crucial moments in the film, Alex's relationship to Catherine (played by Theresa Russell) is depicted through the foregrounding of a screen. Early in the film, when Alex has collected a series of photographs of Catherine in various identities and with different husbands, she projects the images side by side on the blank wall of her apartment. Alex approaches the makeshift screen with a considerable aura of wonder about her, if not at the zero degree of Uncle

Josh, then at the very least with a sense of discovery of a heretofore unknown (or unacknowledged) fascination. She assumes a variety of positions in relation to the images of Catherine. At one point she stands in the position of a husband, at another her hands touch the image in a way strikingly similar to the boy at the beginning of *Persona,* and finally she poses her body in such a way that her hand literally blends with the image of Catherine's hand. This screen play isolates and combines with dizzying rapidity three modes of desire: substitution (for the husband), merging (in the child's fantasy of fusion), and narcissistic identification. While the slides are still flashing on the wall, Alex moves to the bathroom and looks at herself in the mirror, and after turning back to look at the slides again, she pulls back her hair, as if attempting to imitate the appearance of Catherine. The substitution of the mirror for the screen situates Alex's fascination within the realm of the "surveyed female," but the traces of other kinds of desire are in no way dissipated.

Later in the film, after Alex has followed Catherine to Seattle, the site of her latest conquest, Alex visits the local police station to present her evidence. The scene opens with a shot of a group of policemen watching a film entitled "Survival Shooting Techniques" on a small portable movie screen. The projected image is not properly aligned with the small screen, and the men yell for the screen to be fixed. The sound track of the film contains gunfire and music, and as the camera moves forward toward the police officer's office located behind the screen, and separated from the makeshift "screening room" by a glass window, we hear an authoritative voice-over in the film-within-the-film warning that "just because you can't see a suspect doesn't mean he can't see you." Inside the office, a frustrated Alex cannot convince the police officer with her evidence. She stands in front of his desk, and behind her we see, in a kind of "rear projection," the continuation of the movie. Framed by the screen and the incredulous police officer, Alex is as improperly aligned with the law as the projected image was with the screen.

Yet a connection is drawn between Alex and the law, on the one hand, and Alex in her desire for Catherine, on the other. And it will be the work of the film to draw the projected image—Alex's fascination with Catherine—into proper alignment with the law. *Black Widow* is an example of a film that wants to have it both ways; that is, a film which wants to articulate desire between two women and yet remain within the conventions of classical narrative by drawing a line between "normal" and "abnormal" behavior. Hence, when Alex follows Catherine to Hawaii after the Seattle husband is disposed of, a number of more conventional devices of the representation of cinematic desire come into play— most notably, a male surrogate voyeur (a private detective hired by both women) and a male love interest, Paul, shared by both women. In this section of the film,

Catherine's capacity for manipulation is marked all the more strongly (she kills the private detective, and arranges for her next husband-to-be to sleep with Alex so as to facilitate her own marriage to him). In addition, several scenes are quite explicit in their delineation of lesbian attraction.

These disruptions are "managed," as it were, in a somewhat silly conclusion whereby Paul's death is faked, Alex is arrested, and Catherine unknowingly acknowledges all in a final visit to Alex in jail. Throughout the film, there is the (homophobic) suggestion that Alex's obsession with Catherine is the result of her own absence of a social life—i.e., "a man." While the film does not go so far as to pair Alex with an appropriate male significant other at the conclusion of the film, it does seal her marriage with the law, while Catherine is escorted off to prison. *Black Widow* may offer pleasures that are more frequently marginalized or invisible in commercial mainstream film, but it remains a film wholly part of the institutions of commercial cinema. At the same time that *Black Widow* suggests female investment in the processes of ambivalent identification, the possibilities of that investment are closed down with something of a vengeance. I turn now to a group of films that explore, on several levels, how relationships between women function in the creation of alternatives to patriarchal institutions, and how the figure of the screen might function as a trope for women's cinema that refuses to be married to the law.

2. Screen Tests

Black Widow **demonstrates the difficulty of reconciling the**
demands of resolution in the classical Hollywood cinema with figures of ambivalence. Most significantly, *Black Widow* demonstrates the radically different
stakes of ambivalence when the subject is a woman. In this chapter, I will
examine four contemporary films by women directors which might seem, initially to have little in common—Helke Sander's *The All-Round Reduced Personality
(Redupers)* (West Germany, 1977), Julie Dash's *Illusions* (U.S., 1982), Patricia
Rozema's *I've Heard the Mermaids Singing* (Canada, 1987), and Yvonne Rainer's *The Man Who Envied Women* (U.S., 1986). As the different sites of
geographical origin suggest, these films respond to quite different cultural
contexts, and even the two films from the U.S. are radically different in this
sense. There is, however, a thematic relationship between the four films, in that
they take as their central premise the relationship between women and image-
making: the female protagonists of *Redupers* and *I've Heard the Mermaids
Singing* are still photographers; *Illusions* is about two women who work in the
film industry, one as an executive and the other as a "dub" singer; and *The Man
Who Envied Women,* while less invested than the other films in the conventions
of plot and protagonists, focuses as well on the relationship between women and

49

image-making. In other words, these films share a preoccupation with the difficulty and complexity of the relationship between women and cinematic representation.

These four films explore the particular instances of that relationship, through women's "alternatives" to the bureacracy of both the state and the art world *(Redupers)*, race and racism in relation to the commercial cinema *(Illusions)*, sexual identity and the commercialization of art *(I've Heard the Mermaids Singing)*, and intellectual discourse and gentrification *(The Man Who Envied Women)*. All of the films discussed in this book are preoccupied with the relationship between female subjectivity and the cinema; what makes this group of films distinct is, first, their attention to the institutionalized forces that shape any attempts to create female alternatives to patriarchal cinema. This is not to say that this group of films is more "political" than others to be discussed in subsequent chapters; rather, these four films are particularly attentive to the pressures of institutions insofar as they regulate the very possibility of alternative networks and representations.

These films negotiate the tensions between ambivalence and contradiction, on the one hand, and the political institutions which tend to render ambivalence moot, on the other. They articulate a pointed ambiguity about the relationship between the mainstream and the margins, an ambivalence which takes the form of a narrative structure that simultaneously acknowledges and critiques the conventions of the classical cinema. Such an impressive body of feminist literature has been devoted to the exploration of how women filmmakers have reread, deconstructed, or otherwise put into question the codes and conventions of the classical Hollywood cinema, that it might seem a bit disingenuous to isolate these particular films as doing something which, as some feminist critics might put it, is the most basic definition of any alternative women's cinema.

The most dominant critical assumption operative in feminist readings of the classical cinema has been that if the Hollywood cinema is structured upon the hierarchy of the gaze, then women filmmakers will "return" the gaze. But feminist criticism that focuses primarily on the "return of the gaze" runs directly into the limitations of the assumption that the classical cinema is governed exclusively by the sexual hierarchy of the look. As I have suggested in the previous chapter, the lure of film spectacle is not simply the possession of the image, but rather the simultaneity of mastery and the breakdown of the oppositions upon which mastery is based, of merging and disavowal, of passage and obstruction. Figures of the screen in *Uncle Josh at the Moving Picture Show, The Cheat,* and *The Big Sleep* portray this tension, the contradictory ways in which film spectacle operates. Finally, then, what connects the four films I will discuss in this chapter is the trope of the ambivalent screen surface. *Redupers,*

Illusions, I've Heard the Mermaids Singing, and *The Man Who Envied Women* differ in their inquiries into the convergence and nonconvergence of women and the classical cinema, but in each of these films, the figure of the screen emerges as the embodiment of ambivalence, as the site at which cinema both resists and gives support to the representation of female agency and female desire.

There is another common structure in each of these films, and that is the foregrounding of the female voice as it embodies the complexities of female narration. In *Illusions* and *I've Heard the Mermaids Singing,* the voice is identified with the female protagonist, whereas in *Redupers* the female voice-over is anonymous, thus implicitly affiliated not only with the heroine of the film but with a variety of other sources as well. *The Man Who Envied Women* is undoubtedly the most radical experimentation to date of the female voice in relation to female narration, since the voice is quite literally disembodied. Recently, long-overdue critical attention has been paid to the function of the voice in film, and in women's cinema in particular.[1] In this group of films, the female voice does destabilize the conventional symmetry whereby the register of vocal authority is presumed to be male, the realm of the visible, female; but more significant are the narrative strategies created in these films in which the female voice functions in relationship to the figure of the screen.

Redupers tells the story of Edda Chiemnijewski (portrayed by Helke Sander herself), a resident of West Berlin, the mother of a young daughter, a free-lance photographer, and a member of a women's photography group. As a free-lance photographer, Edda is expected to produce photojournalism. Early in the film we see her as she photographs a state-sponsored party for elderly citizens. She stands on a stage, and in her "official" capacity photographs a speaker who mouths platitudes about "one big, happy family," while spectators look on. So much for the kind of photographs Edda is paid to produce. Within her professional work, Edda looks for other possibilities that depart from the official, professional routes. And so, in the next shot, we see her talking to the elderly women, conversing with them about the social rituals of parties. In her official capacity, Edda conveys official trivia, performing a rote gesture that is of a piece with the passive audience response. But in the space which she manages to open up a bit, Edda comes down off the stage to have a chat with the women. This juxtaposition of images suggests the possibility of the everyday mode of narration embodied in chitchat to ironize the official spectacle of taking care of the elderly—in other words, narrative problematizes spectacle.

Redupers opens with a lengthy tracking shot of the city of Berlin, showing us the wall, buildings, and passersby. The movement slows down at some points, and rounds a corner, making clear that we are observing the city as if from the vantage point of a car in motion. We hear a variety of urban noises, including airplanes and automobiles, and we hear bits and pieces of radio programs in a variety of languages. The beginning of the film introduces us, then, to the public sphere of Berlin, a public sphere made up of detached voices speaking in different tongues, a wall that was (at the time the film was made) as naturalized a part of the urban environment as office buildings and graffiti, and the constantly moving perspective of a car in motion. For the moment, the spectator is transported by the camera, afforded no depth but only lateral and continuous movement. Similar tracking shots of the city reappear throughout the film, and the public sphere of the city is evoked throughout as well by the radios which are a continuous element of the sound track. Of particular importance to *Redupers* is the continuous return to the space of the city, and the attendant desire to read that urban public sphere in a critical way.

When the tracking shots are repeated in the course of the film, they are most frequently accompanied by the voice of a female narrator. This narrator's voice is as unanchored in time and space as the numerous radio voices heard throughout the film. Radio voices insinuate themselves into the spaces and cracks between everyday activities; the radio allows you to go about your business and still listen to the news. The voice of the female narrator also insinuates itself into the cracks of everyday life. But the narrator differs from the radio voices in that she functions to articulate both private and public voices. The female voice-over personalizes the tracking shots of the city, describing the history of the women's group and the strategies the women have to use to get their project funded. The voice also functions as a narrator in the strictest sense of the term when it introduces and summarizes scenes. At an antirape demonstration, for example, the voice explains that Edda does not think that enough of her socially conscious photographs are purchased, and thus in this context the voice functions as a third-person narrator, perceiving events from an unspecified, external vantage point.

Yet at the same time, the female voice seems to narrate from "inside," and frequently the female voice slides between the registers of objectivity and subjectivity. Over a series of still photographs of a conference that Edda is photographing, for instance, the voice says: "For years Edda had been struck by the following: that the aesthetic imagination was the passion for things alien. The sorrows and fortunes of others, the fate of a leather ball. Passion for that without meaning. One should at least be able to choose freely those things alien." Here the voice articulates fantasies and desires that are repressed within the single image. And the voice also articulates the kind of facts that are repressed within the image as well, for in the same sequence, it describes in detail Edda's monthly income and expenses. The female voice in *Redupers* does not provide authoritative commentary, however; rather, the voice emphasizes shifting perspective and a plurality of vantage points.

While the female voice-over is one of the most important elements in *Redupers,* its function is better assessed in relationship to the larger preoccupation in the film with permeability and connection. *Redupers* is concerned primarily, not with the female *voice* as the most appropriate metaphor for a feminist definition of image-making and representation, but rather with the metaphor of the screen, both in the sense of a frame of vision and as the common denominator of the various barriers—sonoric, visual, ideological—that determine patterns of meaning and opposition. In this sense, of course, the encounter between a group of women artists and the city of Berlin becomes quite emblematic. Edda's group got money for a photographic project, the female narrator's voice explains, because there was pressure on the government to prove its interest in women's issues, but also—and primarily—because this group applied for less money than any other.

At a meeting of the women's group, Edda shows a series of photographs that illustrate the similarities between East and West Berlin: an owner's pride in his car, a subway, graffiti. In each pairing of images, there is in fact little to distinguish the capitalist from the socialist public sphere. Although the question is asked in the film (somewhat ironically) whether the worker's state changes much in the status of women, it would be mistaken to see *Redupers* as a film that seeks to underscore hopeless similarities between capitalism and socialism. The point, rather, is that the Berlin Wall creates a false dichotomy between two entities united by their urban common denominator. For Edda, the wall is ideological to the extent that it is symptomatic of a mode of consciousness in which slashes and divisions mark absolute and hierarchical differences. "Where does the wall have openings?" Edda asks, and she holds up a photograph of two apartment buildings on either side of the wall between which "full eye-contact is still possible."

The two major projects which Edda's group executes in the course of the film are, precisely, attempts to "screen" the Berlin Wall, to shake it free of its obstinate permanence, to transform a rigidified "image" into a surface which functions in complex and contradictory ways, rather than as a purely referential structure of one-dimensional meaning. Their projects evolve from their perception of "chinks" in the Berlin Wall. They take a huge mounted photograph of the wall, with a single car parked next to it, to a variety of places in the city, and finally to the site photographed, creating a peculiar mise-en-abyme effect (see Figure 7). The women also set up a curtain on one of the platforms from which

Figure 7. Helke Sander's *Redupers* (Museum of Modern Art)

West Berliners can gaze onto the East. The opening of the curtain enhances the act of seeing, as if the sight of East Berlin were indeed a spectacle to be eagerly consumed by the West.

On one level, these projects correspond to a kind of feminist aesthetics of everyday life. Thus the city of Berlin becomes a huge apartment in need of tasteful decoration, and billboards become picture frames containing the city's equivalent of family photographs. Curtains transform the gaping space of a platform into a window, so that looking from West to East imitates the conditions of looking from inside to outside. There is a moment in the film when Edda is seen in her apartment pulling back large curtains to look outside; the match between this "domestic" image and the mise-en-scène on the Berlin Wall is unmistakable.

The risk of a feminist aesthetics of the everyday is in romanticizing, rather than contesting, the conditions of female servitude and the attendant split between the private and the public; it is the risk, in other words, of failing to address the problem of recuperation. But in *Redupers,* there is no sense in which the women triumph in a radical new vision of the wall or the city; theirs is no "alternative" vision in any simple sense. Rather, the risk of co-optation is ominously present. The women move the billboard from one site to another out of frustration, not out of commitment to a shifting signifier, and while the women want to execute the billboard project on a much larger scale, they worry at the same time that their images will be dwarfed and contained by the proliferation of billboard advertising. Similarly, there is something about the curtained platform that reiterates, rather than challenges, the division between West and East Berlin, with the attendant implication alluded to above—the East as a spectacle to be consumed by the West.

Despite all of the evidence that the film offers of the ways in which the wall is less absolute a dividing line than it might appear, *Redupers* does not suggest that the desired chinks, eye contact, or analogies are in any way easy or simplistic alternatives. Far from compromising the feminist visions offered by the film, this is, it seems to me, one of its most compelling features. For *Redupers* is informed by the recognition that fantasies of interconnectedness and permeability exist within a context where such fantasies can easily have unintended results, where they can backfire. I have suggested that in the group of films discussed in the previous chapter, the screen emerges as a figure that embodies simultaneously the possibility of separation and connection, of obstacle and threshold. The Berlin Wall functions in these terms in *Redupers,* but as a critical figure of ambivalence. The film itself articulates that ambivalence in one of its preferred techniques, the tracking shot of the city and in particular of the wall, a tracking shot that embodies both distance and contemplation.

The preoccupation with the Berlin Wall in *Redupers* suggests a feminist desire for a representation of the contradictory movements embodied in the screen. In one of the most unusual scenes in the film, this desire extends beyond the specific social and cultural connotations of the Berlin Wall. Throughout *Redupers,* there are citations from a variety of sources, and the writings of Christa Wolf are particularly significant and privileged texts. However, the most unusual quotation in the film occurs when three small screens appear, one after the other, over the image of a newspaper. In each screen we see a segment from a contemporary woman's film: a close-up of a woman from Ursula Reuter-Christiansen's *The Executioner* (Denmark, 1972); the beach scene from Yvonne Rainer's *Film about a Woman Who* . . . (U.S., 1974), in which a man, a woman, and a child rearrange themselves as if for a series of snapshots; and a kitchen scene from Valie Export's *Invisible Adversaries* (West Germany, 1976), in which a woman cuts up a fish and insects and opens a refrigerator to reveal a baby inside.

These films are concerned not only with the juncture between the rituals of everyday life and female subjectivity, but also with an examination of the cinematic and cultural codes through which such a juncture can be examined.

The only sound heard during the segment is the female voice-over which announces: "Obsessed by daily life as other women see it." The voice continues, quoting a letter from "Aunt Kate Chiemnijewski." The letter contains the kind of fragmented logic sometimes typical of letters, suggesting quite strongly a fore-grounded link between this particular narration of everyday life and the language of dreams. Like the previous sequence, in which Edda works on photographs while she listens to the radio, this scene juxtaposes the "news" (though the newspaper here is distanced, "cited," far more than the radio is) with women's images (similarly, they are much more cited in a very literal sense, as they are drawn from outside the immediate context of the film). The newspaper becomes an object quite literally read between the lines, but more important, it is transformed into a surface, a screen, while the miniature movie screens recall the billboards which the women want to cover with their photographs of the city.

It does not require too much imagination to see photography and the cinema as interchangeable insofar as the film's interrogation of women and image-making is concerned, particularly since *Redupers* features Helke Sander herself in the role of Edda. Yet while the image track, in this particular scene of quotation, draws attention to a contemporary context for women's filmmaking, the sound track emphasizes further the "fiction" of the film, but in a letter that "could be" the filmmaker's own. On one level, the film draws connections between the sophisticated, experimental film practice of the three directors who are cited, and the everyday narration of the fictional aunt. But on another level, the film steps out of its fictional context in this scene more obviously than at any other point.

This may seem a peculiar assertion about a film that is so caught up in the interchange between the fictive and the real, particularly insofar as Sander's own identity as a feminist filmmaker and critic is concerned; but it is in this scene that the sharpest break, the most abrupt shift, in the film occurs. True, *Redupers* is characterized overall by a sense of fragmentation, but its various pieces and fragments cohere around the cityscape of Berlin and the women's desire to speculate on the connections between East and West. The films cited here have no visible or apparent connection with either the cityscape or the women's activities—except in the larger sense that all are concerned with the artifice of cinematic conventions (particularly marked in the segment from Yvonne Rain-er's film) and their relationship to female activities. This scene is, as well, the portion of the film that stands apart for its visual experimentation; that is, the citation of women's cinema inspires another mise-en-scène, another scene, another representation of image and text.

Visually, the quotations are most striking in terms of the aesthetics of the screen surface: the newspaper itself becomes a screen (emphasized in particular by the disappearance of the three miniature screens at the scene's close, leaving the newspaper as the surface of the image, with a subsequent fade to a dark, blank screen), and the appearance of the three screens dramatizes the definition of the cinema as the illusion of depth and pure surface simultaneously. That three screens appear makes for a somewhat asymmetrical structure. It is tempting to assume that the blank space which one expects to be occupied by a fourth screen functions as a space of projection for the viewer. Yet it is a space which, by virtue of its blankness, emphasizes all the more that contradictory nature of the cinema.[2]

This citation of three women's films implies a feminist desire for affiliation. Yet the nature of the citation suggests simultaneously that this desire can never be a one-dimensional connectedness, an affirmation of a sororal model of cinematic cross-referencing to substitute as a simple alternative for the presumably patriarchal model of oedipal rivalry and claims for originality.[3] For the citation is as difficult to "read" as the newsprint that forms the background for the individual screens, so that the fact of allusion becomes more significant than the specific genealogy drawn. Put another way, the style of the citation is most significant, for it is "thick" in several senses of the term—in the obvious sense that there are several levels to the citation, but also in the sense that the very tissue of the citation is the screen surface that both reflects and obscures. This scene condenses the preoccupation with the difficulty of threshold space evidenced throughout *Redupers*.

Particularly significant in this respect are the quotations of the writings of Christa Wolf, not only because Wolf herself is so preoccupied with the difficulty and the necessity of connection, but also because the cinema has functioned, in Wolf's writing, as an emblematic form of a reified consciousness. In "The Reader and the Writer," Wolf says: "We seem to need the help and approval of the imagination in our lives; it means playing with the possibilities open to us. But something else goes on inside us at the same time, daily, hourly, a furtive process hard to avoid, a hardening, petrifying, habituation, that attacks the memory in particular." Wolf speaks of "miniatures," the easily summoned bits and pieces of past experience which we have arranged in our minds as if on shelves, and film belongs to the realm of miniatures. Writing, however, is a "strenuous movement" requiring an active engagement with the past rather than the observation of miniatures. Wolf writes: "Prose should try to be unfilmable. It should give up the dangerous work of circulating miniatures and putting finished pieces together. It should be incorruptible in its insistence on the one and only experience and not violate the experiences of others; but it should give them the courage of their own experiences."[4]

It is tempting to see Wolf's "miniatures" as corresponding to the classical, dominant cinema, but in Sander's appropriation of Wolf's writing, the tendency toward "miniatures" seems to be constantly negotiated, and this is a part of alternative cinema as well. The women in the photography group are wary of co-optation; they are concerned that their photographs will also become yet another means of "circulating miniatures." Even the citation of other women filmmakers resists ironically the miniaturization of film, by a proliferation of miniatures. The dialogue with Christa Wolf that is entertained in *Redupers* is a crucial component of the film's screen metaphor. At the film's conclusion, we see an image of Edda walking into the distance. The female voice-over reads from an essay by Christa Wolf on diaries:

> I don't want to go any further. Anyone who asks about a person's diary must accept the fact more is concealed than said. It was not possible to speak about plans, clearly set forth in the diary, that have arisen, been changed, dropped again, come to nothing, or were carried out, unexpectedly suddenly there, complete. And it wasn't possible to bring into focus through strenuous thought the stuff of life that was very near in time. Or the mistakes made in trying to do this. And, of course, no mention of the names that appear once or more often in the diary.[5]

Sander's film can be read on one level as an attempt to replicate the diary form of which Wolf speaks—its hesitation, its attention to questions rather than "exclamation marks," its function as "training, a means to remain active, to resist the temptation to drift into mere consumption."[6] Yet the very nature of the citation of Wolf—here as in the earlier scene of the quotation of women's films—acknowledges simultaneously the difficulty of any simple correlation between different texts and different art forms. Put another way, then, Sander's film cites Christa Wolf but at the same makes such citation "difficult," or in Wolf's words "unfilmable."

In the publicity poster for *Redupers,* the elements constituting the screen narrative of the film are condensed. Sander's face, with a wry expression, is shown in close-up. To the left of her face is the Berlin Wall, with a curtain running its entire length (evoking the women's curtain project). To the right of her face is an apartment building, suggesting one of the buildings referred to in the film where eye contact between West and East is still possible. A small piece of sky is visible, as if emanating from the crown of Sander's head. The Berlin Wall and the building would meet at an invisible vanishing point obscured by Sander's head.[7] At the conclusion of *Redupers,* there is the suggestion of depth, with Edda's disappearance into the background; but in this poster, the illusion of depth is obstructed, just as in the film there is a constant evocation of ambivalence.

Sander's "image" in this poster is as both character and film director. Her face and her look into the camera quite literally obstruct any possible meeting of the two edifices that frame the poster. Rather, the windows on the one side face onto the vast screen surface created by the curtains on the other. *Redupers* takes what has been one of the most persistent metaphors in classical film theory for the film screen, the "window on the world," and subjects it to the scrutiny of a feminist aesthetics whose most significant feature is not simple reversal—whereby the domestic, traditionally female associations of "windows" would be teased out of official film theory—but rather the exploration of ambivalence through a screen surface which can function simultaneously as surface and frame, which can make "chinks" visible while dispelling at the same time the illusion of an image which is fully present to itself.

Julie Dash's *Illusions* is a short (34 minutes) fiction film set in Hollywood in 1942. The date is significant, not only for its wartime setting but also because it is the year when the National Associaton for the Advancement of Colored People met in Hollywood, and many studio heads agreed that it was high time to include black people in greater numbers in roles both in front of and behind the camera.[8] The central character of the film is Mignon Dupree (portrayed by Lonette McKee), an extremely light-skinned black woman who has worked her way up from a secretarial to an executive position at National Studios. Dupree is passing as a white woman to the extent that—as she explains to her mother on the telephone—"they didn't ask me about it and I didn't happen to mention it. . . ." At the outset of the film, Dupree argues for film stories that deal with the lives and struggles of people in everyday situations. The studio she works for, however, is more committed to films that distract and entertain.

The plot of *Illusions* thickens with the connection between two events. First, the consequences of Mignon's position as a black woman in an industry that assumes she is white are explored in a variety of ways, primarily through the flirtatious advances of a white soldier. Her "private" life, and in particular her relationship with a black soldier overseas, are carefully hidden from view. The soldier who flirts (obnoxiously) with Mignon eventually discovers her "secret." Second, Mignon encounters another black woman working in the industry, and whose position dramatizes her own. Ester Jeeter (played by Rosanne Katon) is a singer who dubs her voice for the voices of those actresses whose own singing talents leave something to be desired. A crisis erupts at the studio when it is revealed that footage of the blonde female star of the picture in production has been shot out of sync, and the star is unavailable to reshoot the scene. Ester is called upon to substitute her voice for that of the star. Mignon and Ester strike up a friendship (Ester immediately recognizes that Mignon is black), and Mignon's recognition of herself in Ester leads her to speculate more clearly on the relationship between black women and the film industry. In a conversation with

Ester near the conclusion of the film, Mignon expresses bitterness and frustration
at the ways in which blacks are marginalized within the film industry. When she
returns to her office, she finds the soldier looking through her personal mail; he
has discovered that she is black. An angry confrontation follows, and Mignon's
frustration gives way to an affirmation of the necessity to engage with the
"illusions" of film rather than walk away from them in despair.

On one level, then, *Illusions* is a meditation on the relationship between
black women and the Hollywood cinema specifically, and in more general terms
between black women and cinematic representation that challenges and entertains simultaneously. The film begins with a shot of a figurine spinning slowly
against a black background. As the camera moves closer and closer, the object is
revealed to be an Oscar, symbol of Hollywood at its glittering best. That image is
immediately followed by a series of documentary images of World War II. If this
juxtaposition of images suggests an opposition between the gloss of Hollywood
film and the grit of documentary, it is an opposition somewhat undone by the
development of the film. For later, when Mignon looks at a photograph of Julius
(the man she hopes to marry) and his fellow soldiers, the predominantly black
faces in that image contrast with the documentary images peopled by whites

If *Illusions* thus underscores the marginalization of blacks characteristic of

Figure 8. Rosanne Katon as Ester Jeeter in Julie Dash's *Illusions*
(Women Make Movies)

any film medium—documentary or fiction—it is not entirely clear just how Mignon's own development in relationship to cinematic representation should be understood. At the beginning of the film, over the image of the Oscar, we hear a female voice—perhaps one assumed to be that of the filmmaker at this point, though later revealed to belong to Mignon—which separates action from illusion: "To direct an attack upon Hollywood would indeed be to confuse portrayal with action, the image with reality. In the beginning is not the shadow but the act, and the province of Hollywood is not action, but illusion." In the discussion that eventually takes place between Mignon and Ester, Mignon continues the same line of reasoning, although with more frustration: "People make films about themselves, what they want, what they love, what they fear most. Here we're nothing but props in their stories, musical props, or dancing props, or comic relief. I came into this world of moving shadows and I made this work for me. But I made *what* work? There isn't anything here for me. There's no joy in the seduction of images."

Finally, after her angry encounter with the soldier at the film's conclusion, Mignon does an about-face. After telling the soldier, "I want to do what you do," Mignon speaks the last words of the film: "We would meet again, Ester Jeeter and I. For it was she who helped me see beyond the shadows dancing on a white wall, to define what I had already come to know. To take action without fearing. Yes . . . I wanted to use the power of the motion pictures. For there are many stories to be told, many battles to begin."

Illusions dramatizes Julie Dash's own relationship, as a black woman director, to the film medium, and it attempts to accomplish what remains for Mignon Dupree an aspiration more than a possibility. Given the somewhat triumphant conclusion of *Illusions*—that is, Mignon's hopeful commitment to the possibilities of film to tell stories that had not been told before—it is perhaps tempting to read the film as arguing for the "positive images" approach that is so maligned in contemporary feminist and poststructuralist criticism. While I do not think that *Illusions* offers any simple formulation of the relationship between women, race, and the cinema, the film does take as its point of departure ("the province of Hollywood is not action, but illusion") and conclusion ("I wanted to use the power of the motion pictures") the gap between image and reality. All too often, the white feminist response to such a gap is to "make allowances" for this apparent plea for "better images," a response which by arguing in the name of pluralism ends up being patronizing; or simply to "recognize" that for black women—and by extension, for women who have a "different relationship" to the dominant cinema (the list usually then goes on to include other minorities, lesbians, working-class women)—the outrageous stereotypes perpetrated by the classical cinema make its conquest that more urgent.

In both cases—whether through "making allowances" or "exceptional recognition"—a film such as *Illusions* is marginalized, relegated to the realm of the
theoretically unsophisticated. I would argue, rather, that *Illusions* challenges a
feminist theory that would displace prematurely the tension between action and
illusion. Teresa de Lauretis has written of how there emerges in feminist writing
a notion of *identity* which "is not the fragmented, or intermittent, identity of a
subject constructed in division by language alone, an 'I' continuously prefigured
and preempted in an unchangeable symbolic order." Nor is it, de Lauretis
continues,

> the imaginary identity of the individualist, bourgeois subject, which is male and
> white; nor the "flickering" of the posthumanist Lacanian subject, which is too
> nearly white and at best (fe)male. What is emerging in feminist writings is,
> instead, the concept of a multiple, shifting, and often self-contradictory identity,
> a subject that is not divided in, but rather at odds with, language; an identity
> made up of heterogeneous and heteronomous representations of gender, race,
> and class. . . . [9]

At the same time that *Illusions* can be seen as arguing *for* the appropriation of
Hollywood film to tell "other stories," the film questions that very assumption.
The assumption is questioned, however, not in the name of the inherent corrup-
tion or inevitable co-optation of all film that tells a story, but rather in the name
of the "concept of a multiple, shifting, and often self-contradictory identity" of
which de Lauretis speaks.

The primary device whereby *Illusions* articulates the relationship between
race, gender, and film representation is ironic juxtaposition—whether in the
quotation of other films and film styles, the relationship between sound and
image, or the framing of individual shots and scenes. At the beginning of the
film, after Mignon's voice-over about the difference between action and illusion,
we hear another voice-over, now a male voice who speaks of "the industry's
broad war effort. . . . The fact that no other medium has so adapted to the task of
building national morale on both the fighting and home fronts readily attests to
the motion pictures' essentiality." The pontificatory tone is soon revealed to
belong to the voice of the soldier who constantly comes on to Mignon; he is
dictating a memo. The camera reveals the source of the voice-over after pausing
on a black man cleaning the window of the film office, and women receptionists
who answer the phones, thus opening up a space between his inflated rhetoric
and the racist and sexist assumptions that make it possible.

Julie Dash has described *Illusions* as a film that "poses as one thing, while in
fact it's another. It intentionally mimics the form and conventions of Hollywood
films of the thirties and forties. But by embedding certain foreign objects in the
film—the protagonist Mignon, for example—I've attempted to throw the form

into relief, hopefully making all of the sexist and racist assumptions of that form stick out."[10] Since Mignon is passing, *Illusions* takes as its most obvious point of departure films such as *Imitation of Life*, in which the black woman passing for white is a figure of pity; as Alile Sharon Larkin points out, Dash's film redefines the stereotype of the "tragic mulatto."[11] Although the figure of the tragic mulatto is better known in literature than in film, the questions of visibility raised by the film medium make Dash's exploration of the stereotype particularly relevant to what Hortense J. Spillers has described as the "spectacular and the specular" components of the mulatto subject: "In a very real sense, America's historic mulatto subject plays out his/her character on the ground of a fiction made public and decisive by dimensions of the spectacular and the specular."[12]

The situation that occasions the encounter between Mignon and Ester evokes *Singin' in the Rain* (1952), in which a silent female film star with a horribly grating voice makes the transition to sound by having another woman's voice dubbed for her, as well as *Inside Daisy Clover* (1965), in which the film's heroine, a movie star, cracks under the pressure of her success during a scene in which she must dub her own voice to footage of her in which the sound was improperly recorded. Indeed, the scene in the recording studio where Ester supplies the voice is quite reminiscent of the scene in *Singin' in the Rain* where Debbie Reynolds supplies the voice. At the end of that film, in the optimistic tradition of the backstage musical, Debbie Reynolds becomes a star and gets her man. *Illusions* reveals what is repressed in a film such as *Singin' in the Rain*—i.e., that for the black women who provided these voices there was no possibility of coming out from behind the curtain as Debbie Reynolds does.

At the same time, *Illusions* displaces the formula of singer-gets-her-man with its staging of the recording scene as the encounter between two black women. The film screen becomes a central figure in this scene for that encounter, at times occupying the entire space of the frame, and at others seen through the glass of the recording booth, with Ester to one side as she records and the two (white, male) engineers and Mignon seen as ephemeral reflections in double. The film that is being "repaired," so to speak, is a fluffy musical; one sequence shows two men and the blonde female star of the film as they sing and dance, and the scene that Ester dubs has the woman doing a solo. Ester is situated vis-à-vis the screen image in a position that is evocative both of Uncle Josh at the movies and of the rear-projectionist. While Ester is in no sense the naive spectator that Josh is, she occupies a relationship to the screen that evokes his simultaneous distance and investment.

Later in the film Ester tells Mignon that when she goes to the movies, she fantasizes while hearing her own voice in the theater, as if to suggest that Ester imagines herself into the alien world of (white) cinematic fantasy just as Josh literalizes the fiction of film. But Ester is also on the other side of the screen, in the position of the rear-projectionist, for it is her voice that supplies the illusion, and the disjunction between sound and image that creates the impression of a seamless flow. Ironically, however, the cuts to close-ups of Ester singing make it quite obvious that, whether this is the actress's "real" voice or not, this source of the illusion is also a dubbed voice. When Mignon enters the sound-recording booth, she looks into the window to catch a glimpse of herself and adjust her hair. If the screen is both a passageway to glorious fantasy and a rigid obstacle separating black from white for Ester, then the glass surface of the recording booth takes on a similar contradictory function for Mignon. For through the glass, Mignon witnesses what is represented in the film as a crisis in conscience. Through the glass, Mignon sees herself reflected in Ester, a reflection paradoxically clarified by the distorted images of the two white men, one of whom had earlier made a racist comment to Mignon. Mignon's relationship to the recording scene is not just identification with Ester, for Mignon becomes both observer and participant; the window and the screen become figures for her own contradictory and complex relationship to the apparatus of the cinema.

While *Illusions* does not contain specific citations of a literary source, like Helke Sander's references to Christa Wolf in *Redupers,* the film's emphasis on the significance of relationships between black women is evocative of a similar preoccupation in contemporary fiction by black women authors. The example of Toni Morrison is particularly relevant to *Illusions,* not only because of the thematics of female friendship in Morrison's work, but also because of the significance of vision, sight, and the simultaneous difficulty and exhilaration of a kind of looking rooted in the connection between black women. In Morrison's first novel, *The Bluest Eye* (1970), the fate of Pecora Breedlove is traced through the intertwining relationships in a black community in Lorain, Ohio, particularly the relationship between two sisters, Frieda and Claudia, one of whom supplies the first-person narration with which the novel begins and ends.

Pecora embodies, in extreme form, the bitter desire for blue eyes, the symbol of whiteness which would allow her not only to assume a white identity and therefore become desirable in the eyes of others, but also to see the world through the eyes of white experience.[13] The final result of that desire for Pecora is an internal dialogue with herself that speaks incoherence, rage, and the impossibility of meaningful connection with other human beings. Yet Pecora— whose name is suggestive of Peola, the light-skinned daughter in Fannie Hurst's novel *Imitation of Life*—is not a character easily classified as "mad" or exceptional, to the extent that virtually every woman in the novel responds in some way to the seduction of blue eyes, to the standard of white "beauty."

The women in *The Bluest Eye* live in a world where constant negotiation of the "blue eye," both as a standard of beauty to which to aspire and as an alienating perspective from which to "survey" oneself, is necessary. The novel abounds in these metaphors of "blue eyes," from a Shirley Temple cup, to a white doll, to the white girls in school. Not surprisingly, one such metaphor comes from the cinema.[14] While she is pregnant, Pauline Breedlove, Pecora's mother, finds in the movies a world of illusion both comforting and alien:

> She was never able, after her education in the movies, to look at a face and not assign it some category in the scale of absolute beauty, and the scale was one she absorbed in full from the silver screen. There at last were the darkened woods, the lonely roads, the river banks, the gentle knowing eyes. There the flawed became whole, the blind sighted, and the lame and halt threw away their crutches. There death was dead, and people made every gesture in a cloud of music. There the black-and-white images came together, making a magnificient whole—all projected through the ray of light from above and behind.[15]

The two female protagonists of Morrison's second novel, *Sula,* share a special friendship that is forged in part in their common fantasies, but more specifically in their desire to *share* their fantasies with another. Noting that "it was in dreams that the two girls had first met," Morrison describes the special bond between Nel and Sula as follows:

> They were solitary little girls whose loneliness was so profound it intoxicated them and sent them stumbling into Technicolored visions that always included a presence, a someone, who, quite like the dreamer, shared the delight of the dream. When Nel, an only child, sat on the steps of her back porch surrounded by the high silence of her mother's incredibly orderly house, feeling the neatness pointing at her back, she studied the poplars and fell easily into a picture of herself lying on a flowered bed, tangled in her own hair, waiting for some fiery prince. He approached but never quite arrived. But always, watching the dream along with her, were some smiling sympathetic eyes. Someone as interested as she herself in the flow of her imagined hair, the thickness of the mattress of flowers, the voile sleeves that closed below her elbows in gold-threaded cuffs.[16]

As the "Technicolor" quality of Nel's fantasies suggests clearly, this is a dream-world made to the measure of Hollywood images. If this passage evokes Pauline Breedlove's relationship to the movies in *The Bluest Eye,* however, something has changed as well. For instead of the "gentle knowing eyes" located firmly within the screen fantasies of the movies, and thus distanced from Pauline Breedlove, we have in *Sula* "some smiling sympathetic eyes," now a function of a relationship *to* the screen, and most important, a relationship that is shared with another female observer. The female friendship central to *Sula* thus takes as one of its structuring principles a fantasy of black female spectatorship. Unlike the relationship between female spectator and screen in *The Bluest Eye,* which can function only to underline the black woman's alienation from the ideals of white, patriarchal culture, in *Sula* the bond between the two dreamers emphasizes alienation and empowerment, simultaneously.

"Because each had discovered years before that they were neither white nor male, and that all freedom and triumph was forbidden to them, they had set about creating something else to be."[17] While Morrison does not offer any easy or pat suggestions of what that "something else" may be, the model of female spectatorship, whereby the power of dominant representations is mitigated by the power of the bond between those doing the watching, represents a significant challenge to one-dimensional notions of acculturation or socialization structured by the dichotomies of activity and passivity. In *Illusions,* the relationship between Ester and Mignon continues the exploration of black female spectatorship that figures so strongly in these novels by Morrison. For the relationship between the two women is not a simple act of mirroring, where the extent of their relationship would be Mignon's recognition of herself in Ester. Rather, the two women recognize in each other's relationship to the cinema a shared fantasy that on one level acknowledges the white illusions of the film industry, but on another puts those illusions into question. That the staging of the decisive encounter between Mignon and Ester should take place around the foregrounded figure of the film screen accentuates that sense of discovery, through black female spectatorship, of the cinema as simultaneously resistant yet accessible to the desires and aspirations of black women.

In *The Cheat,* the screen surface becomes a sign of the space separating East and West. In *Illusions,* the surface of the screen is white in several senses of the word. *Illusions* is shot in black and white, and Dash frequently uses light and dark contrast to signify aesthetic and racial opposition simultaneously. Virtually all of the white women who appear in the film are extremely blonde, the point being not a regurgitation of the dark woman/light woman stereotype, but rather a process of defamiliarization whereby the blonde woman, symbol and symptom of the classical Hollywood cinema, becomes an embodiment of otherness, of the constructed standard of female beauty against which all other women, whether recognizably black (like Ester) or not (like Mignon), are measured. The juxtaposition of the white screen, looming centrally in the foreground, with the black woman who provides the voice that will correct the mismatch between sound and image, creates the possibility for the screen to function as a mirror undermining the illusion of a totally white universe rather than supporting it. The dislocation of image and sound matches the separation of the two reflective surfaces, the glass on the sound booth and the surface of the screen.

Initially, Mignon is quite literally caught between the reflected images of the two white men on the one hand, and the blonde actress whose image looms large on the screen. The connection between Mignon and Ester subverts that containment, not through direct communication between the two women but rather through a connection that undermines the equation between white culture and reflective surfaces.[18] One of the unspoken assumptions of the figure of the screen surface in the films I have described is that boundaries can be transgressed, but within certain limits, and only *The Cheat* postulates those boundaries in terms of race. In that film, of course, the Asian man's function as master narrator is demolished. In *Illusions,* the white of the screen and the white conventions of Hollywood are defamiliarized, and the possibility of black female narration is predicated on the relationship between one black woman who simultaneously creates and foregrounds the illusion, and another who watches and contemplates it. The ambivalence of Dash's film involves, then, a relationship between seer and seen in which the overlapping boundaries between white and black, male and female, are explored in an affirmation of black woman's cinema that acknowledges, simultaneously, the limitations of Hollywood representation.

Illusions foregrounds the whiteness of the screen in its overlapping associations of race, gender, and reflective capacities. In Patricia Rozema's 1987 film *I've Heard the Mermaids Singing,* a screen surface emerges as a central figure in the female protagonist's simultaneous fascination with the art world and lesbianism. In *The Big Sleep,* the frosted window which functions as a barrier between Marlowe and Harry Jones suggests something of an imbalance in the heterosexual symmetry so carefully established in other, similarly constructed scenes in the film. Indeed, a crucial component in this film, as well as in *Uncle Josh at the Moving Picture Show* and *The Cheat,* is the encounter of the male protagonist with his like. Although Laura Mulvey describes the relationship between the male spectator and the male protagonist of the Hollywood cinema as analogous to that between subject and ego ideal, the very establishment of that ego ideal often relies on a slippage between the male as subject and as object—on, that is, the possibility of homosexual desire as well as same-sex (and implicitly heterosexual) identification.[19]

While it is crucial, within the terms of what Monique Wittig calls the heterosexual contract, that such eruptions of male homoerotic desire remain isolated moments that can be superseded by the assumption of presumably "adult" heterosexual identification, it is not always clear that the hierarchy is articulated clearly or firmly.[20] To be sure, Philip Marlowe and Vivian Rutledge are set up as the couple-emerging-victorious, but the very fact that the real-life personae of Bogart and Bacall contribute so significantly to this conclusion can be taken as a sign that within the particular narrative and visual configuration of this film, such extratextual mechanisms function not to affirm what is already there but to supply what otherwise might be lacking.

If the screen motif undermines the clear distinctions between subject and object, then a significant manifestation of that undermining is the simultaneous evocation of homosexual and heterosexual desire, an evocation in which the boundary lines between the "normal" and the "deviant" are not clear-cut. In the films discussed in the previous chapter, however, the boundaries are undermined only insofar as *male* sexuality is concerned. *I've Heard the Mermaids Singing* explores the ramifications of such boundaries insofar as female sexual ambivalence is concerned.

I've Heard the Mermaids Singing is told in a partial first-person point of view, at least to the extent that Polly, the female protagonist (played by Sheila McCarthy), narrates her story by speaking to a video camera set up in her apartment. The close-up, extremely grainy images of her narration alternate with the chronological representation of the events she introduces. Yet another, third level of the film is the representation of Polly's fantasies, often further distinguished from the other two levels by the black-and-white, grainy image. Polly's story, as she tells it, all began when she was hired to work as a temporary assistant at the Church Gallery. After a brief period of time, the elegant owner of the gallery, Gabrielle St. Pères (Paule Baillargeon), offers her a permanent position. For someone who has been described as "organizationally impaired," the opportunity to work for Gabrielle is the highest of compliments.

Yet despite her clumsiness and her awkward persona at the workplace, Polly is depicted—particularly when she leaves work—as a creative, playful individual, and the representation of her fantasies often occurs in this context. She is a photographer (specifically) and a fanciful observer of the world around her (generally). An immediate link between Polly's first-person narration, spoken directly to the video camera, and the events which, once introduced by her narration, are shown in a more conventional narrative style, is the camera. The still camera in Polly's story, and the video camera in her narration, define how she quite literally "sees" the world.

The video camera is one of several figures deployed in the film to render Polly's journey through the complicated intersections of art, power, and sexual desire. The camera is a surveillance device in the gallery, and early in the film we watch Polly and Gabrielle install it in its place, planted atop a mannikinlike female form. Through the video surveillance system, Polly engages in voyeuristic eavesdropping. Polly's adoration of Gabrielle is established firmly from the outset of the film. Polly tells the camera, in one of the early first-person sections, "I just loved how she talked and wanted her to teach me everything." Polly's adoration extends to curiosity, particularly the first time a woman named Mary arrives at the gallery and asks for Gabrielle. The two women go into the gallery, which is separated from the office, and Polly cannot resist the urge to switch on the monitor and eavesdrop.

Figure 9. Sheila McCarthy as Polly in Patricia Rozema's *I've Heard the
    Mermaids Singing* (Museum of Modern Art)

When the women's intimate past is revealed to a perplexed Polly, it is not just lesbianism that provokes her curiosity, but rather the sheer facts of sexuality and personal life themselves, particularly insofar as Gabrielle is concerned. Indeed, this scene marks the first time in the film that Gabrielle's cool, sophisticated exterior crumbles, and at the same time that Mary is revealed as her lover, so is there mention of another recent lover of Gabrielle, a man. In the scene immediately following this one, Polly is seen outdoors, with her still camera, following a heterosexual couple in the woods, attempting—unsuccessfully—to remain unnoticed. Here, too, she is defined as a voyeur, and in both cases, her position on the outside, looking in, is emphasized insofar as *all* sexual relations—and not just lesbian ones—are concerned.

Nonetheless, there is a significant difference between the two kinds of voyeurism, for the one, outdoors, involves the sanctioned if extremely awkwardly executed voyeurism of photographic expression, while the other, in the office, involves a far less sanctioned form of eavesdropping. In both cases, Polly assumes the position of voyeur with considerable discomfort; she dangles awkwardly from the tree in which she attempts to hide, and very much in the fashion of Uncle Josh in the early cinema, she stretches her head to the side of the monitor in the office when Gabrielle and Mary kiss just off camera, hopeful of seeing more. Again, however, there is a difference between the two scenes, for lesbian sexuality remains less representable in conventional terms than heterosexuality, so that the eavesdropping in the office, and the subsequent play on what is shown and what is concealed, speak much more forcefully to narrative and visual intrigue. Put another way, the interplay between display and secrecy central to narrative and visual momentum is engaged in the film in relationship to lesbian, rather than heterosexual, desire.

Polly is presented as a naive neophyte in a world of adults, and the plot of the film thickens as she develops a crush on Gabrielle which hovers between attraction and identification. Polly's discovery of Gabrielle's sexuality (bisexual or lesbian, but with the lesbianism definitely emphasized since the only lover of hers we see is a woman) is complicated and compounded by the delayed discovery that forms the climax to the intrigue of the film. Polly arrives late at a birthday party for Gabrielle, and finds the Curator drunk and sad. She speaks to Polly about her frustrated desire to create beautiful, immortal paintings, and tells her that even when she applied for admission to an adult art class, she was told that her work was "simple-minded." Polly asks to see her paintings, and Gabrielle leads her to a small room where a series of luminous white panels are hung. Eventually, the paintings are revealed to be Mary's work, not Gabrielle's. Polly takes one painting home with her, and then to the gallery, where a critic sees it—all of this unbeknownst to Gabrielle. Once Gabrielle does discover what

Polly has done, she does not exactly willfully conceal the truth, but neither does she dispel the illusion that has been created, particularly once Mary has insisted that they are partners in a "victimless crime." Mary detests the art world in which Gabrielle moves so comfortably, and so she encourages Gabrielle to present her paintings as her own.

When Polly brings the painting home, she sets it against a wall in her apartment that is covered with her own photographs. Clearly inspired by Gabrielle's simultaneous insecurity and confession, Polly decides to send some of her photographs, under a "pseudo-name," to Gabrielle at the gallery. When Gabrielle receives the photographs, she does not respond as Polly had hoped, but rather exclaims on their deficiency: "She just doesn't have it. . . . God, look at this—the trite made flesh." Gabrielle uses the same phrase—"simple-minded"—to describe Polly's photographs as the art teacher had used to describe her own work. Polly's subsequent humiliation and misery lead her to burn her photographs and toss away her camera.

Polly discovers the truth when Gabrielle and Mary enter the gallery surreptitiously with more paintings, and Polly—unbenownst to them—is lying on one of the benches, somewhat drunk. This scene plays upon the mode of reversal common in the film, since Polly occupies the position of Gabrielle in the earlier scene when the paintings were first introduced. Polly overhears their conversation in which the ruse is revealed, and she peeks at the new paintings they have brought in, only to be stunned, even momentarily blinded, it would appear, by the bright light. The paintings are wrapped, not coincidentally, in a comforter which Polly had given Gabrielle as a birthday gift. Polly's anger leads to an angry outburst, and she throws hot tea on Gabrielle's face. Polly's disillusionment with Gabrielle has less to do with the public fraud than with the personal one, that is, with the fact that Gabrielle let Polly assume that Mary's paintings were her own.

The conclusion of this scene is the first of several conclusions that the film offers. Polly conducts an imaginary orchestra, and a slow zoom onto her as she triumphantly assumes the music transforms the painting into an ethereal background, no longer contained by its borders. It would appear, then, that Polly has switched sides, as it were, shifted from the position of adoring spectator of the painting to powerful creator in her own right, an equivalent of Uncle Josh tearing down the screen, and an assumption of the role of the rear-projectionist as well. That one critic described the screen/painting as the closest thing to music approximated in a painting contributes to the sense of the realization of a fantasy. Ultimately, the film would have Polly's vision—buttressed by Mary, the "true" artist—win out, a vision, that is, based on the pure pleasure of creation rather than its exchange value. For Mary, like Polly, aspires not necessarily to artistic greatness and renown but to creation for its own sake, and significantly, Mary disputes Gabrielle's opinion of Polly's photographs (and without knowing that they are Polly's).

I've Heard the Mermaids Singing has difficulty coming to a firm conclusion, evidenced in particular by the fact that the film provides a series of endings. After Polly has completed her "conductor" fantasy, she takes the video camera and leaves the gallery. The film returns to her first-person narration (the placement of the video camera in her apartment thus explained), and Polly says, "There it is. That's what happened." As she moves toward the camera—to shut it off, one assumes—the final credits are intercut with the images of her. But her narration continues as she shifts positions, both literally and figuratively. Having changed the position of the camera, she speaks, apparently to a different audience than previously, about practical matters—leaving town, renting her apartment. She hears a knock at the door; Gabrielle and Mary enter. Now it is Gabrielle's (and Mary's) turn to make a discovery—that the photographs sent anonymously were in fact Polly's. The intercut credits images continue, over one of which Polly's voice-over is heard, "C'mon, I'll show you some more." The next image shows Polly opening the door to a golden wonderland of trees, inviting Gabrielle and Mary to join her. Before going through the door herself, Polly leans over and turns off the camera. While this final image appears to be a continuation of Polly's first-person narration, the image quality is like the more conventional narrative of the film. In fact, this final image is a fusion of the three narrative elements that have remained more or less separate in the film—Polly's first-person narration to the camera, the "events" that led up to her narration, and her fantasy life (here suggested by the golden landscape).

While this difficulty of, or resistance to, closure could be read as a sign of open-endedness, it is also a sign of confusion, having to do in part with the strain between self-expression and the "public" function of art, which the film cannot resolve. When Gabrielle and Mary come to Polly's apartment and see the display of her photographs, Polly is now identified in the role of teacher that Gabrielle previously held. When Polly informs her guests that she has many more images to show them, and opens the door to a wonderland of autumn foliage, the couple moves in awe, as if seeing the world for the first time.[21] This conclusion does seem a bit idealistic, with its uncomplicated affirmation of Polly's vision, its mode of simple reversal (in which Polly is now the "real artist," Gabrielle the apprentice), and its neat tying together of all three narrative and visual modes of the film. At the same time, however, there is a strong sense in the film that the series of endings do not necessarily work so seamlessly in unison. In other words, a sense of the difficulty of resolution is presented in an extremely provocative and productive way—in a way, that is, that calls for a reading of the relationship between the ambivalence posed by the film and the necessity for closure.

Kay Armatage has described the video camera sculpture as "the pivotal visual object of the movement of narrative, signifying system, and sexual identity. . . ." "The 'woman's look,' " says Armatage, "is thus technological, aesthetic, knowledge producing, and functional in the protagonist's self-revelation." For Armatage, the consolidation of a number of threads in the "clever conceit" of the video sculpture suggests the function of lesbianism in the film as idealized, romanticized, and unproblematically set forth as the decisive moment of passage for Polly. Describing the final scene of the film, Armatage refers to the "paradisaical bower of egalitarian bliss" evoked by the forest, with Polly's smile at the camera a consolidation of "the movement . . . through representation to a vision of feminine sexuality in full possession of its own knowledge."[22]

While the conclusion of the film does suggest romanticization, I do not think it is lesbianism that is being romanticized here, but rather the position of innocence that Polly embodies. This "final, really final ending" (as Armatage refers to it) seems to me quite different in tone and gesture from the way that Polly's journey is conveyed in the film. If the development of *I've Heard the Mermaids Singing* were shaped uniquely or primarily by the camera, particularly in the fusion of the fanciful observation of the still camera with the confessional of the video camera, then one might rightly criticize the film for a simplified access to fully adequate vision, complete unto itself. But the instruments of vision function in relationship to the figure of the screenlike surface which is just as central to the film's narrative. The camera sculpture, as Armatage suggests, condenses a number of threads in the film, and taken on its own terms perhaps does suggest a kind of total assumption of knowledge, authority, and control. But the figure of the camera sculpture needs to be seen in relationship to the equally compelling figure of the painting, ostensibly executed by Gabrielle but really done by Mary, that is presented to Polly.

The painting, to which Polly responds with awe and wonder, is a luminous, white, almost quivering surface which becomes a metaphoric screen in the film, and acquires the functions of simultaneous passage and threshold. Indeed, Polly's innocent fascination with the art world, with Gabrielle, and with lesbianism is evocative of Uncle Josh's naive apprehension of the cinema screen. In Polly's case, the video camera sculpture is—as Armatage says—appropriated and used, more integrated to Polly's own vision and story than it is to the consumerist stereotype of female beauty upon whose neck it rests. But there is a split in Polly's trajectory, between the camera which *is* appropriated and the painting, the screen surface, which remains at a distance, a mysterious object which inspires equally mystified awe. Unlike the camera, which Polly can take outside the gallery and adapt to her own storytelling ends, the painting inspires the opposite desire—the desire to put it on display, to engage in the very circuit of fetishized artifice which, on other levels, Polly resists.

I have mentioned the fantasy sequences which embody Polly's vision and are set off from the rest of the film, whether through black-and-white imagery, extreme graininess, or unconventional relationships between sound and image. Sometimes these fantasies involve Polly in superhuman feats, such as scaling a building or flying through the city. Sometimes they suggest Polly's simultaneous fascination with and fear of the world she discovers through Gabrielle and the art gallery. In one black-and-white sequence that occurs after Polly has learned of Gabrielle's lesbianism, for instance, Polly and Gabrielle are dressed in old-fashioned frilly costumes, complete with wide-brimmed hats and parasols. Polly holds forth on sexuality and desire. "I believe that gender is irrelevant to matters of the heart," she says, and goes on to cite the notion of polymorphous perversity. Gabrielle nods approvingly and deferentially throughout Polly's exposition. If the series of endings of *I've Heard the Mermaids Singing* speaks to an ambivalence about the relationship between art in its personal and public manifestations, the same might be said about the film's relationship to lesbianism. While Gabrielle's sexuality is part of Polly's attraction to her, whether lesbianism constitutes a distinctly alternative sexuality is left open to question. Polly's fantasy of polymorphous perversity suggests simultaneously a desire for a different sexuality and a desire for no sexuality at all.

After Polly has brought the white, screenlike painting home to her apartment, a black-and-white fantasy depicts her in the same type of somewhat old-fashioned clothing, riding in a bus to an isolated setting by the ocean. The sound track consists of a series of melodic female voices, laughing and singing—one of several instances in the film which are inflections of the singing mermaids of the film's title.[23] Polly gazes at the sky and the ocean with the same sense of wonder that characterized her response to the painting. A dissolve within the fantasy to a white screen creates, momentarily, a parallel between the screen surface of the film (more specifically, of Polly's consciousness) and the luminous white painting which she had just previously discovered. The figure of the screen functions here as a quite literal foregrounding of what Bruce Kawin calls "mindscreen," the representation of a character's consciousness.[24] The parallel between the painting and Polly's "mindscreen" suggests further that in Polly's mind, the painting captures both a feeling of connectedness to the natural world, and the essence of creation. At the same time, however, the very fact of the *difference* of the fantasy prevents the easy assumption that Polly's fantasy life is fully and wholly of a piece with the rest of the film.

However, in the conclusions, Polly's fantasy life *does* become integrated and connected with the other realms represented. When Polly conducts the imaginary orchestra in the gallery near the conclusion of the film, two different levels of the narration, the fantasy sequences and the recounting of the events leading up to the acquisition of the video camera, are fused. Polly, standing in front of the painting and framed by its aura, is nonetheless still situated within the fiction of the film, while the musicians, located in the reverse field of her vision, are portrayed in the black and white associated with her fantasies. That the final conclusion joins all three narrative levels (the two already "fused" in the orchestra fantasy, as well as the first-person narration) suggests a romantic vision of artistic completion, wherein the screen and the camera (whether still or video) have become equally joined in a fantasy of beauty, wholeness, and integrity.

Juxtaposed with the orchestra fantasy, however, is the acquisition of the video camera, which undoes somewhat the easy resolution of the music fantasy by recalling the position of voyeur that Polly has assumed throughout the film. In other words, the "conclusion" of the fantasy in relation to the screen is one that the film undermines, and with it any easy assumption of an unqualified position of authority. Through Polly, then, the relationship between Uncle Josh and the movie screen is not replicated with a female substitute, but rather is fundamentally rewritten in such a way that the very desire to "get inside the image," to transgress the boundary separating screen and audience, is rethought. The look and the surface, the camera and the screen, here do not function as simple or self-evident supports for one another; rather, Polly's wonder and awe in front of the luminous surface serve as counterpoint to her eager assumption of the voyeur's role.

In an essay published in 1987, a year after the release of *The Man Who Envied Women*, Yvonne Rainer raises a series of questions concerning the devices and strategies appropriate to women's cinema. She concludes with this question:

> Should a film whose main project is to restore the voice and subjectivity of a previously ignored or suppressed person or segment of the population, should such a film contain argument, contradiction, or express the director's ambivalence within the film either directly, through language, or indirectly, through stylistic intervention? Obviously, we can't afford to be prescriptive about any of this.[25]

The films discussed in this chapter are concerned, precisely, with the difficult relationship between the politics of restoration (to use Rainer's term) and ambivalence and contradiction. Yet, the films discussed thus far are quite different from *The Man Who Envied Women*, which is far more explicitly theoretical in its focus, and more concerned with the limits of language and representation in relationship to sexual politics. In no way, however, does *The Man Who Envied Women* establish a rigid distinction between the realm of the political and the artistic; it does not "abandon" the political for the sake of the avant-garde, nor does it affirm contradiction and ambiguity at the expense of political reflection.

Indeed, while virtually all of Rainer's films prior to *The Man Who Envied Women* are concerned with questions central to feminist representation and theory, this film is nonetheless unique in the way it interweaves different levels of the political—from the politics of heterosexual relationships to gentrification in New York City to American intervention in Central America—with analyses and evaluations of sound and image, representation, and narrative. In feminist film studies, *The Man Who Envied Women* has acquired a privileged status; as Lucy Fischer says, Rainer's film "constitutes a virtual catalogue of the major tendencies in feminist cinema and criticism of the 1970s and 1980s."[26] Thus many feminist film critics have found in the film crucial articulations of issues central to feminist film theory, including female spectatorship, dialogic discourse, space, the difficulty of heterosexual relations, and language and the gaze.[27]

The Man Who Envied Women creates a radical sexual division. Of the man and woman whose break-up initiates the soon-to-be-disrupted narrative thread of the film, one (the man) not only is excessively visible but is portrayed by two actors, and the other (the woman) exists primarily as a disembodied voice, performed by the choreographer and dancer Trisha Brown. Throughout the film, the figure of the screen embodies ambivalence and contradiction, not in opposition to the political but rather as a political question in its own right. The title of this chapter—"Screen Tests"—is borrowed from one of the most striking tropes in *The Man Who Envied Women*. The film begins as Jack Deller, the male protagonist, speaks, ostensibly to his psychiatrist, while a film screen behind his body displays the title "Screen Tests," and shows the opening shots of Luis Bunuel's and Salvador Dali's film, *Un Chien Andalou,* in which preparations for the famous eye-slitting scene occur.[28] Throughout the film, this psychoanalytic scene is repeated with a variety of film clips projected, the majority of them from classical Hollywood films, but with a small dose of avant-garde films as well. These screen images function most obviously as quite literal projections of the patriarchal imagination of Jack Deller.

At the same time, the mise-en-scène operates a disjunction, since Deller entertains no direct engagement with the screen as either viewer or projectionist.[29] The screen functions specifically, then, as a projection of a patriarchal unconscious about women, but it has a more active function in return, and as a result there is no simple, one-directional movement. Rather, the screen comments on Jack Deller as much as it reflects him. The notion of "screen tests" suggests, then, the conventional sense of a sample performance to be judged by standards of evaluation, but the object of the tests shifts between Jack Deller and the film clips. At the same time, of course, the questioning of the very notion of a "test," of standards of evaluation that are fixed, knowable, and conventional, is central to *The Man Who Envied Women*. There is a deeper ambiguity and playfulness in the notion of "screen tests" that informs the film as well, since it is the screen itself, as the conventional ground and surface for film projection, that is "tested," prodded, stretched, and foregrounded in a variety of ways.[30]

Jack Deller's "therapy sessions" become one of the most significant threads in the film. There is virtually always a disjunction between what Deller says and what the screen shows, in the sense that his voice might be heard while the sound track is suppressed, or vice versa.[31] From the outset, however, the film insists upon a direct relationship between the man and what is projected on the movie screen. At the very beginning, when the opening scenes of *Un Chien Andalou* are projected, for example, there is a symmetry between Jack Deller, puffing on a cigarette and facing screen left, and the figure of Luis Bunuel, similarly smoking (and facing screen right) as he prepares for the famous eye-slitting scene. Later, Jack comments on the absurdity of his female companion referring to herself as a "good girl," after which the film which had been projected silently *(Dark Victory)* is accompanied with sound, and we hear a discussion between Bette Davis and George Brent in which she describes herself precisely as a "good girl." The screen does not function simply as the projection of Jack Deller's patriarchal fantasies, but rather becomes the site for the projection of the unconscious of the film.

In the essay cited earlier, Rainer observes that the distinction between political and avant-garde women's films is one of many "useless oppositions" which serve to divide and conquer, and thus attempts to rethink the standard opposition between the conventional and the avant-garde in feminist thinking about film.[32] This desire to reexamine conventional oppositions while simultaneously finding a place to represent contradictions and ambiguities is one of the most crucial principles of *The Man Who Envied Women*. The film clip from *Dark Victory* is interrupted, for instance, by a clip from Hollis Frampton's *Otherwise Unexplained Fires,* and the camera zooms forward so that the projection screen fills up the entire frame. The "scene" of the avant-garde has the power to disrupt the (already disrupted) relationship between spectator and screen that the film has established.

Similarly, later in the film a clip from Michael Snow's *Wavelength* appears, humorously inserted among images of New York lofts in various stages of repair. Again, the avant-garde cinema has the capacity to enter into the fabric of *The Man Who Envied Women* without the necessary "framing" of the psychoanalytic session. In the course of the film, however, any such opposition between the "uses" of the dominant and the avant-garde cinema are broken down. A clip from *Gilda* appears outside the confines of the therapy session, for instance, and several of the Hollywood films are subjected to formal interrogation. A scene from *In a Lonely Place* is projected at fast-forward speed, and then repeated at normal speed; and a scene from *The Night of the Living Dead* is repeated again and again, while the camera moves back to reveal Jack Deller sitting on a stage in a movie theater, with a group of spectators in front of him who become increasingly agitated as the film clips are repeated.

There is, however, one experimental film which does occupy a privileged place in *The Man Who Envied Women*. The therapy session that "climaxes" with the crowd reaction to *Night of the Living Dead* begins with a projection of *Watermotor*, by Trisha Brown and Babette Mangolte. The clip features Trisha Brown dancing in slow motion. *Watermotor* could be seen in relationship to the other films "quoted" in *The Man Who Envied Women*, in that like the Hollywood films it features a woman as the object of inquiry, and like the experimental films it features an unconventional use of the cinematic apparatus (here, the use of slow motion). Yet *Watermotor* is also unlike virtually every other film cited in Rainer's film, since however experimental, it nonetheless focuses on the female form; since—unlike the Hollywood films—it focuses on a woman alone, un-defined by the codes of Hollywood romance; and since it is the only film by women directors (and for that matter, the only codirected film) cited in the film.

This is the only time when we are afforded a "look" at Trisha Brown, whose voice provides the central narration of the film. (We presumably "see" Trisha early in the film as she departs from Jack's apartment, but even this brief representation of Trisha is "performed," since "she" is portrayed by someone else.) The appearance of Trisha Brown within the screen tests serves to reiterate the divided quality of female narration in the film. It is somewhat tempting to argue that as *image*, the female narrator becomes more exposed to the possibili-ties of co-optation and containment by the discourse of the male, since this is quite literally what happens during the session where *Watermotor* is projected. In a monologue that embodies most forcefully the "envy" of the film's title, Jack describes himself, via the description of him by his former sister-in-law, as "the most wonderful husband a woman ever had." Jack continues to speak of his love for "all gracious and tender women," with Trisha's obviously graceful and perhaps tender body serving as counterpoint in the background screen.

To be sure, the representation of Jack's envy ("I suppose that a man who was married for almost twenty-one years to a woman he adored becomes in a sense a lover of all women, and is forever seeking, even though he doesn't know it, for something he has lost") is ironic; in no way could the match between sound

Figure 10. Jack Deller (William Raymond) and Trisha Brown in Yvonne
Rainer's *The Man Who Envied Women* (courtesy of Yvonne Rainer)

and image be read as seamless. At the same time, there is a match, a symmetry,
between the footage of Trisha and Jack's commentary, like other parallels that
have been drawn in the course of the film. It would be much too simple to argue,
however, that as *voice* the female narration is assured a capacity for interrogation
not available through the overdetermined quality of the image. Rather, *The Man
Who Envied Women* creates female narration by a different relationship between
woman as image and woman as voice, and not by the mere suppression of the
woman as image. That an image of Trisha "returns" to the scene of the film, via
the therapy session, via the screen, speaks to the necessity of such a reinterroga-
tion, rather than the simple reversal of hierarchies.

The preoccupation with the screen in *The Man Who Envied Women*, and
with attendant processes of repression, projection, and otherness, takes as its
most obvious form the therapy scenes that recur in the film. At the same time,
however, there is visible throughout the film a preoccupation with the liminal
quality of screen surfaces, now in the sense of permeable surfaces, of threshold
effects. From the very outset, "connection" in *The Man Who Envied Women*
relies on surfaces which simultaneously block and open up. After the opening
"therapy session" of the film, accompanied by Trisha's voice-over, we cut to a
reverse tracking shot in a coffee shop—another scene which is repeated several
times. There is a pun on "cut" here, since the last image of the "therapy session"

shows the close-up, in *Un Chien Andalou,* of an eye being slit open. The shot in the coffee shop begins on a metal surface, which is not polished enough to be a mirror but not dull enough to be read simply as a wall, and in its capacity as somewhere in between the two it also is suggestive of the surface of the screen.

The next scene is a tracking shot of a series of windows, all of which are so brightly lit that it is nearly, although not completely, impossible to see what lies beyond them—suggestive, again, of the translucent, threshold effect of the screen. The tracking shot concludes with a dark screen in place of the last window. The next shot shows a man peering from behind a screen—an image that will recur much later in the film, when Yvonne Rainer herself, during a dream sequence, peers from behind a doorway. Connecting these various introductions to *The Man Who Envied Women,* then, is a series of match cuts based on translucent boundaries, and visual continuity thus explores the borderlines of spatial division. Throughout the film, translucent surfaces are foregrounded, from the windows and glass bricks in the loft where Jack Deller delivers a pretentious lecture on theory, to the folding screen in his apartment, to the movie screen itself.[33]

At the same time that *The Man Who Envied Women* is preoccupied with these threshold spaces, with boundaries that are nonetheless permeable—or may be made to be so—another point of return suggests a rather different kind of preoccupation. A series of magazine articles and images are tacked to the white wall in Deller's loft, and they are rearranged and commented upon throughout the film. Many critics have noted that the structure of Rainer's film is a collage effect, quite like this collection of images and texts described as "Trisha's art work" by Deller.[34] The most sustained dialogues in the film occur around these images and texts—dialogues between Trisha and Jack, between Trisha and Yvonne Rainer, and between video artist and critic Martha Rosler and Rainer. The collage is first shown early in the film, shortly after the departure of the "woman" who will be known from here on in as a voice, and consists of four images: a Sunday *New York Times Magazine* cover of a man's face, with the words "How I Was Broken by the KGB"; a page from the "About Men" section of the *Times Sunday Magazine,* with a drawing of a male figure with a tear on its cheek; a full-color cigar advertisement, with the legend "The Sweet Smell of Success," and a photograph of a man in a country setting with two dogs; and a color photograph of decapitated corpses and severed heads, with a handwritten legend underneath it. The images are rearranged in a variety of ways throughout the film, whether literally, in their placement on the wall, or figuratively, through the conversations that are heard as the camera shows them. Eventually, another image is added, this one an advertisement from a medical journal for a hormone treatment for menopausal women, featuring a close-up of a woman's face in obvious pain.

Figure 11. Yvonne Rainer's *The Man Who Envied Women*
(courtesy of Yvonne Rainer)

This collage is a surface which is the opposite of the screen in the therapy session, and the visual opposition parallels the opposition between the man's voice and the woman's voice. For the man's voice, so dominant during the therapy sessions (literally in Jack Deller's pronouncements, figuratively in the patriarchal "voice" that speaks in the representations of women), is muted during most of the conversations that take place around the series of images on the wall. To be sure, Jack Deller's voice is heard discussing the images, but it carries much less narrative authority than in the therapy scenes in front of the screen. The collage is not so anchored to the consciousness of one individual man, as the movie screen is. Yet, at the same time, the two surfaces—the movie screen and the wall—have much in common. Both become screen surfaces through which some kind of opening is possible—the collage through conversation, the movie screen through ironic commentary.

Indeed, in the course of *The Man Who Envied Women*, ironic commentary becomes another form of conversation. But there is another difference between the two surfaces, in terms of what they show. The movie screen is largely a funiction of the patriarchal unconscious, and so the manipulation of the image, and its relationship to Jack Deller, become means for the female subject of disrupting patriarchal hegemony. There is another kind of return of the repressed in the collage: the horrible image of the corpses and severed heads, a brutal reminder of a political reality which may well be patriarchal, but in relationship to which the female voice-over is potentially complicit, to the extent that she is white, North American, and, even in her presumably marginal status as an artist, complicit with the gentrification of New York neighborhoods.

The Man Who Envied Women threatens at many moments to "break down"; that is, one of its most distinct characteristics is the disruption of any possibility of seamless flow. Nonetheless, there is one particularly crucial disruption in relationship to the "screen tests" performed by the film. The first conversation between Martha Rosler and Yvonne Rainer about the collage comes to a halt as Rosler comments on the photograph of decapitation ("It's really hard to look at this picture. . . . It's really awful . . .").[35] It is interesting in this context that the final spoken words of the film belong to Martha Rosler. In response to Yvonne Rainer's question (spoken, of course, in voice-over) "If this were an art work, how would you critique it?" Rosler responds in a contradictory way. On the one hand, she says, she would feel manipulated by the progression of images, suggesting as they do that "the problems of daily life are only a veneer over the truth that the state destroys people." What such a manipulation of images masks, says Rosler, is that "it *is* a matter of interest whether men are or are not presented as hard surfaces that exude the smell of success from their very physical appearance. . . ." On the other hand, however, the strength and horror of that one photograph are such that even Rosler's own commentary about the problem of manipulation becomes hopelessly inadequate ("But this image is so strong that I can't . . . I can only wince and it makes it really difficult to think about the other stuff once I get to this").

The "screen tests" of *The Man Who Envied Women* function in several complex ways. The screen is a site for the projection of male fantasies about women, but also for various kneadings, pullings, proddings, and teasings about those fantasies that occur primarily through the female voice but also through the various manipulations of the images. In more general terms, the aesthetic preoccupation in the film with translucent surfaces speaks to the desire to see beyond the frame of immediate and visible projection, the desire for a kind of absent presence. Yet that desire for simultaneous separation and merging does not assume a position of "other" to patriarchal consciousness, and this is where the "conversation" in the film, between the screen and the collage, is so crucial.

For however much *The Man Who Envied Women* may focus on the difficulty, even on the impossibility, of relationships between men and women—on, that is, the various "screens" that separate them—the film articulates as well the alternative possibility of conversation among women as a privileged site of theoretical reflection. In some ways, the different choruses of women's voices in Rainer's film evoke the "citation" of women directors in Helke Sander's *Redupers,* and as in Sander's film, the women who are cited are part of a community of female artists. This is not to say that *The Man Who Envied Women* establishes an opposition between heterosexual and homosocial (if not homosexual) worlds—it resists such neat oppositions. Rather, the opposing fantasies of men and women (which are staged so hilariously and even somewhat poignantly in the extremely dense dialogue between Jack Deller and Jackie Raynal in the last section of the film) can be read, disentangled, although never quite dissected or dispensed with, only through a dialogue among women. Within that female dialogue reside the possibilities for rescreening the fictions of male and female desire.

All four of the films discussed in this chapter propose "screen tests" as visual and narrative figures for female narration. The figure of the screen ranges from the literal film screen foregrounded in *Illusions* and *The Man Who Envied Women,* to the more metaphoric evocations of the screen, through billboard photographs and curtains, in *Redupers,* or through the white painting in *I've Heard the Mermaids Singing.* The screen tests performed by these films embody a desire to engage ambivalence and contradiction, but to do so in a way that resists the dual traps of co-optation and recuperation, on the one hand, endless circulation within and attendant containment by the field of binary opposition, on the other. The signifying power of female-to-female bonds is central to all of the films. But unlike those to be discussed in the next two chapters, which are concerned with the relationship between female authorship and lesbian desire, the group of films discussed in this chapter do not take as their principal point of departure an erotics of female desire.

To be sure, *I've Heard the Mermaids Singing* brings lesbianism center stage in the relationships between women that it foregrounds, but sexual relationships between women are subordinate to how questions of power, authority, and desire are negotiated. Nonetheless, *I've Heard the Mermaids Singing* could be read, among these four films, as occupying one end of Adrienne Rich's controversial lesbian continuum ranging from explicit and exclusive lesbianism to female friendship, with the other three located on other points of the continuum.[36] Yet despite the different placements of these films on such a continuum, they share a bracketing of women's relationships with men. Men appear only as stereotypes, absences, or afterthoughts in *I've Heard the Mermaids Singing, Illusions* (Mignon's lover is in the service; the white soldier is a catalyst), and *Redupers* (Edda appears in only a few perfunctory scenes with her male lover); and while men are excessively visible in *The Man Who Envied Women,* what the film foregrounds first and foremost is precisely the ironic process of bracketing them.

In all of the films, communities of women—from the friendship between the two black women in *Illusions* to the trio in *I've Heard the Mermaids Singing,* from the women's photography group in *Redupers* to the conversations among women in *The Man Who Envied Women*—are explored for their signifying capacities in both aesthetic and political terms. It has become too easy an assumption in feminist theory (particularly that theory desribing itself as "anti-essentialist") that such affirmations of female friendship and female communities entail of necessity an impossible and utopian return to the Lacanian imaginary, or a simple reversal of (male) oedipal priorities in favor of (female) pre-oedipal ones, or a romantic affirmation of the maternal as a refuge from the difficulties of the patriarchal, symbolic universe. I will not claim that the lure of female friendship as a retreat from patriarchy is totally absent, or refuted by these films. More significant is that they acknowledge that lure, and acknowledge simultaneously the irony that relationships between women are at once contained by the (false) symmetries of male/female, paternal/maternal, heterosexual/homosexual identities, and suggestive of other formulations of identity, relationships, and representation. Lesbianism may, of course, be one such formulation, but what characterizes the screen tests of these films is a tentativeness about the possibility of re-placement. A point of great difficulty in feminist theory has been the relationship between female communities and lesbianism.[37] A disavowal of the relationship between the two, and of the necessarily erotic charge in *any* definition of community, smacks of homophobia; while an affirmation of the relationship can deny the very specific struggles of lesbians within female and feminist communities.[38]

To define lesbianism as the entire spectrum of connections between women, or to return to a phrase such as "women-identified women" (which had its political usefulness at a certain historical point within feminism), avoids the tension. At the conclusion of *The Man Who Envied Women*, Trisha articulates the necessity for another way to describe herself in these terms:

> Lately I've been thinking yet again: I can't live without men, but I can live without a man. I've had this thought before, but this time the idea is not colored by stigma, or despair, or finality. I know there will sometimes be excruciating sadness. But I also know something is different now. Something in the direction of unwomanliness. Not a new woman, not non-woman or misanthropist, or anti-woman, and not non-practicing Lesbian. Maybe unwoman is also the wrong term. A-woman is closer. A-womanly. A-womanliness.[39]

While these words evoke a number of tensions and conflicts, particularly interesting in the present context is the ironic fact that in dismissing "non-practicing Lesbian" as a potential name for herself, Trisha here evokes (as de Lauretis, Fischer, and Rainer herself have pointed out) Monique Wittig's claim that "Lesbians are not women."[40] But Trisha's "citation" of Wittig maintains a tension between "a-womanliness" as what is produced between the cracks of patriarchal discourse, on the one hand, and what has been barely nameable, on the other.

This group of films is thus weakest—or strongest, depending upon your point of view—in terms of closure. To be sure, these films are more oriented toward the "process" that has been celebrated in so many variations of contemporary theory and artistic practice; toward, that is, a notion of subject positioning that emphasizes production rather than product. The question of closure, however, seems to me most pertinent in these films, not in the standard opposition of competing notions of subjecthood but rather in terms of how those competing notions of subjecthood coexist within the subject. Put another way, the difficulty of closure in these films speaks, not to a fully coherent "patriarchal subject" against which the female subject is defined, but rather to how the female subject is both complicit with the fictions of patriarchy and resistant to them. This difference is crucial in order to resist facile praise of "open-endedness" as a value in its own right—or, for that matter, ambiguity and ambivalence as qualities to be pursued, whatever their points of reference, whatever their contexts.

Although the terms of the films are different, they share the preoccupation with ambivalence as simultaneously a refusal to prioritize and an inevitable component of female subjectivity under patriarchy. But rather than simply affirm this simulatenous impossibility and necessity, these films attempt to articulate ambivalence in a critical and potentially empowering way. There is nothing resembling an easy "solution," no blueprint, no simple imposition of a Lacanian-inspired "third term" to contain ambivalence within the imaginary order and facilitate passage into the symbolic. That these films take the screen as such a significant figure marks the importance of a feminist practice of cinematic narration in which it is possible to speak simultaneously of what the classical cinema represents and what it represses. For however fractured the narratives of these films, and to whatever differing degrees, they share the desire to appropriate forms of narrative associated with the classical cinema to the representation of female desire.

In her discussion of contemporary women authors and their relationship to the codes of romantic fiction, specifically in relationship to "endings," Rachel Blau DuPlessis writes: "An ending in which one part of a structuring dialectic is repressed is a way of reproducing in a text the sense of juridical or social limits for females of one class, when that class ideology encourages striving behavior for males. Yet when that closure is investigated, the repressed element is present in shadowy form."[41] Although the context to which I refer in this chapter is different, the aims are quite similar. For these "screen tests" explore the limits of the interface between spectacle and narrative, and in so doing seek to "investigate" the elements that are repressed, marginalized, or otherwise displaced in classical film narrative. The metaphor of the screen serves not to replace one sense of "screen" (what is made invisible) with another (the luminous, white space of consciousness) but to produce a kind of narration that can account for both. To "account for both" does not mean to establish a static duality, but rather to account for their interdependence and the tension between them.

Redupers affirms the subversive potential of women's image-making in relationship to the divided city of Berlin, but the potential is held in check by the power of habit and institutions. In Julie Dash's *Illusions,* the friendship between the two black women who share fantasies about the possibilities of motion pictures does not displace or in any way triumph over the politics of the white film industry; rather, it is only in the constant negotiation of both, the film suggests, that any kind of black women's cinema is possible. Rozema's *I've Heard the Mermaids Singing* posits a female world of desire and image-making with specifically lesbian contours, not as an idyllic retreat from the world of men and power but as a complex set of relations of vision and power that exist both within that world and outside it. Rainer's *The Man Who Envied Women* is a theoretical take on the process of appropriation and complicity, resistance and investment central to all of these films. The two kinds of screen surfaces in the film, the movie screen and the collage—like the contradictory meanings of the screen evoked in this group of films—are demonstrations of patriarchal fantasies of femininity, and are at the same time permeable, open to the effects of feminist interrogation.

II.
Female
Authorship

3. Female Authorship Reconsidered

All of the films discussed in the previous chapter take as their central premise and plot the relationship between women and image-making, and may thus be read as explorations of female authorship in the cinema. The importance of female authorship is accentuated by the fact that, with the exception of Julie Dash, the filmmakers themselves appear in their films, from Helke Sander's role as protagonist of *Redupers,* to the more cameolike appearances of Yvonne Rainer (as a voice and briefly on screen) in *The Man Who Envied Women* and Patricia Rozema (in a window as Polly climbs up a building during one of her fantasies) in *I've Heard the Mermaids Singing.* In more general ways, of course, all of the films trace a relationship between women and cinematic production.

In this chapter, I will examine how female authorship has been theorized in feminist film studies, and I will focus in particular on the example of Dorothy Arzner, one of the few women to have been successful as a director in Hollywood in a career that spanned from the late 1920s to the early 1940s. Arzner was one of the early "rediscoveries" of feminist film theory, and she and her work remain to this day the most important case study of female authorship in the cinema. While the most significant work on Arzner's career was done in feminist film studies of the early to mid-1970s, I will suggest that important dimensions of her status as a female author have yet to be explored.

In contemporary feminist literary criticism, inquiries into the nature of female authorship have been shaped by responses to two somewhat obvious assumptions: first, that no matter how tenuous, fractured, or complicated, there is a connection between the writer's gender, her personhood, and her texts; and second, that there exists a female tradition in literature, whether defined in terms of models of mutual influence, shared themes, or common distances from the dominant culture. A wide range of critical practice is held within these assumptions. But insofar as a self-evident category of womanhood may be implicit in the female author defined as the source of a text and as a moment in a female-specific tradition, these seemingly obvious assumptions evoke what has become in contemporary theory a dreaded epithet: essentialism.

A decade or so ago, a friend of mine remarked sarcastically upon the prevalence of "oedipus detectors" at a Modern Language Association meeting, that is, critics eager to sniff out any remnants of oedipal scenarios in work that was ostensibly "progressive," "feminist," or "postoedipal." Contemporary feminist criticism—and feminist film studies in particular—is marked by a similar presence of "essentialist detectors." For virtually any mention of "real women" (especially insofar as authors are concerned) tends to inspire a by-now-familiar recitation of the "dangers" of essentialism—an affirmation of the difference between men and women as given, and an attendant belief in the positive value of female identity which, repressed by patriarchy, will be given its true voice by feminism. While there is obviously much to be said about the risks of essentialism, the contemporary practice of essentialism detection has avoided the complex relationship between "woman" and "women," usually by bracketing the category of "women" altogether.

Even though discussions of the works of women filmmakers have been central to the development of feminist film studies, theoretical discussions of female authorship in the cinema have been surprisingly sparse. While virtually all feminist critics would agree that the works of Germaine Dulac, Maya Deren, and Dorothy Arzner (to name the most frequently invoked "historical figures") are important, there has been considerable reluctance to use any of them as privileged examples to theorize female authorship in the cinema, unless, that is, such theorizing affirms the difficulty of women's relationship to the cinematic apparatus. This reluctance reflects the current association of "theory" with "antiessentialism." In the realm of feminist literary theory and criticism, however, antiessentialism has not had quite the same widespread effects of negation. In the works of critics such as Margaret Homans and Nancy K. Miller, for instance, female authorship is analyzed not in terms of simple categories of agency and authority, but rather in terms of complex textual and cultural processes which dramatize and foreground women's relationships to language, plot, and the institutions of literature.[1] My point is not that feminist film critics have the proverbial "much to learn" from feminist literary critics, but rather that the paradigm of female authorship in literature may provide a useful point of departure to examine the status of female authorship in the cinema.

For such a point of departure, I turn to two anecdotes, one "literary" and one "theoretical," both of which stage an encounter between women's writing and the cinema in similar ways. My first anecdote, the more "literary" one, concerns two contemporary novels by women concerned with the vicissitudes of female writing. In both novels, cinema becomes a persuasive metaphor for the difficult and sometimes impenetrable obstacles that confront the woman writer. Doris Lessing's novel *The Golden Notebook* explores the relations between female identity and artistic production, and a formulation of that relation is represented through the cinema. Woman is the viewer, man the projectionist, and the whole viewing process a form of control and domination. Writer Anna Wulf describes her vision of events from her own past as films shown to her by an invisible male projectionist. The films represent what Anna calls the "burden of recreating order out of the chaos that my life had become." Yet Anna is horrified by this vision of cinematic order:

> They were all, so I saw now, conventionally, well-made films, as if they had been done in a studio; then I saw the titles: these films, which were everything I hated most, had been directed by me. The projectionist kept running these films very fast, and then pausing on the credits, and I could hear his jeering laugh at *Directed by Anna Wulf*. Then he would run another few scenes, every scene glossy with untruth, false and stupid.[2]

Lessing's cinematic metaphor is informed by a relationship between viewer and image, and between projectionist and screen, that is profoundly patriarchal in the sense that separation, hierarchy, and power are here synonymous with sexual division. The conventionality and gloss of untruth of the films are complicit with Anna Wulf's alienation from her name that appears on them. If, for Lessing, the conditions of film viewing suggest patriarchal domination, then the most immediate terms of that metaphor are the simultaneous evocation and denial of female authorship. Cinema embodies distance from the self—or at least, distance from the *female* self, a distance produced by the mockery of female authorship in the titles of the film. As evoked in *The Golden Notebook* within the context of the female narrator's relationship to language and to experience, cinema functions as a particularly and peculiarly negative inflection of the female authorial signature.

In her novel *The Quest for Christa T.*, Christa Wolf evokes the cinema as a form of illusory presence, as a fantasy control of the past. The female narrator of *The Quest for Christa T.* describes her search for Christa, as well as for the very possibility of memory: "I even name her name, and now I'm quite certain of her. But all the time I know that it's a film of shadows being run off the reel, a film that was once projected in the real light of cities, landscapes, living rooms."[3] Film may create images of the past, but the images are contained by a reified memory. The cinema thus suggests a past that has been categorized, hierarchized, and neatly tucked away.[4] Like Lessing's Anna Wulf, the narrator of *The Quest of Christa T.* searches for the connections between female identity and language. While less explicit in its patriarchal configuration, Wolf's metaphor nonetheless posits cinema as resistant to the process of active searching generally, and female self-expression specifically. The female narrator in *The Quest for Christa T.* is engaged, in Wolf's words, in a search for "the secret of the third person, who is there without being tangible and who, when circumstances favor her, can bring down more reality upon herself than the first person: I." As in *The Golden Notebook,* cinema obstructs the writing of female self-representation, thus embodying what Wolf calls "the difficulty of saying 'I.' "[5]

If we are to take Lessing's and Wolf's metaphoric representations of the cinema at their word, then the difficulty of saying "I" for the woman filmmaker is far greater than for the woman writer. Feminist interrogations of the cinema have supported Lessing's and Wolf's metaphors, for the narrative and visual staging of cinematic desire relies, as most theoretical accounts would have it, on the massive disavowal of sexual difference and the subsequent alignment of cinematic representation with male-centered scenarios. To be sure, one could argue—with more than a touch of defensiveness—that such metaphoric renderings of the cinema suggest the strategic importance of the works of women filmmakers. For if the cinema is symptomatic of alienation (Lessing) and reification (Wolf), then the attempts by women directors to redefine, appropriate, or otherwise reinvent the cinema are crucial demonstrations that the boundaries of that supremely patriarchal form are more permeable, more open to feminist and female influence, than these film-inspired metaphors would suggest. At the same time, it could be argued that the works of women filmmakers offer reformulations of cinematic identification and desire, reformulations that posit cinematic metaphors quite different from those in the passages from Lessing and Wolf cited above. In other words, the "difficulty of saying 'I' " does not necessarily mean that female authorship is impossible in the cinema, but rather that it functions differently than in literature.

If Lessing's and Wolf's formulations reflect the spirit of much feminist writing about film, suggesting that the cinema is peculiarly and forcefully resistant to the female creator, yet another obstacle to the theorizing of female authorship in the cinema emerges when the literary comparison is pursued in another direction. My second, more properly "theoretical" anecdote of the relationship between female authorship in its literary and cinematic forms is drawn from the introduction to *Revision,* a collection of essays on feminist film theory and criticism. The editors of the volume note that feminist film critics have "reason to be envious" of those feminist critics working in literature who "were able to turn to a comparatively substantial canon of works by women writers." Unlike literature, the cinema has no such evidence of a female-authored cinema to which feminist critics might logically turn to begin to elaborate the components of women's cinema or of a feminist film aesthetic. "For where in the classic cinema," the editors ask, "do we encounter anything like an 'autonomous tradition,' with 'distinctive features' and 'lines of influence'? And if, with some difficulty, we can conceive of Lois Weber and Dorothy Arzner as the Jane Austen and George Eliot of Hollywood, to whom do they trace their own influence?"[6]

While feminist literary critics have their own disagreements about the validity of the concept of a "female tradition" (autonomous or not) or a female "canon" (substantial or not), it is true that feminist film critics simply do not have the body of evidence to suggest how and in what ways female-authored cinema would be substantially different from cinema directed and created by men. The absence of this body of evidence notwithstanding, however, it seems to me that the reluctance of many feminist critics to speak, as feminist literary critics do, of a "female tradition" in cinema had to do with a number of other factors, ranging from theoretical frameworks in which any discussions of "personhood" are suspect, to the peculiar status of authorship in the cinema. Particularly insofar as the classical Hollywood cinema is concerned, the conventional equation of authorship with the role of the film director can repress or negate the significant ways in which female signatures *do* appear on film. For instance, consideration of the role of the often-forgotten, often-female screenwriter might suggest more of a female imprint on the film text; and the role of the actress does not always conform to common feminist wisdom about the controlling male gaze located in the persona of the male director—witness Bette Davis as a case in point.[7]

The reluctance to speak of a "female tradition" has perhaps been most influenced, however, by the fear of essentialism—the fear, that is, that any discussion of "female texts" presumes the uniqueness and autonomy of female representation, thus validating rather than challenging the dualism of patriarchal hierarchy. However, the act of discarding the concept of female authorship and of an attendant female tradition in the cinema as necessarily compromised by essentialist definitions of woman can be equally dualistic, in assuming that the only models of connection and influence are unquestionably essentialist ones. Sometimes it is assumed that any discussion of authorship is a throwback to the era of biographical criticism, to the text as transparent and simple reflection of the author's life. While the limitations of such an approach are obvious, purely textual models of cinematic representation have their own limitations insofar as the narrative strategies of many contemporary women's films are concerned, for these strategies frequently involve an inscription of authorship in literal terms, with the director herself a performer in her film.

Any discussion of female authorship in the cinema must take into account the curious history of definitions of cinematic authorship in general.[8] It was not really until the 1950s that "auteurism" became a fixture of film theory and criticism. The French term did not connote then, as French terms have in the past two decades of film studies, a particularly complex entity. For *auteurism* refers to the view that the film director is the single force responsible for the final film, and that throughout the films of a given *auteur* a body of themes and pre-occupations will be discernible.[9] The obviousness of these claims is complicated, rather, by the fact that the object of inquiry for auteurist critics was primarily the Hollywood cinema. To speak of a "Hitchcock" or a "John Ford" or a "Nicholas Ray" film as opposed to an "MGM" or a "John Wayne" film was, if not a necessarily radical enterprise, then at least a historically significant one, in that a shift was marked in the very ways in which one speaks of film. For the corporate industrial model of film production was being challenged by a liberal humanist one, and "Hitchcock" does not carry quite the same capitalist, industrial, or corporate baggage as "MGM."

Despite the opposition between the industry and the creative individual from which auteurism emerges, however, the terms do not differ all that much in their partiarchal connotations; "MGM" and "Hitchcock" may be patriarchal in different ways, but they share a common ground. The cinematic *auteur* was identified as a transcendental figure resistant to the leveling forces of the Hollywood industry; to use Roland Barthes's words, the *auteur* theory in cinema reinstated the "formidable paternity" of the individual creator threatened by the institutions of mass culture of which the cinema is a paradigmatic and even privileged example.[10] Thus it does not require too much imagination to see Alexandre Astruc's famous equation of the camera with a writer's pen, in his phrase "caméro-stylo," as informed by the same kind of metaphorical equivalence between pen and penis that has defined both the Western literary tradition (symptomatically) and feminist literary history (critically).[11] The phallic denominator can be read several ways, most obviously as a denial of the possibility of any female agency. Conversely, it can be argued that the privileging of female authorship risks appropriating, for women, an extremely patriarchal notion of cinematic creation. At stake, then, is whether the adjective *female* in female authorship inflects the noun *authorship* in a way significant enough to challenge or displace its patriarchal and proprietary implications.

Whether authorship constitutes a patriarchal and/or phallocentric notion in its own right raises the specter of the "Franco-American Dis-connection" (to use Domna Stanton's phrase) that has been the source of much critical debate, or confusion, depending upon your point of view, in contemporary feminist theory.[12] The position usually described as "American"—and therefore empirical and historical—would claim female authorship as basic to the goals of a feminist appropriation of (cinematic) culture, and the position described as "French"—theoretical and deconstructive—would find "authorship" and "appropriation" equally complicitous in their mimicry of patriarchal definitions of self, expression, and representation.[13] Although it is a commonly held assumption that contemporary film studies, especially as they developed in England, are virtually synonymous with "French theory," the fate of auteurism, particularly in relationship to feminist film theory, has not followed such an easily charted or one-directional path. In a famous 1973 essay, for example, Claire Johnston argued against the dismissal of the *auteur* theory. While acknowledging that "some developments of the *auteur* theory have led to a tendency to deify the personality of the (male) director," Johnston argues nonetheless for the importance of auteurism for feminism. She notes that "the development of the *auteur* theory marked an important intervention in film criticism: its polemics challenged the entrenched view of Hollywood as monolithic, and stripped of its normative aspects the classification of films by director has proved an extremely productive way of ordering our experience of the cinema."[14]

Johnston's argument recalls Peter Wollen's writings on *auteur* theory, where the cinematic *auteur* is defined less as a creative individual and more as a figure whose imprint on a film is measured by the repetition of sets of oppositions and the network of preoccupations, including unconscious ones.[15] Her analysis needs to be seen in the context of a certain moment in feminist criticism, when notions of "good roles" for women (and therefore "positive" versus "negative" images) had much critical currency. Johnston turns that critical currency on its head in a comparison of Howard Hawks and John Ford. She argues that the apparently more "positive" and "liberated" heroines of Hawks's films are pure functions of male desire. For John Ford, women function in more ambivalent ways. Whereas in Hawks's films woman is "a traumatic presence which must be negated," in Ford's films woman "becomes a cipher onto which Ford projects his profoundly ambivalent attitude to the concepts of civilisation and psychological 'wholeness.' "[16] Defined as a narrative and visual system associated with a given director, Johnston's auteurism allows for a kind of analysis which goes beyond the categories of "good" and "bad" (images or roles) and into the far more productive critical territory of symptom and contradiction.

While Johnston's analysis seems to stress equally the importance of auteurism and of "symptomatic readings," her work is read today far more in the context of the latter. As with Peter Wollen's work on authorship, one senses that perhaps the auteurist part is a backdrop upon which more significant critical and theoretical assumptions are projected—those of structuralism and semiotics in the case of Wollen, and those of Althusserian-based critical readings in the case of Johnston. The kind of analysis for which Johnston argues—analysis of the position of "woman" within the narrative and visual structures of the cinema— has by and large been pursued without much direct consideration for the *auteur* theory, or for *auteurs*.[17] Despite the importance of auteurism in staking out what Johnston would call progressive claims for film criticism, the analysis of the kinds of structures to which Johnston alludes in the films of Hawks or Ford has been pursued within the framework of textual and ideological analyses of that ubiquitous entity, the classical Hollywood cinema, rather than within the scope of authorship.

By and large, the preferred mode of textual analysis, given its particular attention to unconscious resonances within narrative and visual structures, has had little room for an exploration of auteurism. One notable exception is Raymond Bellour's analyses of Hitchcock's role as "enunciator" in his films, which nonetheless define authorship in explicitly literal and narrow textual terms—i.e., the fact that Hitchcock's famous cameo appearances in his films occur at crucial moments of the exposition and/or resolution of cinematic desire.[18] More frequently in contemporary film studies, one speaks of a "Hawks" film or a "Ford" film in the same way one would speak of a "horror" film or a "film noir"—as a convenient categorization of films with similar preoccupations and similar stylistic and narrative features. Such a demystification of authorship might well be more progressive than Johnston's defense of authorship. Conversely, authorship itself may have assumed a symptomatic status, in which case it has not been demystified so much as concealed within and displaced onto other concerns, evoking a process similar to what Nancy K. Miller has observed in the field of literary studies, where the concept of authorship has been not so much revised as it has been repressed "in favor of the (new) monolith of anonymous textuality."[19]

In film theory and criticism of the last decade, auteurism is rarely invoked, and when it is, it is more as a curiosity, as a historical development surely influential, but even more surely surpassed. In this context, Kaja Silverman has suggested that a curious slippage occurs in feminist discussions of the avant-garde works of women filmmakers, for the concept of authorship—largely bracketed in textual analysis—reappears, but in an extratextual way.

> The author often emerges . . . as a largely untheorized category, placed definitively "outside" the text, and assumed to be the punctual source of its sounds and images. A certain nostalgia for an unproblematic agency permeates much of the writing to which I refer. There is no sense in which the feminist author, like her phallic counterpart, might be constructed in and through discourse—that she might be inseparable from the desire that circulates within her texts, investing itself not only in their formal articulation, but in recurring diegetic elements.[20]

Silverman recommends a theorization of female authorship that would account for a diversity of authorial inscriptions, ranging from thematic preoccupations, to the designation of a character or group of characters as a stand-in for the author, to the various enunciative strategies (sonoric as well as visual) whereby the film *auteur's* presence is marked (whether explicitly or implicitly), to the "fantasmatic scene" that structures an author's work.[21]

The concept of female authorship in the cinema may well have a currency similar to categories of genre or of style. But can female authorship be so easily assimilated to the existing taxonomy of the cinema? Present categories of authorship are undoubtedly much more useful in analyzing the configurations of "woman" on screen than in coming to terms with the ways in which women directors inflect cinematic practice in new and challenging ways. The analysis of female authorship in the cinema raises somewhat different questions than does the analysis of male authorship, not only for the obvious reason that women have not had the same relationship to the institutions of the cinema as men have, but also because the articulation of female authorship threatens to upset the erasure of "women" which is central to the articulation of "woman" in the cinema. Virtually all feminist critics who argue in defense of female authorship as a useful and necessary category assume the political necessity for doing so. Hence, Kaja Silverman urges that the gendered positions of libidinal desire within the text be read "in relation to the biological gender of the biographical author, since it is clearly not the same thing, socially or politically, for a woman to speak with a female voice as it is for a man to do so, and vice versa."[22] The notion of female authorship is not simply a useful political strategy; it is crucial to the reinvention of the cinema that has been undertaken by women filmmakers and feminist spectators.

One of the most productive ironies of feminist theory may be that, if "woman" and "women" do *not* coincide (to borrow Teresa de Lauretis's formulation), they also connect in tenuous and often complex ways. It is customary in much feminist film theory to read "subject" to "object" as "male" is to "female." But a more productive exploration of female authorship insofar as "woman" and "women" are concerned may result when subject-object relationships are considered within and among women. Visions of "woman" that appear on screen may be largely the projections of patriarchal fantasies, and the "women" who make films and who see them may have problematic relations at best with those visions. While it is tempting to use de Lauretis's distinction as an opposition between traditional cinematic representations of "woman" and those "women" filmmakers who challenge and reinvent them, the gap, the noncoincidence are better defined by exploring the tensions within both "woman" and "women."[23]

One such strategy has been directed toward the "reading against the grain" of traditional cinematic representations of women, demonstrating how they can be read in ways that contradict or otherwise problematize their function within male-centered discourse.[24] Surprisingly little comparable attention has been paid, however, to the function and position of the woman director. Central to a theorizing of female authorship in the cinema is an expanded definition of textuality attentive to the complex network of intersections, distances, and resistances of "woman" to "women." The challenge of female authorship in the cinema for feminist theory is in the demonstration of *how* the divisions, overlaps, and distances between "woman" and "women" connect with the contradictory status of cinema as the embodiment of both omnipotent control and individual fantasy.

The feminist rediscovery of Dorothy Arzner in the 1970s remains the most important attempt to theorize female authorship in the cinema. Arzner may not be feminist film theory's answer to George Eliot, but her career as a woman director in Hollywood with a significant body of work (and in whose work—true to the most rudimentary definitions of film authorship—a number of pre-occupations reappear) has posed issues most central to a feminist theory of female cinematic authorship. As one of the very small handful of women directors who were successful in Hollywood, particularly during the studio years, Arzner has served as an important example of a woman director working within the Hollywood system who managed, in however limited ways, to make films that disturb the conventions of Hollywood narrative.

The significance of this argument, advanced primarily by Claire Johnston and Pam Cook, in which Arzner is defined as a director "critical" of the Hollywood cinema, needs to be seen in the context of the development of the notion of the film *auteur*. Arzner was very definitely *not* one of the directors for whom auteurist claims were made in the heyday of auteurist criticism. For despite the core themes and preoccupations visible across her work, Arzner does not satisfy any of the specific requirements of cinematic authorship as they were advanced on either side of the Atlantic—there is little of the flourish of mise-en-scène that auteurists attributed to other directors, for instance, and the preoccupations visible from film to film that might identify a particular signature do not reflect the life-and-death, civilization-versus-the-wilderness struggles that tended to define the range of more "properly" auteurist themes.[25]

Given the extent to which feminist analysis of the cinema has relied on the distinction between dominant and alternative film, the claims that can be made for an alternative vision that exists within and alongside the dominant cinema will be crucial in gauging the specific ways in which women directors engage with "women's cinema" as divided between representations that perpetuate patriarchal definitions of femininity, and representations that challenge them and offer other modes of identification and pleasure. One can read in responses to Arzner's work reflections of larger assumptions concerning the Hollywood cinema. At one extreme is Andrew Britton's assessment of Arzner, in his study of Katharine Hepburn, as the *auteur* of *Christopher Strong* (1933), the film in which Hepburn appears as an aviatrix who falls in love with an older, married man.

That *Christopher Strong* functions as a "critique of the effect of patriarchal heterosexual relations on relations between women" suggests that the classical cinema lends itself quite readily to heterogeneity and conflicting ideological allegiances, whether the "critique" is the effect of the woman director or the female star.[26] At the opposite extreme, Jacquelyn Suter's analysis of *Christopher Strong* evolves from the assumption that whatever "female discourse" there is in the film is subsumed and neutralized by the patriarchal discourse on monogamy.[27] If the classical cinema described by Britton seems remarkably open to effects of subversion and criticism, the classical cinema described by Suter is just as remarkably closed to any meanings but patriarchal ones, and one is left to assume that female authorship is either a simple affirmation of agency, or virtually an impossibility as far as Hollywood cinema is concerned.

In contrast, Claire Johnston's analyses of Arzner are reminiscent of Roland Barthes's description of Balzac as representative of a "limited plurality" within classical discourse.[28] For Johnston suggests that the strategies of her films open up limited criticisms of the Hollywood cinema. Johnston's claims for female authorship in Arzner's films rely on notions of defamiliarization and dislocation, and more precisely on the assumption popularized within film studies, primarily by Jean-Louis Comolli and Jean Narboni, that there exists within the classical Hollywood cinema a category of films in which realist conventions are criticized from within, generating a kind of internal critique. Claims for this "progressive" text have been made from a variety of vantage points, virtually all of them concerned with ideological value—with, that is, the possibility of a Hollywood film that critiques the very values that are ostensibly promoted, from the literal dark underside of bourgeois ideology "exposed" in *Young Mr. Lincoln* to the impossibility of familial ties for women in *Mildred Pierce*.[29] For Johnston, female desire is the *auteurist* preoccupation that generates a critique of patriarchal ideology in Arzner's films.

Initially, Johnston's analysis of Arzner appears to rely on a definition of the classical cinema that allows for more heterogeneity and more articulation of contradiction than is the case in those analyses that posit a rigid distinction between the classical cinema and its alternatives. However, Arzner's films can be identified as "progressive" only in relationship to a norm that allows for no divergences from purely classical filmmaking. More problematical within the present context, there is nothing in this kind of analysis to suggest what these marks of dislocation and critique have to do with distinctly *female* authorship. Many "woman's films" are motivated by the representation of female desire, and feminist critics have shown how these films might also be read as driven by such an internal—if often unconscious—critique.[30] It is not clear, in other words, to what extent the fact of female authorship gives a particular or distinct inflection to the representation of female desire.

The "political" reasons for insisting on the relevance of the author's gender are not adequate in and of themselves, for they can easily harden into an idealized abstraction, and the name "Dorothy Arzner" would thus become just one more signature to add to the pantheon of (male) directors who critique the conventions of Hollywood cinema from within. While the importance of Arzner's signature in extratextual terms is undeniable, stressing that importance should not be a substitute for an examination of the textual ramifications of female authorship. Yet Johnston's approach to those textual ramifications in Arzner's work seems torn between female authorship understood ("politically") as agency and self-representation, on the one hand, and as a negative inflection of the norms of classical cinema, on the other.[31] This ambivalence—which could be read in terms of the conflicting claims of the so-called American and French positions—is not particularly productive, for the agency thus affirmed dissolves into negation and the impossibility of a female position, evoking Julia Kristéva's extremely limited hypothesis that "women's practice can only be negative, in opposition to that which exists, to say that 'this is not it' and 'it is not yet.' "[32]

Noting that structural coherence in Arzner's films comes from the discourse of the woman, Johnston relies on the notion of defamiliarization, derived from the Russian formalists' *priem ostranenie,* the "device of making strange," to assess the effects of the woman's discourse on patriarchal meaning: "the work of the woman's discourse renders the narrative strange, subverting and dislocating it at the level of meaning."[33] Johnston discusses in this context what has become the single most famous scene from any of Arzner's films, when Judy (Maureen O'Hara), who has played ballet stooge to the vaudeville performer Bubbles

(Lucille Ball) in *Dance, Girl, Dance* (1940), confronts her audience and tells them how *she* sees *them*. This is, Johnston argues, the only real break between dominant discourse and the discourse of the woman in Arzner's work, and it is a break that is quickly recuperated within the film, for the audience applauds Judy, and she and Bubbles are quickly dispatched to center stage, where they engage in a catfight, to the delight of the audience. The moment in *Dance, Girl, Dance* when Judy faces her audience is a privileged moment in feminist film theory and criticism, foregrounding as it does the sexual hierarchy of the gaze, with female agency defined as the return of the look, thus "citing" the objectification of woman.[34]

The celebrity accorded this particular scene in Arzner's film needs to be evaluated in the context of feminist film theory in the mid-1970s. Confronted with the persuasive psychoanalytically based theoretical model according to which women either did not or could not exist on screen, the discovery of Arzner, and especially of Judy's "return of the gaze," offered some glimmer of historical hope as to the possibility of a female intervention in the cinema. To be sure, the scope of the intervention is limited, for as Johnston herself stresses, Judy's radical act is quickly recuperated within the film when the audience gets up to cheer her on, and she and Bubbles begin to fight on stage. But the need to revise Johnston's model of authorship is most apparent in this reading of recuperation, for it is informed by the assumption that such a "break" can be only a brief eruption, and can occur in classical cinema only if it is then immediately contained within the laws of male spectatorial desire.

Only one kind of look (Judy's return of the look to her audience) and one kind of spectacle (where men are the agents of the look and women its objects) have received attention in *Dance, Girl, Dance*. In other words, the disruptive force of female desire central to Arzner's work exists primarily within the symmetry of masculinity and femininity.[35] However, I would suggest that female authorship acquires its most significant contours in Arzner's work through relations between and among women. The female gaze is defined early on in the film as central to the aspirations of women as they are shaped within a community of women. Madame Basilova, the older woman who is in charge of the dancing troupe of which Judy and Bubbles are a part, is seen gazing through the rails of a stairway as Judy practices her ballet, and the gaze of Judy herself is isolated as she looks longingly at a rehearsal of the ballet company which she wishes to join. Even Judy's famous scolding of the audience is identified primarily as a communication, not between a female performer and a male audience (the audience is not, in any case, exclusively male) but between the performer and the female member of the audience (secretary to Steven Adams, the man who will eventually become Judy's love interest) who stands up to applaud her.[36] And the catfight that erupts between Judy and Bubbles on stage is less a recuperative move—i.e., transforming the potential threat of Judy's confrontation into an even more tantalizing spectacle—than the claiming by the two women of the stage as an extension of their conflicted friendship, rather than as the alienated site of performance.

To be sure, the men—promoters as well as onlookers—eagerly consume the spectacle of Judy and Bubbles in a catfight. But I see this response less as a sign of pure recuperation by the male-centered system of looks and spectacles, and more as the dramatization of the tension between performance and self-expression which the film attempts to resolve. Although Johnston is more concerned with the devices that give Arzner's films "structural coherence," it is tempting to conclude from her analysis that Judy functions as a metaphoric rendering of the woman filmmaker herself, thus establishing something of a homology between Arzner's position vis-à-vis the classical Hollywood cinema and Judy's position on stage.[37] The stage is, in other words, *both* the site of the objectification of the female body *and* the site for the theatricalizing of female friendship. This "both/and"—the stage (and, by metaphoric implication, the cinema itself) is an arena simultaneously of patriarchal exploitation and of female self-representation—stands in contrast to the more limited view of Arzner's films in Johnston's work, where more of a "neither/nor" logic is operative—neither patriarchal discourse nor the "discourse of the woman" allows women a vantage point from which to speak, represent, or imagine themselves.

Reading Arzner's films in terms of the "both/and" suggests an irony more far-reaching than that described by Johnston. Johnston's reading of Arzner is suggestive of Shoshana Felman's definition of irony as "dragging authority as such into a scene which it cannot master, of which it is *not aware* and which, for that very reason, is the scene of its own self-destruction. . . . "[38] The irony in *Dance, Girl, Dance,* however, does not just demonstrate how the patriarchal discourse of the cinema excludes women, but rather how the cinema functions in two radically different ways, both of which are "true," as it were, and totally incompatible. I am borrowing here from Donna Haraway's definition of irony: "Irony is about contradictions that do not resolve into larger wholes, even dialectically, about the tension of holding incompatible things together because both or all are necessary and true."[39] This insistence on two equally compelling and incompatible truths constitutes a form of irony far more complex than Johnston's analysis of defamiliarization.

Johnston's notion of Arzner's irony assumes a patriarchal form of representation which may have its gaps and its weak links, but which remains dominant in every sense of the word. For Johnston, Arzner's irony can be only the irony of negativity, of puncturing holes in patriarchal assumptions. Such a view of irony has less to do, I would argue, with the limitations of Arzner's career (e.g., as a woman director working within the inevitable limitations of the Hollywood system) than with the limitations of the film theory from which it grows. If the cinema is understood as a one-dimensional system of male subjects and female objects, then it is not difficult to understand how the irony in Arzner's films is limited, or at least would be *read* as limited. While rigid hierarchies of sexual difference are indeed characteristic of dominant cinema, they are not absolute, and Arzner's films represent other kinds of cinematic pleasure and desire.

An assessment of Arzner's importance within the framework of female authorship needs to account not only for how Arzner problematizes the pleasures of the cinematic institution as we understand it—e.g., in terms of the voyeurism and fetishism reenacted through the power of the male gaze and the objectification of the female body—but also for how, in her films, those pleasures are identified in ways that are not reducible to the theoretical clichés of the omnipotence of the male gaze. The irony of *Dance, Girl, Dance* emerges from the conflicting demands of performance and self-expression, which are linked in their turn to heterosexual romance and female friendship. Female friendship acquires a resistant function in the way that it exerts a pressure against the supposed "natural" laws of heterosexual romance. Relations between women and communities of women have a privileged status in Arzner's films. To be sure, Arzner's films offer plots—particularly insofar as resolutions are concerned—that are compatible with the romantic expectations of the classical Hollywood cinema; communities of women may be central, but boy still meets girl.

Claire Johnston claims that the conclusion of *Dance, Girl, Dance,* where Judy is embraced by Steven Adams, destined for a fusion of professional mentoring and romance, is marked by Judy's defeat. This strikes me more as wishful feminist thinking than as a convincing reading of the film's conclusion, which "works" within the conventions of Hollywood romance. Noting Judy's final comment as she is in Steven's arms—"when I think how simple things could have been, I just have to laugh"—Johnston says that "this irony marks her defeat and final engulfment, but at the same time it is the final mark of subversion of the discourse of the male."[40] If the "discourse of the male" is subverted in *Dance, Girl, Dance,* it has less to do with the resolution of the film and more to do with the process of heterosexual initiation which the film has traced. Judy's attractions to men are shaped by substitutions for women and female rivalry—Steven Adams is a professional mentor to substitute for Basilova, and Jimmie Harris is an infantile man who is desirable mainly because Bubbles wants him too.[41] Therefore, the heterosexual romance provides the conclusion of the film, but only after it has been mediated by relationships between women.

A controversial area in feminist theory and criticism has been the connection between lesbianism and female friendship in those fictional worlds which, like Arzner's, take communities of women as their inspiration. Barbara Smith's suggestion that the relationship between Nel and Sula in Toni Morrison's novel *Sula* can be read in lesbian terms has been provocative to say the least, particularly given Toni Morrison's own assertion that "there is no homosexuality in *Sula*."[42] But the case of Arzner is somewhat different. What is known about Arzner implies that she herself was a lesbian.[43] But this assertion raises as many questions as it presumably answers, concerning both the responsibility of a critic vis-à-vis an individual who was presumably in the closet, and the compulsion to define lesbianism as something in need of proof.[44] Bonnie Zimmerman has suggested that "if a text lends itself to a lesbian reading, then no amount of biographical 'proof' ought to be necessary to establish it as a lesbian text."[45] The point is well taken, but in Arzner's case another "text" mediates the relationship between director, her films, and their reception. For Arzner's films are virtually no longer read independently of her persona—an issue to which I will return momentarily. Nonetheless, if relationships between and among women account for much more narrative and visual momentum than do the relations between men and women in Arzner's work, then one begins to wonder about the perspective that informs these preoccupations.

For all of the attention that has been given to Arzner's work, one striking aspect of her persona—and of her films—has been largely ignored. Although the photographs of Arzner that have accompanied feminist analyses of her work depict a woman who favored a look and a style connoting lesbian identity, discussions of her work always stop short of any recognition that sexual identity might have something to do with how her films function, particularly concerning the "discourse of the woman" and female communities, or that the contours of female authorship in her films might be defined in lesbian terms. This marginalization is all the more notable, given how *visible* Arzner has been as an image in feminist film theory. With the possible exception of Maya Deren, Arzner is more frequently represented visually than any other woman director central to contemporary feminist discussions of film. And unlike Deren, who appeared extensively in her own films, Arzner does not have the reputation of being a particularly self-promoting, visible, or "out" (in several senses of the term) woman director.

Sarah Halprin has suggested that the reason for this omission is, in part, the suspicion of any kind of biographical information in analysis of female authorship:

> most discussions of Dorothy Arzner's films, especially those by the English school, carefully avoid any mention of Arzner's appearance in relation to some of

the images in her films. Lengthy analyses of *Dance, Girl, Dance* ignore the fact that while the "main" characters, Judy and Bubbles, are recurrently placed as immature within the context of the film, there are two "minor" characters who both dress and look remarkably similar to Arzner herself (i.e., tailored, "mannish," in the manner of Radclyffe Hall and other famous lesbians of the time) and are placed as mature, single, independent women who are crucial to the career of young Judy and who are clearly seen as oppressed by social stereotyping, of which they are contemptuous. Such a reading provides a whole new way of relating to the film and to other Arzner films, encouraging a discussion of lesbian stereotypes, relations between lesbians and heterosexual women as presented in various films and as perceived by any specific contemporary audience.[46]

Indeed, one of the most critical aspects of Arzner's work is the way in which heterosexuality is assumed equivocally, without necessarily violating many of the conventions of the Hollywood film.

In his book on gay sexuality and film, Vito Russo quotes another Hollywood director on Arzner: "an obviously lesbian director like Dorothy Arzner got away with her lifestyle because she was officially closeted and because 'it made her one of the boys.' "[47] An interview with Arzner by Karyn Kay and Gerald Peary gives some evidence of her status as "one of the boys," at least insofar as identification is concerned, for in discussing both *Christopher Strong* and *Craig's Wife,* Arzner insists that her sympathies lie with the male characters.[48] However, one has only to look at the photographs of Arzner that have accompanied essays about her work in recent years to see that this is not a director so easily assimilated to the boys' club of Hollywood. Arzner preferred masculine attire, in the manner, as Halprin says, of Radclyffe Hall. Two dominant tropes shape the photographic mise-en-scène of the Arzner persona. She is portrayed against the backdrop of the large-scale apparatus of the Hollywood cinema, or she is shown with other women, usually actresses, most of whom are most emphatically "feminine," creating a striking contrast indeed.

Both tropes appear in the photograph on the cover of the collection edited by Claire Johnston, *The Work of Dorothy Arzner: Towards a Feminist Cinema.* We see Arzner in profile, slouching directorially on a perch next to a very large camera; seated next to her is a man. They both look toward what initially appears to be the unidentified field of vision (Figure 14). When the pamphlet is opened, however, the photograph continues on the back cover: two young women, one holding packages, look at each other, their positions reflecting symmetrically those of Arzner and her male companion (Figure 15). It is difficult to read precisely the tenor of the scene (from *Working Girls* [1930]) between the two women: some hostility perhaps, or desperation. The camera occupies the center of the photograph, as a large, looming—and predictably phallic—presence (Figure 16). The look on the man's face suggests quite strongly the clichés of the

Figure 12. Dorothy Arzner (Museum of Modern Art)

male gaze that have been central to feminist film theory; from his perspective the two women exist as objects of voyeuristic pleasure. Arzner's look has quite another function, however, and one that has received very little critical attention, and that is to decenter the man's look, and to eroticize the exchange of looks between the two women.[49]

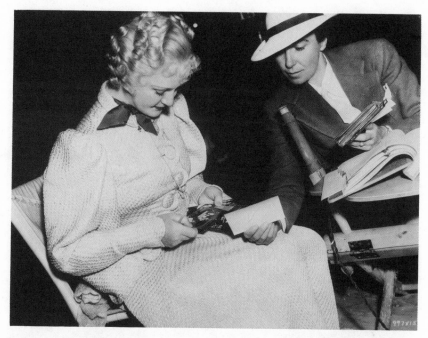

Figure 13. Dorothy Arzner and Billie Burke (Museum of Modern Art)

While virtually none of the feminist critics who analyze Arzner's work have discussed lesbianism, a curious syndrome is suggested by this use of "accompanying illustrations." The photograph on the covers of the pamphlet edited by Claire Johnston speaks rather literally what is unspoken in the written text, in a teasing kind of way. Johnston's and Cook's essays are reprinted in a recent collection of essays on feminist film theory, not one of which discusses erotic connections between women.[50] Yet on the cover of the book is a photograph of Arzner and Rosalind Russell exchanging a meaningful look with more than a hint of female homoeroticism. One begins to suspect that the simultaneous evocation and dispelling of an erotic bond between women in Arzner's work is a structuring absence in feminist film theory. Like any good symptom it rather obsessively draws attention to itself. Arzner's lesbian persona may not be theorized in relationship to her films, but her visibility in feminist film criticism suggests that one of the mechanisms cited most frequently as central to male spectatorial desire informs feminist film theory, too. I am referring, of course, to fetishism.

To be sure, any parallel between a classical, male-centered trajectory such as fetishism and the dynamics of feminist theory can be made only tentatively.[51]

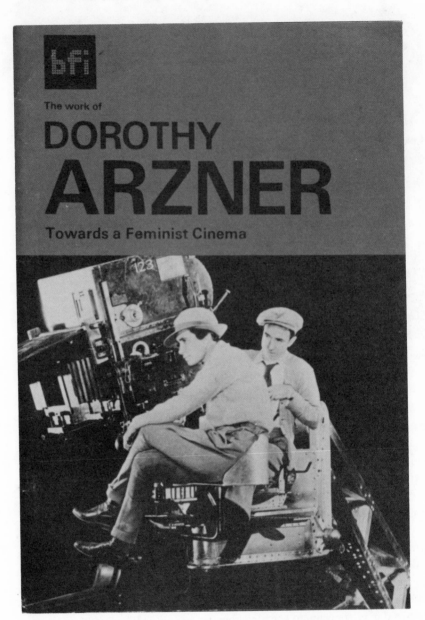

Figure 14

Figure 15

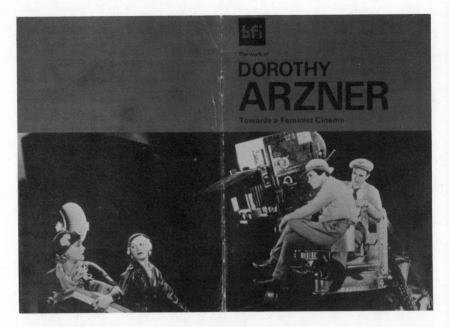

Figure 16

But there is nonetheless a telling fit between Octave Mannoni's formula for disavowal ("I know very well, but all the same . . . "), adapted by Christian Metz to analyze cinematic fetishism, and the consistent and simultaneous evocation and disavowal of Arzner's lesbian persona.[52] A heterosexual master code, where any and all combinations of "masculinity," from the male gaze to Arzner's clothing, and "femininity," from conventional objectification of the female body to the female objects of Arzner's gaze, has shaped discussions of Arzner's work. The narrative and visual structures of her films are praised for their "critique" of the Hollywood system, but the critique is so limited as to only affirm the dominance of the object in question.

The photographs of Arzner are interesting not only in the biographical terms suggested by Sarah Halprin, but also in textual terms. For one of the most distinctive ways in which Arzner's authorial presence is felt in her films is in the emphasis placed on communities of women, to be sure, but also in the erotic charge identified within those communities. If heterosexual initiation is central to Arzner's films, it is precisely in its function as rite of passage (rather than natural destiny) that a marginal presence is felt—an authorial presence that is lesbian, as well as female. Consider, for instance, *Christopher Strong*. Katharine Hepburn first appears in the film as a prize-winning object in a scavenger hunt, for she can

Figure 17. Katharine Hepburn as aviatrix Cynthia Darrington in Dorothy
Arzner's *Christopher Strong* (Museum of Modern Art)

Figure 18. Katharine Hepburn and Colin Clive in *Christopher Strong*
(Museum of Modern Art)

claim that she is over twenty-one and has never had a love affair. Christopher Strong, the man with whom she will eventually become involved, is the male version of this prize-winning object, for he has been married for more than five years and has always been faithful to his wife. As Cynthia Darrington, Hepburn dresses in decidedly unfeminine clothing and walks with a swagger that is masculine, or athletic, depending upon your point of view. Hepburn's jodhpurs and boots may well be, as Beverle Houston puts it, "that upper-class costume for a woman performing men's activities."[53] But this is also clothing that strongly denotes lesbian identity, and which (to stress again Sarah Halprin's point) is evocative of the way Arzner herself, and other lesbians of the time, dressed.

Cynthia's "virginity" becomes a euphemistic catchall for a variety of margins in which she is situated, both as a woman devoted to her career and as a woman without a sexual identity. The film traces the acquisition of heterosexual identity, with some peculiar representations of femininity along the way, including Hepburn dressed as a moth. I am not arguing that *Christopher Strong,* like the dream which says one thing but ostensibly "really" means its mirror opposite, can be decoded as a coherent "lesbian film," or that the real subject of the film is the tension between gay and straight identities. The critical attitude toward heterosexuality takes the form of inflections, of bits and pieces of tone and gesture and emphasis, as a result of which the conventions of heterosexual behavior become loosened up, shaken free of some of their identifications with the patriarchal status quo.

Most important, perhaps, the acquisition of heterosexuality becomes the downfall of Cynthia Darrington. Suter has described *Christopher Strong* in terms of how the feminine discourse, represented by the various female characters in the film, is submerged by patriarchal discourse, the central term of which is monogamy. The proof offered for such a claim is, as is often the case in textual analysis, convincing on one level but quite tentative on another, for it is a proof which begins from and ends with the assumption of a patriarchal master code. Even the "feminine discourse" described by Suter is nothing but a pale reflection of that master code, with nonmonogamy its most radical expression. The possibility that "feminine discourse" in *Christopher Strong* might exceed heterosexual boundaries is not taken into account.[54] As should be obvious by now, I am arguing that it is precisely in its ironic inflection of heterosexual norms, whether by the mirroring gesture that suggests a reflection of Arzner herself or by the definition of the female community as resistant to, rather than complicitous with, heterosexual relations, that Arzner's signature is written on her films.

These two components central to female authorship in Arzner's work— female communities and the mirroring of Arzner herself—are not identical. The one, stressing the importance of female communities and friendship among women, may function as a pressure exerted against the rituals of heterosexual initiation, but is not necessarily opposed to them. This foregrounding of relationships among women disturbs the fit between female friendship and heterosexual romance, but the fit is still there, the compatibility with the conventions of the classical Hollywood cinema is still possible. The representation of lesbian codes, as in the mirroring of Arzner's—and other lesbians'—dress, constitutes the second strategy, which is more marginal and not integrated into narrative flow. These two authorial inscriptions—the emphasis on female communities, the citing of marginal lesbian gestures—are not situated on a "continuum," that model of continuity from female friendship to explicit lesbianism so favored in much contemporary lesbian-feminist writing.[55] Rather, these two strategies exist in tension with each other, constituting yet another level of irony in Arzner's work. Female communities are compatible with the classical Hollywood narrative; the lesbian gesture occupies no such position of compatibility, it does not mesh easily with narrative continuity in Arzner's film.

Thus, in *Dance, Girl, Dance,* Arzner accentuates not only the woman's desire as embodied in Judy and her relationships with other women, but also secondary female figures who never really become central, but who do not evaporate into the margins, either—such as the secretary (who leads the applause during Judy's "return of the gaze" number) and Basilova (the dance teacher and director of the troupe). That these figures do not simply "disappear" suggests even more strongly their impossible relationship to the Hollywood plot, a relationship that *is* possible insofar as Judy is concerned. In *Craig's Wife,* however, there is more of an immediate relationship between marginality and female communities, although in this case, the marginality has less of a lesbian inflection, both dress- and gesturewise. Julia Lesage has noted that in *Craig's Wife,* Arzner rereads George Kelley's play, the source of the film, so that the secondary women characters are treated much more fully than in the play.[56]

Craig's Wife—preoccupied with heterosexual demise rather than initiation—shows us a woman so obsessively concerned with her house that nothing else is of interest to her. Harriet Craig (Rosalind Russell) married as "a way towards emancipation. . . . I married to be independent." If marriage is a business contract, then Harriet Craig's capital is her house. Indeed, Harriet's sense of economy is pursued with a vengeance. And the men in the film are the victims, explicit or not, of her obsession. It is Harriet's husband who married for love, not money, and in a subplot of the film, a friend of Walter Craig is so obsessed by his wife's unfaithfulness that he kills her and then himself.

At the conclusion of the film, virtually everyone has cleared out of Harriet's house. Her niece has left with her fiancé, her servants have either quit or been fired, and Walter has finally packed up and left in disgust. Harriet seems

Figure 19. Billie Burke and Rosalind Russell in Dorothy Arzner's
        Craig's Wife (Museum of Modern Art)

pathetically neurotic and alone. The widow next door (Billie Burke) brings
Harriet some roses. In Kelley's play, Harriet has become a mirror image of her
neighbor, for both are portrayed as women alone, to be pitied. But in Arzner's
film, the neighbor represents Harriet's one last chance for connection with
another human being. Thus the figure who in Kelley's play is a pale echo of
Harriet, becomes in the film the suggestion of another identity and of the
possibility of a female community. The resolution of Arzner's *Craig's Wife* has
little to do with the loss of a husband, and more to do with situating Harriet
Craig's fantasy come horribly true alongside the possibility of connection with
another woman. And while Billie Burke is hardly evocative of lesbianism (as
Basilova is in *Dance, Girl, Dance*), she and Rosalind Russell make for a play of
contrasts visually similar to those visible in photographs of Arzner with more
"feminine" women.[57]

To be sure, Arzner's authorship extends to an ironic perspective on patriarchal institutions in general, and in this sense her films do not require or assume a
lesbian audience, as if this was or is likely to happen within the institutions of the

Hollywood cinema. At the same time that the irony of Arzner's films appeals to a wide range of female experiences, and is thus readable across a wide spectrum, ranging from lesbian to heterosexual and from female to feminist, the marks of female authorship in her work do not constitute a universal category of female authorship in the cinema. The female signature in Arzner's work is marked by that irony of equally compelling and incompatible discourses to which I have referred, and the lesbian inflection articulates the division between female communities which do function within a heterosexual universe, and the eruptions of lesbian marginality which do not. This lesbian irony taps differing and competing views of lesbianism within contemporary feminist and lesbian theory. Lesbianism has been defined as the most intense form of female and feminist bonding, on the one hand; and as distinctly opposed to heterosexuality (whether practiced by women or men), on the other. In Arzner's own time, these competing definitions were read as the conflict between a desexualized nineteenth-century ideal of romantic friendship among women, and the "mannish lesbian" (exemplified by Radclyffe Hall), defined by herself and her critics as a sexual being.[58] Arzner's continued "visibility" suggests not only that the tension is far from being resolved, but also that debates about lesbian identity inform, even (and especially!) in unconscious ways, the thinking of feminists who do not identify as lesbians.

I see, then, several points to draw from the example of Dorothy Arzner as far as female authorship in the cinema is concerned. The preoccupations with female communities and heterosexual initiation are visible and readable only if we are attentive to how the cinema, traditionally and historically, has offered pleasures other than those that have received the most sustained critical and theoretical attention in recent years. Female authorship finds an inadequate metaphor in the female gaze as it returns the ostensibly central and overriding force of the male gaze. Other forms of the female gaze—such as the exchange of looks between and among women—open up other possibilities for cinematic meaning and pleasure and identification. In addition, a female signature can take other forms besides the gaze—costume and gesture, and the strategies of reading "marginality" in the case of Arzner. Textually, the most pervasive sign of female authorship in Arzner's film is irony, and that irony is most appropriately described as the confrontation between two equally compelling, and incompatible, discourses.

I am suggesting, of course, that lesbian irony constitutes one of the pleasures in Arzner's films, and that irony is a desirable aim in women's cinema. Irony can misfire, however.[59] It has been argued that in Jackie Raynal's film *Deux Fois,* for instance, the ironic elaboration of woman-as-object-of-spectacle is rendered decidedly problematic by the fact that it is only in offering herself as an object of spectacle that the category of woman-as-object-of-spectacle can be criticized; it is only by affirming the validity of patriarchal representation that any critique is possible.[60] I have in mind here another kind of misfiring, when the ironic reading of patriarchal conventions collides with other coded forms of representation which may serve, quite disturbingly, as a support for that irony.

In *Dance, Girl, Dance,* for instance, racial stereotypes emerge at three key moments in the narrative of the film. In the opening scenes, at a nightclub in Akron, Ohio, the camera moves over the heads of the members of the audience as it approaches the stage where the female dance troupe is performing. Intercut is an image of the black members of the band, who are smiling like the proverbially happy musicians. While an equivalence seems to be established between women and blacks as objects of spectacle, I see little basis for any "critical" use of the racist stereotype. Later in the film, when Judy watches longingly the rehearsal of the ballet company, another stereotype emerges. The performance number portrays the encounter between ballet and other forms of dance and body language within the context of the city. At one point in the performance, the music switches suddenly to imitate a jazzy tune, and a white couple in blackface struts across the stage. During one of the concluding scenes of the film, when Judy and Bubbles resolve their friendship in a court of law, the ostensibly "amusing" conclusion to the scene occurs when the clerk announces the arrival of a black couple whose names are "Abraham Lincoln Johnson" and "Martha Washington Johnson."

However disparate these stereotypes, they do emerge at crucial moments in the deployment of irony and performance. In each case, the racial stereotype appears when the sexual hierarchy of the look is deflected or otherwise put into question. The black performers at the beginning of the film are defined securely within the parameters of objectification when it is apparent—much to Bubbles' irritation and eventual attendant desire—that Jimmie Harris, one of the spectators in the audience, is totally unengaged in the spectacle on stage. The appearance of the white couple in blackface occurs when the centrality of Judy's desire, as defined by her longing gaze at the performance, is affirmed. In the courtroom scene, Judy assumes aggressively and enthusiastically the court as her stage, and the racist stereotype of "Mr. and Mrs. Johnson" appears once the rivalry between the two women is on the verge of resolution.

In each of these instances, the stereotype affirms the distinction between white subject and black object just when the distinction between male subject and female object is being put into question. While there is nothing in *Dance, Girl, Dance* that approximates a sustained discourse on race, these brief allusions to racist stereotypes are eruptions that cannot be dismissed or disregarded as mere background or as unconscious reflections of a dominant cinematic practice that was racist. The marks of authorship in *Dance, Girl, Dance* include these racist clichés as well as the ironic inflection of the heterosexual contract. I want to stress that female irony is not just a function of sexual hierarchy, but that virtually all forms of narrative and visual opposition are potentially significant. To ignore, in Arzner's case, the intertwining of sexual and racial codes of performance is to claim female authorship as a white preserve. The racist stereotypes which serve as an anchor of distinct otherness in *Dance, Girl, Dance* speak to a more general problem in female authorship. While Arzner's films suggest other forms of cinematic pleasure that have been relatively untheorized within film studies, these forms cannot be posited in any kind of simple way as "alternatives." I think it is a mistake to assume that the racist clichés are symptomatic of the compromises that inevitably occur with any attempt to create different visions within the classical Hollywood cinema. Such clichés are possible within virtually any kind of film practice.

Dorothy Arzner has come to represent both a textual practice (consciously) and an image (less consciously) in feminist film theory, and the relationship between the textual practice and the image suggests an area of fascination, if not love, that dares not speak its (her) name. The preferred term *sexual difference* in feminist film theory can slide from the tension between masculinity and femininity into a crude determinism whereby there is no representation without heterosexuality. Challenging that implicit homophobia would be reason enough to read the marks of lesbian authorship in Arzner's work. There are two other issues which the designation of lesbian authorship crystallizes in particularly important ways. First, female authorship cannot be a useful concept if it perpetuates the notion of a monolithic essentialist identity, with a feminist inflection, perhaps, but no less problematic for that. Feminists have said frequently enough that when unchallenged, the notion of the "human subject" refers inevitably to a subject that is white, male, and heterosexual.

Similarly, the unexamined female subject may not be male, but is usually assumed to be nonetheless white and heterosexual. To be sure, there is much "female bonding"—to use the preferred phrase whereby lesbianism is usually repressed—in Arzner's films, but that female bonding takes many forms, one of which is lesbian; and it is the lesbian inflection where Arzner's authorial signature is most in evidence. Second, lesbianism raises some crucial questions concerning identification and desire in the cinema, questions with particular relevance to female cinematic authorship. Cinema offers simultaneous affirmation and dissolution of the binary oppositions upon which our most fundamental notions of self and other are based. In feminist film theory, one of the most basic working assumptions has been that in the classical cinema, at least, there is a fit between the hierarchies of masculinity and femininity on the one hand, and activity and passivity on the other. If disrupting and disturbing that fit is a major task for filmmakers and theorists, then lesbianism would seem to have a strategically important function. For one of the "problems" that lesbianism poses, insofar as representation is concerned, is precisely the fit between the paradigms of sex and agency, the alignment of masculinity with activity and femininity with passivity.

It is perhaps "no coincidence" that one discourse in which the "problem" of lesbianism is thus posed most acutely is psychoanalysis. For reasons both historical and theoretical, the most persuasive as well as controversial accounts of cinematic identification and desire have been influenced by psychoanalysis. Laura Mulvey's classic account of sexual hierarchy in narrative cinema established the by-now-familiar refrain that the ideal spectator of the classical cinema, whatever his/her biological sex or cultural gender, is male. Many critics have challenged or extended the implications of Mulvey's account, most frequently arguing that for women (and sometimes for men as well), cinematic identification occurs at the very least across gender lines, whether in transvestite or bisexual terms.[61] However complex such accounts, they tend to leave unexamined another basic assumption common both to Mulvey's account and to contemporary psychoanalytic accounts of identification, and that is that cinematic identification not only functions to affirm heterosexual norms but finds its most basic condition of possibility in the heterosexual division of the universe.

While feminist film theory and criticism have devoted extensive attention to the function of the male gaze in film, the accompanying heterosexual scenario has not received much attention, except for the occasional nod to what seems to be more the realm of the obvious than the explorable or questionable. Even David Bordwell, Kristin Thompson, and Janet Staiger's *The Classical Hollywood Cinema*—a model of historical and formal precision—characterizes heterosexual love as a theme that links cinema with other historical forms in a very simple way. "Almost invariably," writes David Bordwell, one of the main lines of action in the classical Hollywood cinema "involves heterosexual romantic love. This is, of course, not startling news." Bordwell goes on to specify that in the sample of 100 films used in the study, "ninety-five involved romance in at least one line of action, while eighty-five made that the principal line of action."

Thus, Bordwell concludes, "in this emphasis upon heterosexual love, Hollywood continues traditions stemming from the chivalric romance, the bourgeois novel, and the American melodrama."[62] The unbroken narrative connecting chivalric romance and Hollywood plots suggests, quite accurately of course, that heterosexual love is common to both forms. But this is a bit like saying that the *Iliad* and *Citizen Kane* are alike in that they both explore the relationship between the individual and society—true, perhaps, but only in the most a-historical way.

When feminists criticize heterosexual scenarios, or, to use Monique Wittig's phrase, the "heterosexual contract," it is rarely heterosexuality as a simple "attraction to the opposite sex" that is under scrutiny, but rather the absolute equation between one kind of heterosexuality, drawn as the norm against which all differences are measured as "perversions," and cultural meaning. Or as Wittig puts it, the heterosexual contract "produces the difference between the sexes as a political and philosophical dogma."[63]

An impressive body of feminist writing has been devoted to the exploration of how—following Luce Irigaray—heterosexuality functions as a ruse, a decoy relation to mask male homosocial and homosexual bonds. "Reigning everywhere, although prohibited in practice," Irigaray writes, "hom(m)o-sexuality is played out through the bodies of women, matter, or sign, and heterosexuality has been up to now just an alibi for the smooth workings of man's relations with himself."[64] Comparatively little attention has been paid to how heterosexual economies work to assure that any exchange between women remains firmly ensconced within that "hom(m)osexual" economy. To be sure, male and female homosexualities occupy quite different positions, and given the logic of the masculine "same" that dominates the patriarchal order, female homosexuality cannot be ascribed functions that are similar to male homosexuality. However, the two homosexualities share the potential to disrupt, in however different ways, the reign of the "hom(m)osexual." Irigaray speaks of the "fault, the infraction, the misconduct, and the challenge that female homosexuality entails." For lesbianism threatens to upset the alignment between masculinity and activity, and femininity and passivity. Hence, writes Irigaray, "the problem can be minimized if female homosexuality is regarded merely as an imitation of male behavior."[65]

Irigaray's discussion of the disruptive potential of female homosexuality emerges from her symptomatic reading and rewriting of Freud. In the Freudian text that occasions Irigaray's remarks on the "problem" of female homosexuality within psychoanalysis, "The Psychogenesis of a Case of Homosexuality in a Woman" (1920), questions of narration and identification, masculinity and femininity, and dominant and alternative practice are posed in ways that are particularly relevant to lesbian authorship in the cinema. Jacqueline Rose has said of the case history that here, Freud "is in a way at his most radical, rejecting the concept of cure, insisting that the most psychoanalysis can do is restore the original bisexual disposition of the patient, defining homosexuality as nonneurotic."[66]

In the case history, Freud describes the brief analysis of a young woman who was brought to him by her parents after her unsuccessful suicide attempt. This "beautiful and clever girl of eighteen" pursued with great enthusiasm her attraction to a woman ten years older than she, and her parents (and her father in particular) were particularly distressed by her simultaneous brazenness ("she did not scruple to appear in the most frequented streets in the company of her questionable friend") and deception ("she disdained no means of deception, no excuses and no lies that would make meetings with her possible and cover them").[67] The suicide attempt occurred when these two factors that so distressed her parents coincided in full view of her father. After the young woman and her female companion were greeted by the woman's father with extreme displeasure as his path crossed theirs on the street one day (as Freud notes, the scene had all the elements of a mise-en-scène planned by the young woman), the young woman threw herself in desperation over a railway fence.

Despite the apparent gravity of the suicide attempt, Freud saw little hope for successful analysis, for the woman—while not necessarily hostile to analysis, as was Dora, to whom this patient has frequently been compared—was nonetheless brought to analysis of a will other than her own.[68] In addition, Freud saw little actual illness in the young woman, at least as far as her sexuality was concerned; rather than resolving a neurotic conflict, Freud was being asked to assist in "converting one variety of the genital organization of sexuality into the other" (p. 137). As Freud proceeds to untangle the various threads of the young woman's lesbian attachment, a somewhat confusing and often contradictory portrait of homosexuality emerges.[69]

The woman's sexuality is read through a variety of oppositions which form the territory of psychoanalysis—body and mind ("in both sexes *the degree of physical hermaphroditism is to a great extent independent of the psychical hermaphroditism*" [p. 140]); masculine and feminine desire ("She had thus not only chosen a feminine love-object, but had also developed a masculine attitude towards this object" [p. 141]); maternal and paternal identification (written before Freud hypothesized more extensively about the importance of the pre-oedipal phase for women, the case history nonetheless acknowledges the maternal object as, if not on the same level of importance as the oedipal scenario, then at the very least constitutive of her sexual identity). The case history is written within the field of these opposing terms, but there are shades of a breakdown of opposition, and the subsequent interdependence of the opposing terms. Hence, Freud speculates that the woman to whom the analysand was so intensely attracted evoked two love objects, her mother and her brother.

> Her latest choice corresponded, therefore, not only with her feminine but also with her masculine ideal; it combined gratification of the homosexual tendency with that of the heterosexual one. It is well known that analysis of male homosexuals has in numerous cases revealed the same combination, which should warn us not

to form too simple a conception of the nature and genesis of inversion, and to keep
in mind the extensive influence of the bisexuality of mankind. (p. 143)

Indeed, this case history occasions some of Freud's most famous pronouncements on the importance of bisexuality. Speculating that rage toward her
father caused the young woman to turn away from men altogether, Freud notes
that "in all of us, throughout life, the libido normally oscillates between male and
female objects; the bachelor gives up his men friends when he marries and
returns to club-life when married life has lost its savour" (p. 144).

But the "bisexuality of mankind" posited in the case history takes two
distinctly different forms. On the one hand, it is posited as an originary force, a
kind of biological given from which a variety of factors—Freud sometimes
privileges predisposition, and sometimes environment—will determine one's
choice of sexual aim and sexual object. On the other, bisexuality emerges in a
much more challenging and disturbing way as the violent play of warring forces,
as evidenced most particularly in the young woman's suicide attempt. For the
desperate jump over the railroad wall is no quivering oscillation, and it is far
from the kind of serial bisexuality alluded to in the above quotation about
bachelors, marriage, and club-life. Rather, in the suicide attempt the battle of
maternal and paternal objects attains crisis proportions and provokes a parallel
crisis in representation. There are two divergent conceptions of bisexuality in the
case history—one that assures that the young woman is either really like a man
(in her choice of role) or really like a heterosexual (in her choice of love object),
and the other which suggests, rather, a deeper tension between the desire to be
seen by the father and the desire to construct an alternative scenario of desire
altogether.

Despite its reputation as a more successful exploration of questions posed in
the case history of Dora, "The Psychogenesis of a Case of Homosexuality in a
Woman" does not read as a particularly convincing narrative in its own right.
The "problem" of the case history centers on the woman's self-representation, on
her desire, not simply for the loved object but for a certain staging of that desire.
In the event of the attempted suicide, it is not clear to what extent it was an
unconscious attempt to put an end to parental—and particularly paternal—
disapproval by literal self-annihilation, or rather an equally unconscious attempt
to dramatize her conflicting allegiances by creating a scene where she is at once
active subject and passive object (Freud notes frequently that the young woman's
amorous feelings took a "masculine" form). The suicide attempt is best described
as both of these simultaneously—one a desire for resolution, the other a desire
for another language altogether whereby to represent her conflicted desires.[70] Put
another way, the suicide attempt crystallizes the position of "homosexuality in a
woman" as a problem of representation and of narrative.

Freud discusses the young woman's case in ways that suggest quite strongly the pressure of lesbianism against a system of explanation and representation. Throughout the case history, the young woman's "masculinity" is the inevitable frame of reference. Masculinity acquires a variety of definitions in the course of the essay, at times associated with the biological characteristics of men (the young woman favored her father in appearance), and at others equated with the mere fact of agency or activity (she displayed a preference for being "lover rather than beloved" [p. 141]). But "masculinity" never really "takes" as an explanation, since throughout the case history the woman remains an embodiment of conflicting desires. The suicide attempt turns upon what has become, in the cinema, a classic account of the activation of desire, the folding of spectacle into narrative. However, in the standard account, woman leans more toward the spectacle with man defined as the active agent. Here, the woman's desires to narrate and to be seen collide, leading her to make quite a spectacle of herself, but without a narrative of her own to contextualize that spectacle. As the young woman recounted the scene, the disapproving gaze from her father led her to tell her female companion of his disapproval, and her companion then adopted the opinion of the father and said that they should not see each other again. The sudden collapse, the identity between lover and father, the erasure of tension, seem to precipitate the woman's quite literal fall. The woman's desire for self-annihilation occurs, in other words, when her desire becomes fully representable within conventional terms.

What I am suggesting, then, is that the conditions of the representability of the lesbian scenario in this case history are simultaneously those of a tension, a conflict (which is "readable" in other than homosexual terms), *and* those of a pressure exerted against the overwhelmingly heterosexual assumptions of the language of psychoanalysis, a desire for *another* representation of desire. Or as Wittig puts it, "Homosexuality is the desire for one's own sex. But it is also the desire for something else that is not connoted. This desire is resistance to the norm."[71] Expanding on Irigaray, de Lauretis writes: "Lesbian representation, or rather, its condition of possibility, depends on separating out the two contrary undertows that constitute the paradox of sexual (in)difference, on isolating but maintaining the two senses of homosexuality and hommo-sexuality."[72] The irony in Arzner's signature suggests the division to which de Lauretis refers, between a representation of female communities and an inscription of marginality. That irony stands in (ironic) contrast to feminist film theory's division of Arzner into a textual hommo-sexual (in print) and a visible homosexual (in pictures).

Given Arzner's career in Hollywood, and the realist plots central to her films, her influence would seem to be most apparent among those filmmakers who have appropriated the forms of Hollywood cinema to feminist or even lesbian ends—Susan Seidelman *(Desperately Seeking Susan),* Donna Deitch *(Desert Hearts).* A more notable connection, however, exists with those contemporary women filmmakers whose films extend the possibilities of lesbian irony while revising the components of the classical cinema and inventing new cinematic forms simultaneously. I turn now to two films which are remarkable explorations of the desire, so succinctly expressed in the case history, to see and to be seen, to detach and to fuse, to narrate one's own desire and to exceed or otherwise complicate the very terms of that narration.

4. Mistresses of Discrepancy

The text of Dorothy Arzner's signature comprises a variety of interconnecting factors—a foregrounding of female friendship and references to marginal women in her films, and the assumption of a style that suggests both "masculinity" and lesbianism. Arzner's importance in contemporary feminist film theory may seem to lie exclusively at the level of a textual practice isolated from the woman's life and style. But the fact that Arzner has also functioned so consistently as an image for feminist film theorists suggests the significance of the difference embodied in that image. The fact that this image has been largely untheorized suggests a set of questions insufficiently addressed. The ironic lesbian signature finds a contemporary echo in two films which, while more explicit in their representation of lesbianism, also elaborate on the strategies present in the simultaneous and ironic evocation of female friendship and lesbian marginality in Arzner's films.

Writing about the complex ways in which the lesbian styles of butch and fem have appropriated heterosexual culture, Joan Nestle notes that "it is easy to confuse an innovative or resisting style with a mere replica of the prevailing custom." The confusion of which Nestle speaks has been one of the most challenging areas of feminist analysis, since contradiction is far more difficult to theorize than either pure recuperation or absolute novelty. But much contemporary feminist theory takes contradiction as its point of departure and return, particularly since the limitations of totalizing discourses—woman as either absolute victim or innocent exile—have become abundantly clear. Lesbian representation highlights contradiction in particularly strong ways, for lesbianism is both lure and threat for patriarchal culture as well as for feminism, and it challenges a model of signification in which masculinity and activity, femininity and passivity, are always symmetrically balanced. Nestle suggests that "lesbians should be mistresses of discrepancies, knowing that resistance lies in the change of context."[1] It is just such a "change of context" that characterizes the irony of Arzner's signature.

The two contemporary women's films to which I turn in this chapter both cite and disturb the heterosexual codes of cinema, and offer quite stunning demonstrations—even exhibitions—of the female authorial signature. While neither film takes butch and fem relationships as its point of departure, both exemplify the "discrepancies" to which Nestle refers. In Chantal Akerman's 1974 film *Je tu il elle,* heterosexual and lesbian attachment are baldly juxtaposed in relation to an "I" whose speaking self is somewhat detached from her corporeal self, a bodily presence marked by the intertwining activities of eating and writing. Ulrike Ottinger's 1979 film *Bildnis einer Trinkerin [Ticket of No Return]* traces the itinerary of a woman who comes to Berlin with the intention of performing a drinker's tour of the city. Her primary encounters are with women, while the few men who do appear in the film function primarily to evoke and quickly dismiss clichés of male spectatorial desire. In these films, the change of context to which Nestle refers engages controversial material, for both films tap not only heterosexual codes but also dominant stereotypes of lesbianism.

These films are concerned, in different yet interrelating ways, with the elaboration of the relationship between the act of self-representation and the vicissitudes of desire between women. These are not in any obvious or self-evident way lesbian films, as that term would be relevant to the films of Barbara Hammer, for instance, which appropriate the language of experimental cinema to the representation of the lesbian body, or to a recent film such as *Desert Hearts* which adapts the romantic codes of the Hollywood cinema to lesbian ends.[2] *Je tu il elle* and *Ticket of No Return* are less concerned with affirmative representations of lesbian experience than with explorations of the simultaneous ambivalence and pressure of lesbianism with regard to the polarities of agency and gender. This could of course be taken to mean that Akerman's and Ottinger's films are, because less "explicitly" lesbian in their focus, less lesbian, period. But these films do not reflect the tendency visible in some women's films to allude to lesbianism from within the securely defined boundaries of female bonding and friendship.

That tendency is quite pronounced in Diane Kurys's films, particularly in *Coup de foudre [Entre nous* (1983)], in which two women, Léna (played by Isabelle Huppert) and Madeleine (played by Miou-Miou), living in post–World War II provincial France, discover an attraction for each other (an attraction that is definitely erotic though never explicitly sexual) and eventually leave their husbands to live together.[3] As was widely publicized at the time of the film's release, the friendship of the two women has a strong autobiographical significance, for it corresponds to the experience of Kurys's own mother. At the conclusion of the film, when Léna (Kurys's mother) asks Michel (Kurys's father, played by Guy Marchand) to leave, their daughter—i.e., the fictional representation of Kurys herself—is seen watching them. Over the final shot of the film, of Madeleine walking with the children on the beach, a title appears, a very literal authorial signature: "My father left at dawn. He never saw my mother again. It's now been two years since Madeleine died. I dedicate this film to the three of them."[4]

All of Kurys's films are marked by the connection between storytelling and a female bond that wavers between the homosocial and the homoerotic. Somewhat surprisingly, perhaps, that connection is most strongly marked in what appears to be, on the surface, the film that departs the most sharply from the distinctly female world central to Kurys's other films. In *A Man in Love* (*Un Homme amoureux* [1987]), the plot centers upon a young actress, Jane (played by Greta Scacchi), whose affair with a narcissistic American movie star, Steve Elliot (played by Peter Coyote), is interwoven with her relationship with her mother (played by Claudia Cardinale), who suffers from and eventually dies of cancer. While the film follows Jane as its central protagonist, it is not until approximately two-thirds of the way through that her voice emerges, quite literally, as the voice of the film, through voice-over commentary. The voice-over is the major component of the film's mise-en-abyme; in the concluding scenes, Jane begins writing—"A Man in Love." The first appearance of the voice-over occurs immediately after a scene in which Jane, in bed with her lover, Steve, speaks—seemingly at his behest—a fantasy of lesbian lovemaking.

Hence, the conditions of the emergence of the female narrator's voice are bound up, narratively, with the lesbian fantasy, a fantasy which offers, within the logic of the film, the possibility of combining two spheres otherwise separate—heterosexual passion, on the one hand, and the maternal bond, on the other. The association of the female narrator in *A Man in Love* with a lesbian fantasy suggests the kind of connection between lesbianism and cinematic representation that is explored in *Je tu il elle* and *Ticket of No Return,* not from the point of view of the heterosexual woman *(A Man in Love)* or the child *(Entre Nous)* but from the point of view of a female author whose desire for other women is central to her work. Kurys's films also make for interesting counterpoints to the narrational and authorial strategies in Akerman's and Ottinger's films. The self-representation of Kurys herself (in *Peppermint Soda* and *Entre Nous* in particular) is wrapped in a fiction of the author that is totally compatible with the fictions of narrative cinema. In *Je tu il elle* and *Ticket of No Return*, however, Akerman and Ottinger both appear in ways that expose and undermine those fictions, not only because of the explicit lesbian desire which defines the relationship of both authors to their film texts, but more specifically because of how that desire is represented, through the exposition of pain, narcissism, infantilism, and neediness.

Chantal Akerman's *Je tu il elle* consists of three parts, each of which turns centrally on the separation between the woman as a narrating subject and as object. The first section of the film begins with an image of a young woman—portrayed by Akerman herself—seated in a room surrounded by a bed and furniture, over which we hear Akerman's voice (" . . . et je suis partie"/" . . . and I left"). Akerman's voice and body are discontinuous—that is, she speaks only in the disembodied, nonsynchronized voice on the sound track. During the course of the first section, the woman strips the room of its furniture until only her mattress remains. She writes, and she eats powdered sugar from a paper bag. Much of her writing consists of a letter addressed to a person, a lover one assumes, whose gender is unspecified; but given so-called normal viewing expectations, one assumes the indirect object of unspecified gender, "lui," to be a man. She takes off her clothes, submitting her body to the same process of unmasking as the room.

There is a ritual quality to this section of the film, an almost meditative tone of quiet contemplation that characterizes Akerman's movements and the fit between her voice and her gestures. Yet there is, simultaneously, undeniable obsessiveness as well, particularly insofar as the compulsive eating of the sugar is concerned. The scene suggests both calm and torment, peaceful solitude and turbulence. As a result, here as throughout *Je tu il elle* there is an unsettling quality, a sense that the film is torn between conflicting moods and emotions. Aside from the young woman, the only other human presences during this section of the film are children's voices heard from outside the windowed door to the apartment, and a passerby in a raincoat—one assumes it is a man, although the face is not visible—who peers into her room while Akerman lies naked on the mattress. The voice-over continues throughout the sequence, and while it ostensibly provides a running commentary on her activities, more frequently it alludes to what is seen on the image track without necessarily describing accurately what we see. Also, the voice-over is often out of sync with the image track, and as a result, events are alluded to on a delayed basis.

The first section of the film concludes when Akerman, after examining herself in the reflection of the windowed door, dresses and leaves the apartment with the door slightly ajar. The second section begins with an abrupt change from the enclosed space of the room, for here we see Akerman in a high angle shot on a highway, as her voice-over describes getting a ride from a trucker. There are alternations between the interior of the truck cab, shot in very grainy, often hand-held close-ups, and the restaurants and bars where the two stop to eat. Akerman sleeps occasionally in the rear of the cab. Akerman's voice is heard less frequently here; rather, it is the truck driver who offers extensive monologues, ranging from instructions for the hand job that Akerman gives him (she is located off screen when this occurs) to a description of his wife and children. His meditations alternate with images accompanied by noise—the sounds of television, radio, music—rather than by human speech. In several instances these background sounds are drawn from American television and radio, hence giving this section of the film—and perhaps the entire film by extension—the feel of being rooted in no specific place, that is, neither the United States (for every person in the film is French-speaking) nor Europe. While the trucker does most of the talking, there is very definitely a strong communicative bond between the two, but I do not think it entirely accurate to describe that bond as conventionally sexual. Rather, their mutual fascination is conveyed most strongly in those scenes where no words are spoken—their somewhat awkward avoidance of eye contact during a long scene in a restaurant, for instance, or Akerman's fascination with the male rituals of shaving and urinating in a restroom.

The final section of the film begins when Akerman arrives at the apartment building of her woman lover. The woman announces immediately that Akerman cannot stay, and the first part of this section of the film is a ritual of the two women's simultaneous attraction to and distance from each other, as Akerman puts on her coat and stands next to the elevator, seemingly waiting for her lover to tell her to stay. Throughout *Je tu il elle,* food plays a crucial role, and here food marks the transition from speechless communication to sexual encounter. Akerman delays her departure by announcing that she is hungry, and proceeds to eat, fairly voraciously, the sandwich the woman prepares for her. She asks for more, and once the woman has prepared yet more food, Akerman pushes it away and reaches for her. The two women make love, and during the three lengthy shots that represent their lovemaking, there is a sense of a return to the room in which the film began.

The three shots reflect in miniature the three-part structure of the film. And

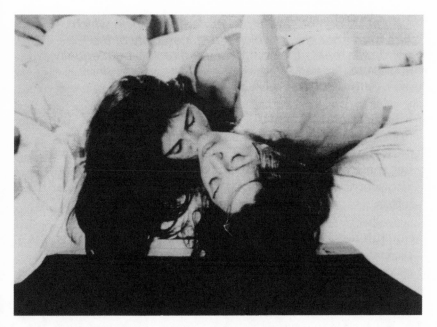

Figure 20. Chantal Akerman's *Je tu il elle* (World Artists)

as in *Je tu il elle* as a whole, there is little linearity in the progression of the scene. In the first shot, the two women roll around energetically; in the second shot, their faces are isolated as they kiss. Finally, in what one might assume to be the climactic shot, the lover separates Akerman's legs to engage in oral sex. However, throughout all three of these shots, little separates the initiator from the recipient; little, that is, isolates active subject from passive object. The representation of the lovemaking departs absolutely from the codes of pornography, so that there is no cutting from "subject" to "object," no isolation of a breast or genitalia as the fetishized object, no simulation of sexual frenzy.[5] If neither Akerman nor the lover can be situated neatly within the pole of subject or object, in other words, neither is there a clearly marked place for the spectator.[6] In the concluding scene of the film, Akerman leaves her lover's bed and exits the apartment. The film concludes with a children's song sung by a female voice with a children's chorus.

There is hardly a single moment in *Je tu il elle* when Akerman's presence is not marked, either by her literal presence on screen or by the presence of her voice. Indeed, one could hardly find a contemporary woman's film more saturated with authorial signature than *Je tu il elle*. What are we to make of this extensive presence of Akerman in the film, a presence that seems at times to achieve a kind of narcissistic frenzy? The "je" of the film traces the difficult encounter between female subjectivity and cinematic authorship. If, for the female "I" of the film, there is a fundamental connection between orality and self-expression, the marks of cinematic authorship indicate simultaneously the divisions within female identity and possible realignments of those divisions, both within the female subject and between her and others.[7] Hence the separation of voice and body in the representation of Akerman.

Perhaps the most telling scene in this context is the single instance in the film where Akerman is absent from the frame—where, that is, her fictional persona and her role as filmmaker "behind" the camera are fused. This is when Akerman, located offscreen, gives the truck driver a hand job. After he has ejaculated, he looks briefly and somewhat self-consciously at the camera. Aside from the obvious function of breaking the illusion of cinematic distance, which is not particularly notable in a film that has persistently departed from any of the conventional modes of representing distance, this brief glance at the camera is an explicit acknowledgment of what we know, that the fictional character within the film is identical to the filmmaker. Akerman as the female subject of *Je tu il elle* occupies, in this scene, the same metaphorical position, behind the camera as it were, as the cinematic author.

It is somewhat curious that this acknowledgment, this fusion of character and author, should occur during a scene of sexual servicing of the man, particularly in a film that concludes with lesbian lovemaking. Indeed, the contrast between the two sexual encounters is striking. The two participants are separate in the one, and quite enmeshed, to the point that it is not always clear which body is which (and this despite the difference in coloring and body type between the two women), in the other; a close-up is used in one, medium shots in the other; speech dominates the one and is totally absent from the other; a clear linear movement toward climax structures the one, whereas such movement is absent from the other. And in contrast to the scene with the man, where Akerman appears to occupy positions on both sides of the camera simultaneously, in the scene with the woman she is quite definitely situated within the frame.[8]

The separation between Akerman as subject and Akerman as object is achieved in the most obvious way by the distance between the voice-over and the images and sounds that appear on screen. This distance is most marked in the first section of the film, where the voice at times describes actions that have not been seen on screen, or in some cases that could not be "seen" even if they were shown (at the beginning of the film, the voice announces that she repainted all the furniture blue . . . and then announces that she painted it all again, but green; the film is in black and white). The separation occurs in other ways as well. There is a preoccupation in *Je tu il elle* with space, with the relationship between interior and exterior space, and in particular with thresholds, with moments of connection or obstruction between connecting spheres. Again, this is most apparent in the first section of the film, where the space outside the room is associated with sounds—the sounds of the highway, or of children playing—or with the intrusion of the gaze of a passerby. The windowed door to the apartment serves a complex function in this respect, for it is both a literal mirror into which Akerman gazes at herself, and the passageway outside the room.[9]

The spatial opposition between inside and outside is maintained throughout *Je tu il elle,* though with different configurations from what is seen in the room at the beginning of the film. I have noted that in the second section of the film, the interior of the truck cab is set off from the space surrounding it by the graininess of the image. While the truck cab could hardly be said to occupy the same function as the private space of the room in the first part of the film, it does acquire some of the attributes of Akerman's room, particularly given that Akerman is seen a number of times sleeping in the back of the cab. In this section of the film, however, it becomes more difficult to distinguish between what is part of Akerman's spoken reality—that is, the reality created through her gestures in the room and her voice-over commentary—and what is more properly associated with the realm of a separate, public sphere. Divisions are maintained with the passage from the first to the second parts of the film, but they are broken down simultaneously. In the last section, this spatial opposition seems to dissolve. Except for the children's song—which is purely extradiegetic, in contrast to the children's voices heard in part one, which one assumes to be at least spatially contingent—the world inhabited by the two women is initially very self-enclosed. Yet the spatial opposition does not so much disappear as it becomes displaced, for in the encounter with the woman the precarious balance between one's position as subject and as object, between the inner and outer worlds, is affirmed.

Akerman is defined both as contained by—and occasionally even imprisoned by—the space that surrounds her, and as a powerful controller of that space. There is a difference in this context between the first and last sections of the film, for in the first Akerman seems more contained by her surroundings, and in the last she exercises more control over them. In the second section of the film, her position is somewhere between the two extremes, for she is both a passive recipient of the driver's speech and an active observer of his actions and gestures.[10] To be sure, one of the most important ways in which the film maintains the distinction between the woman as subject and the woman as object is by virtue of the fact that the young woman is played by Akerman herself.

Je tu il elle is a significant film in terms of female and lesbian authorship in the cinema, not merely because Akerman functions so centrally as its narrative and visual center, but also because of the specific way in which her role materializes. For Akerman's role is staging and restaging of the components of female cinematic authorship. The process traced in *Je tu il elle* is one of the very conditions of representation and representability for the female subject. I use the term *subject* advisedly, for what is affirmed in Akerman's film is a position for the female subject vis-à-vis the cinema that affirms her visibility and her readability in terms irreducible to—and perhaps even independent of—the overlapping paradigms of gender and agency. This affirmation of female subjectivity in the cinema occurs in several ways: through the connections between different forms of orality (eating, speech, sex), and between the literal and the figurative; through a movement back and forth from the positions of spectator to actor to writer; and through a series of resonances whereby the desire of the woman is linked to those of the child and the adult, to the desire to see and to be seen, to the desire to speak and to write.

I have said that this is not a film that sits comfortably withn the category of the "lesbian film," that is, that *Je tu il elle* does not take as its obvious point of departure the address to a lesbian audience or the direct affirmation of lesbian identity. The film does affirm sexual desire between women as a complex source of creativity and as a difficult—difficult in the productive rather than prohibitive sense—question of representation. The structure of *Je tu il elle* is not linear, so that it is quite difficult to read the film as a progression from part one, where the woman is seated alone, sealed within the hermetic space of her own narcissism just as she is contained within her room, to the woman in part two who becomes a sexual being through her interactions with the trucker, to part three, where the woman arrives finally at a more satisfactory, more complete, more successful sexual identity with her woman lover. *Je tu il elle* brackets heterosexuality in the sense that it is not accorded the privileged status that one has come to expect after decades of films, classical or otherwise, which take as their unquestionable assumptions variations on the boy-meets-girl story. Rather, the heterosexual dialogue—which in this film is undoubtedly more accurately described as a male monologue—is represented as one possible configuration of the pronouns that compose the film's title.

However, there is no lesbian triumphalism in the film, and little sense in which the lovemaking with which the film concludes is posited as the culmination of that configuration of pronouns. To be sure, there is more passion in the lovemaking between the two women than there is between the truck driver and the young woman as she gives him a hand job. But the encounter with the truck driver is not at all represented as the negative alternative, but rather as an alternative way of engaging critically with the heterosexual formula of cinematic representation, without falling ino the trap of "heterosexual = bad, lesbian =

good," the trap, that is, of reversing the duality without questioning it. Rather, the heterosexual encounter of the second part of the film is represented as a series of observations. Given Akerman's departure at the conclusion of the film, and the first words uttered by her voice in the first section of the film (". . . et je suis partie" [" . . . and I left"]), it is tempting, rather, to see the process of departure, isolation, and return as the trajectory of desire that the film inscribes.[11]

However, some elements of *Je tu il elle* do evoke the radical otherness of lesbian identity and lesbian sexuality. Throughout the film, an emphasis is placed on orality in a very literal sense, as a desire for food. Akerman's obsessive ingestion of powdered sugar in the first section has all the contours of an eating disorder. During the second section the hunger disappears—Akerman gives food from her plate to the trucker—and only thirst remains, although the way in which she drinks evokes little of the compulsive eating seen in the first section of the film. Only in the last section of *Je tu il elle,* when Akerman has arrived at her lover's apartment, does the hunger reappear, now appeased temporarily by the sandwich that her lover prepares for her and which Akerman devours, and the thirst as well, quenched when the lover brings her a bottle of wine. After asking for more food, Akerman pushes it away and reaches for her lover, stressing the obvious link between orality and sexuality. More specifically, the link created in the film between food and sex evokes clinical diagnoses of homosexuality as regressive, as arrested development, as the desire—for women—to fuse with the maternal object. In virtually all of Akerman's films, maternal identification is central, from the dislocated yet enormously profound conversation between mother and daughter in *News from Home* to the patient observation of the mother's rebellion in *Jeanne Dielman, 23 Quai du Commerce, 1080 Bruxelles.*[12] In *Je tu il elle,* Akerman affirms the significance of "regressive" orality as informative of, rather than working against, female representation and creativity—whether these take the form of writing a letter or making a film.

I seem to be arguing myself into a corner as far as *Je tu il elle* is concerned. I have said that it does not inhabit comfortably the category of "lesbian film." The problem of naming *Je tu il elle* is difficult, and compounded by the fact that naming is—as the very title of the film suggests—central to its direction and structure. It may well be that what *Je tu il elle* works with and through is precisely the difficulty of naming, and my own reluctance to categorize the film may be less a function of the film's own resistance to naming than a reflection of the fact that there exist, in the taxonomy of film types, no categories which adequately describe what *Je tu il elle* is. The film's title is, then, an appropriate place from which to consider how lesbian representation inhabits the processes of naming and of cinematic address. The "je," the "il", and the "elle" of the title have obvious designations in the film—"je" is Akerman herself, "il" is the trucker, and "elle" the woman lover. That "il" and "elle" are intended to have some kind of symmetrical balance in their status as third-person pronouns is indicated by how the title of the film appears: each word is handwritten, appearing consecutively down the left side of the screen, until "elle" appears on the right side of the screen, alongside "il." Yet the "elle" could be read in the opposite way as well, for however symmetrically it might sit with the "il" alongside it, the "elle" creates an imbalance between the two columns, strains the linear rectitude of pronouns.

The "tu" of the film's title is decidedly more ambiguous, which is most obvious in the fact that virtually all of the subjects in the film, including Akerman herself, occupy the position of "tu" at one point or another. In the first section of the film, there is only one literal reference to "tu." Akerman's voice-over says, "When I lifted my head suddenly, there were people walking in the street. I still waited for them to leave or for something to happen. For me to believe in God or for you [*tu*] to send me a pair of gloves so I could go out in the cold".[13] One assumes, of course, that this "tu" is the same person addressed in the letters, a "tu" who remains unspecified.

The word *tu* lends itself to other ambiguities aside from those concerning the actual person to whom Akerman addresses her thoughts and her letters. The past tense of the verb *taire* (to render silent) is *tu,* and Akerman's voice-over refers at one point to her silencing of herself: "The eighth or ninth day, I started the second letter over again, and I ate a lot of powdered sugar for eight pages. And I crossed out . . . marked out . . . a few lines remained. I stopped eating and kept quiet [*je me suis tu*]."[14] And if *tu* is the second-person singular, it is also, at least phonetically, the singular form of the verb *tuer,* to kill *(je tue, tu tues, il/elle tue),* and it has been suggested that the title of Akerman's film could also be read (ungrammatically) as "je tue il, elle."[15] While Akerman is present during the entire film, it is only at the conclusion, with the appearance of the final credits, that she is given a fictional name—Julie. Interestingly, the name Julie appears by itself, along with the names of the actors who play the roles of the truck driver and the lover. The first syllable of "Julie" suggests, of course, both "je" and "tu," and the name contains "il" and even "elle" (or "el") in reverse. This combination of pronouns occurs only in the *written* name; as a speaking subject, Akerman/ Julie is divided across the pronouns of the film's title.

As "Julie," as "je" and "tu" and "il" and "elle" simultaneously and con-currently, Akerman attempts nothing less than the rewriting of the cinematic scenario that prescribes formulaic relations between those terms along the lines of heterosexual symmetry. Akerman shares with Monique Wittig an insistence upon pronouns as stubborn knots both contained by and resistant to patriarchal logic, and the "I" of *Je tu il elle* is quite suggestive of the divided "I," the "j/e" of Wittig's *The Lesbian Body*.[16] But while there is an obvious connection to be made between Akerman and Wittig's work, Akerman's "je" is shaped by tensions which pull in several directions, one of which is embodied in Wittig's practice. Elaine Marks has described the project of *The Lesbian Body* in the following terms:

> The physical exchange between J/e and Tu is reminiscent at times of a *pas de deux*, at times of a boxing match, at times of a surgical operation. But destruction of one order of language and sensibility implies creation of a new order. The J/e of *Le Corps lesbien* is the most powerful lesbian in literature because as a lesbian-feminist she reexamines and redesigns the universe. Starting with the female body she recreates through anecdote and proper names a new aqueous female space and a new female time in which the past is abolished.[17]

The divided, utopian lesbian subject of Wittig's novel is a horizon for Akerman's film, but the "new order" of the film addresses the female subject as both within and outside patriarchal culture. *Je tu il elle* explores the possibilities of rewriting the relationship between the female subject, sexuality, and representation, by reformulating the pronouns in relation to *other* kinds of desire.

Like Akerman's protagonist (at least until the final credits), the central woman character in Ulrike Ottinger's *Ticket of No Return* is unnamed. The film follows the journey of the woman (portrayed by Tabea Blumenschein) through the city of Berlin. It begins with her arrival at the airport, and a female voice-over describes the woman's desire to perform a drinker's tour of the city, to "live her passion undisturbed—live to drink, drink to live, a drunken life, life as a drunk." The young woman is an embodiment of the clichés of female beauty, for she exhibits the kind of preoccupation with self-presentation and masquerade commonly associated with the most stereotypical definitions of femininity. As in Akerman's film, there is a disjuncture between the bodily presence of the woman and her voice. She rarely speaks, and when she does there is a disruption of the fit between body and voice.

At the beginning of the film, for example, we see the woman's hands at a desk as she purchases her plane ticket. When the male clerk asks her what kind of ticket she wants, a female voice which we presume to be Blumenschein's responds "aller, jamais retour" ("ticket of no return," the name given to the film in English); however, there is no simultaneous image of her face to ground the voice. But whereas in Akerman's film the division between voice and body, between sound and image, occurs primarily within the single female protagonist, in *Ticket of No Return* that division occurs, rather, across a multiplicity of female figures. The female voice-over at the beginning of the film, for instance, is in no way assumed to be the voice of Blumenschein; rather, it is a voice that adopts a kind of free indirect style of referring to Blumenschein in the third person.

Although I have specified that neither *Je tu il elle* nor *Ticket of No Return* functions obviously as a "lesbian film," I suspect that my discussion of Ottinger's film within the context of lesbian representation will be seen by some as requiring more "justification." The lesbian lovemaking at the conclusion of *Je tu il elle* may not provide a simple resolution to the film, but it does validate a lesbian reading—as if the feminist insistence on the distinction between sexuality and sexual act had not yet sunk in. In contrast, *Ticket of No Return* offers even fewer clearly marked guideposts to authorize a reading of lesbian representation. Ottinger's film is concerned just as centrally as *Je tu il elle* with the connections between authorship, thresholds, and desire between women. But the focus is somewhat different, emphasizing the erotic connections between women more than explicitly sexual ones.

The plot and structure of *Ticket of No Return* follow the woman's movements through the city as her desire to drink leads to some obvious sites—bars and clubs—as well as to some not-so-obvious ones—a skating rink, a subway station. The entire social landscape is seen as a function of her fantasies, her desires. There are occasional shifts in the film, from a realistic city scene to more fantastically inspired scenes, including an enchanted garden. However, when seen as components in the journey of the woman, these shifts seem less abrupt and more a function of her own narcissism, whereby little distinguishes the world of her fantasies from the world outside them. Indeed, much of what occurs in *Ticket of No Return* is an attendant breaking down of the boundaries between self and other. This disintegration occurs on one level within the character portrayed by Blumenschein herself. As she first appears in the film, she is a prototype of the woman-as-object as theorized by feminist film theory: she has no voice of her own (there are some rare exceptions to this rule later in the film, but they are so stylized as to problematize the fusion of body and voice), she embodies the fetishism of clothing and costuming to an extreme degree, and her narcissism is defined quite literally in the unquenchable thirst and oral rage of her alcoholism.

Yet however much she embodies the woman-as-object, the polarity of the quintessential subject/object division of the cinema, Blumenschein's drinker is also the subject of the film, even if in sometimes indirect and fractured ways. *Ticket of No Return* explores, then, the possiblity of the woman-object as woman-subject, with the polarities of subject and object interwoven and interdependent. Blumenschein's drinker may follow from the categories of woman as constructed by patriarchy, but *Ticket of No Return* explores how woman, and women, function as objects for each other. This exploration does not always sit comfortably with feminism, however, for *Ticket of No Return*'s woman drinker is no female hero, and the interdependence of subject and object explored in the film postulates as much pain as pleasure, and female agency emerges as a contradictory entity. If Blumenschein's drinker figures the desire to be subject and object simultaneously, to see and to be seen, that desire leads to her own self-destruction.

The woman drinker functions on another level as a catalyst to break down other oppositions particularly relevant to women. Throughout the film, Blumenschein's drinker encounters three women, the "houndstooth ladies," named individually as "Social Question," "Common Sense," and "Accurate Statistics." Ostensibly in Berlin to attend a conference, these women are first seen at the airport at the beginning of the film. Whereas Tabea Blumenschein's heroine is a most unusual tourist with an equally unusual itinerary, these women are tourists in the most conventional sense. Their movements through the city intersect constantly with those of the woman drinker. The three ladies seem initially to be in total opposition to the woman. To be sure, their coordinated houndstooth costumes are as stunning in their way as Blumenschein's own, but they are nonetheless uniforms. Where Blumenschein's heroine does not speak, these women talk incessantly, and what they say mirrors in a narrow sense the names they are given. The houndstooth ladies can be read as caricatured super-egos to the woman drinker as id, as comic reality principles that collide with the fantasy principle embodied in the woman drinker.

Blumenschein also has repeated encounters in the film with a bag lady, Lutze. Their first meeting occurs when Lutze cleans the windshield of the car in which the woman drinker is riding, hoping, one assumes, for a small tip. The woman drinker is captivated by Lutze from the outset; she stares at the bag lady with fascination. Lutze becomes a companion to Blumenschein, as she joins her on her drinking expedition and engages in a relationship with her that is at times playful, at times childish, and at times erotic.

If *Ticket of No Return* is shaped by the woman drinker's tour of the city of Berlin, then her itinerary is shaped in turn by a universe defined primarily by women. Put another way, *Ticket of No Return* is concerned with positions of desire and agency, subject and object, looking and being looked at, as they exist between and among women. This is not to say that men or figures of masculinity are totally absent from the film; rather, they are afforded only a marginal status. One of the clubs where the woman drinker and Lutze stop on an evening's outing, for instance, features punk performer Nina Hagen, perched on a piano, singing a song in a characteristically screechy voice. With her extreme make-up (white skin and black lipstick), Hagen stretches the limits of the woman-as-object-of-spectacle beyond conventional notions of beauty. So does Ottinger's portrayal of her, with a low camera angle and lighting that make her blend into her surroundings. This sequence is one of the rare occasions in the film where attention is drawn to the male spectator, here portrayed in terms just as excessive as Hagen herself is. We see a series of close-up, extremely low angle shots of male spectators, some of whom look directly into the camera. I do not think it would be incorrect to say that there is a certain reversal operative here—that, in other words, the female performer exercises a much more powerful gaze than do the male onlookers, whose spectatorial positions seem as fragmented as women's bodies often are in the traditional cinema. Much more crucial is the bracketing, not only of the conventional male gaze but also of men.

There is, however, one male figure who functions centrally in the film—the midget who appears at the airport at the beginning of the film, and reappears to facilitate passages into a more clearly demarcated world of fantasy, such as the exotic garden or the fountain to which he leads the woman drinker. Narratively and visually, however, this man has a function that is distinct from the more conventional male positions alluded to in the scene described above. While he is a man, the midget has none of the attributes of male power or authority. Rather—and perhaps somewhat ironically—the man is an extension of the woman drinker herself; he is a kind of master of ceremonies for the staging of her own desires. Principles of contrast—social as well as narrative and visual—are applied, rather, to the female figures in the film.

Ticket of No Return thus upsets the conventional wisdom that the opposition between masculine and feminine is collapsed into the difference between men and women as the most pervasive denominator of cinematic narrative. To be sure, there is plenty of opposition in Ottinger's film. *Ticket of No Return* delights in the complicated trajectories of collision, tension, and difference, but with the crucial qualification that virtually all of the oppositions occur among women. In the case of the woman drinker and the houndstooth ladies, the drinker represents a kind of literal return of the repressed, for she is an embodiment of the "problem" of female alcoholism to which they refer in terms of statistics and clichés. The woman drinker embodies what is repressed by those facts and figures—the possibility that the woman disdained is also the woman desired.

The opposition between Blumenschein's woman drinker and Lutze is, on the most obvious level, an opposition of social class. Tabea Blumenschein's character may exaggerate the conventions of femininity, but the excess remains within the boundaries of socially acceptable exoticism. Lutze, however, is unquestionably marginal, her initial bedraggled appearance in total contrast to that of the woman drinker. If the woman drinker figures for what is repressed in the three houndstooth ladies, Lutze embodies a kind of otherness which the woman drinker embraces with great enthusiasm. The woman drinker eventually

Figure 21. Lutze and Tabea Blumenschein in Ulrike Ottinger's
Ticket of No Return (Museum of Modern Art)

dresses Lutze, if not exactly in her own image then at least as an imitiation of her.

On the one hand, then, the encounters between Lutze and the woman drinker are marked by the transgression of boundaries, an alliance forged in a love for alcohol and a common fascination for each other. On the other, the encounters between the woman drinker and the three houndstooth ladies are charcterized by more distance, more objectification. A recurrent motif in *Ticket of No Return* is the breakdown of distance, the transgression of boundaries, particularly insofar as the relation between the three ladies and the woman drinker is concerned. The words uttered by the three ladies function to keep the woman drinker set apart as an other, a symptom of social disintegration. But visually, the relationship between them and the woman suggests something else. Early in the film, for instance, we see Blumenschein in a café, shot frontally through the window, as she orders drink after drink and moves her lips as if speaking to an (invisible) interlocutor. When the three houndstooth ladies enter the café, we are given a broader and more comprehensive sense of the space of the café, as if to reflect the equation between these women and a kind of reality principle. When

Blumenschein is in the frame, the space of the café functions only as a backdrop. From the moment they enter the café, the three ladies occupy a position which in the conventional language of the cinema would be occupied by a man.

The woman drinker listens to the houndstooth ladies as they expound upon the dangers of alcoholism while indulging in huge sundaelike concoctions. She sees Lutze outside the café, and gestures to her to come in. The woman drinker is shot in such a way that her reflection is visible in the café window, and when Lutze first approaches, she assumes the place of that reflection. Lutze and the woman drinker drink, while the chatter of the houndstooth ladies continues in the background. The visual uniformity of the three houndstooth ladies in their almost identical outfits stands in opposition to the strong visual contrast between Blumenschein, dressed in a coordinated yellow outfit, and the bag lady, dressed in rags. Also, two different kinds of orality are contrasted. The houndstooth ladies talk and eat, their obvious relish in devouring their sundaes standing in sharp contrast to the coded vocabulary of social control that charcterizes their speech. In other words, they consume their food with a passion that is regulated in their speech.

The orality of Lutze and the woman drinker possesses no such division; they drink, laugh, and gesture, their bodies totally immersed in the pleasures of consumption. The staging of contrasts between the two groups of women is interrupted when a man and a woman arrive on the scene. Like the male spectators whose bracketed function I referred to earlier, this heterosexual couple has a brief, intrusive function before they evaporate into the margins of the film. As if on cue, Blumenschein throws her drink on the glass window of the café, a gesture quickly imitated by Lutze. The couple, armed with cameras, proceed to take photographs of the scene, while the three ladies gape and stare. A waiter throws the woman drinker and Lutze out of the café, leaving the three hound-stooth ladies to their food and platitudes on the shamefulness of women who get drunk in public.

The gesture which attracts the cameras of the heterosexual couple and which gets Lutze and the woman drinker thrown out of the café is a trope in *Ticket of No Return,* repeated at key moments of desire and recognition. The clear liquid streaked on the window does not, in any substantial way, interfere with the visibility of what lies beyond the window. However, it does call attention to the window as a surface that mediates between the viewer and the object of vision.[18] This trope is first introduced in *Ticket of No Return* when the woman drinker arrives at the airport. The male midget's path crosses hers in the airport terminal, and somewhat eerie music commences, suggesting a shift from the ostensibly "realistic" space of the airport to the space of the woman drinker's fantasies. She proceeds through sliding doors, and we next see her behind a glass window, in medium shot, looking somewhat perplexed. She places her gloved hand on the glass. Another hand enters the screen, and squeezes water over the glass, apparently "liquefying" the image of Blumenschein. In a reverse shot, we see the back of Blumenschein's head in the foreground of the image, and an elderly cleaning woman, her head wrapped in a black scarf, laughing as she continues to wash the glass. As the series of alternating images continues, Blumenschein does not really establish eye contact with the woman, but looks dreamily off into space.

It is not altogether clear whether the woman drinker's fascination has to do with the cleaning woman herself, or with the fact of being looked at by the cleaning woman. In any case, virtually all of the cinematic elements used here—the sound track, the editing, the framing—suggest the enormous significance of the encounter, and it is one of the rare scenes in the film where the conventional shot–reverse shot is used. The encounter with the cleaning woman as it is represented at the airport introduces two themes, one narrative and one visual, that will recur throughout the film. First, there is the encounter with otherness, with a woman separated from the woman drinker by her age, her appearance, her demeanor, and her social class. Second, the water-streaked glass suggests transparence and surface at the same time. The woman drinker's first encounter with Lutze (when Lutze attempts to clean the windshield of the car) is a replay of this scene, with Blumenschein's fascination expressed with the same dreamy look, and the liquid on the car window a repetition of the imagery. The café scene replays the scene as well.

In a more general way, the encounter with the cleaning woman prefigures the preoccupation in *Ticket of No Return* with women as both like and unlike each other, with separation and desire, projection and distance as the forces that determine women's relationships to each other. The woman drinker appears to live entirely and exclusively within the narcissistic world of her own regressive fantasies, but female figures of social marginality function, however briefly and tangentially, as marks of otherness and signs of fascination. On the other end of the social spectrum, the film is equally taken up with how Blumenschein's woman drinker tantalizes and even challenges the less obviously narcissistic but equally self-enclosed world of the three houndstooth ladies. Lutze fascinates the woman drinker in some of the same ways that the woman drinker fascinates the three houndstooth ladies, with the significant difference that the woman drinker, located on the brink between subject and object, is much more susceptible to crossing over those boundaries than the houndstooth trio.

Yet one important example of the transgression of the boundary separating the woman drinker and the three ladies draws on the same elements as the encounter between the woman drinker and the cleaning woman. A section of

Ticket of No Return is devoted to the acting out of the woman drinker's "professional fantasies," including acting in *Hamlet* and performing a daredevil car stunt. She also performs a brief stint as an office worker, during which time she drinks excessively and is berated by her boss, played by Kurt Raab. The three ladies peer through a frosted window to attempt to see what is going on, and their hands press against the window in an imitation of the woman drinker's gestures at the beginning of the film. Their faces are somewhat distorted against the opaque glass, and while the distance marked is considerably greater than that offered by the glass streaking the window in the earlier scene, the effect is quite similar. Between the various denominations of "woman" in *Ticket of No Return*, then, there are a variety of screens, thresholds, and passages, and it is a major goal of this film to explore and define just how those various conduits operate.

Unlike Akerman's *Je tu il elle*, Ottinger's film does not inscribe its fantasies of the complexities of relations between women within the literal representation of lesbian lovemaking. This is not, of course, to say that lesbian representation occurs only in those films that are explicitly sexual, but rather to point out that in *Ticket of No Return*, lesbian representation functions somewhat differently than in Akerman's film. A key scene in *Ticket of No Return* does take place in a lesbian bar, where the paths of the woman drinker, Lutze, and the three hound-stooth ladies cross once again. While the woman drinker drinks and Lutze dances, the three ladies pontificate about the gay subculture, animal experiments, and varying attitudes toward homosexuals. Their pronouncements are interrupted by a woman in black leather who asks one of the ladies to dance. This lesbian flirtation—to which "Exact Statistics" responds in a delighted fashion, while her two companions look on somewhat dumbfounded—is structurally similar to the companionship between the woman drinker and Lutze that intruded on the ladies in the earlier café scene. Here, however, there is a distinct difference, in that the intrusion is welcome.

The bar scene suggests that desire between women is both complicitous with and in sharp distinction from patriarchal culture; the women's interchanges are not unlike the rituals of heterosexual dating, but the flush of discovery that the invitation to dance inspires in the houndstooth lady is connected to a forbidden eroticism. However, the significance of lesbian representation in Ottinger's film has less to do with the explicit frame of reference elicited by the lesbian bar, and more to do with the eroticizing of the thresholds and boundaries that exist among women, the contemplation of which is the dominant movement in the film. Like *Je tu il elle*, *Ticket of No Return* explores the relationship between female desire and the polarities of agency and objectification.

But what of lesbian authorship? I have suggested that Chantal Akerman's display in *Je tu il elle* as "Julie," as je/tu, il/elle simultaneously, inscribes female cinematic authorship as a complex writing and rewriting of cinematic narration. Ulrike Ottinger also appears in *Ticket of No Return,* and while her self-representation is quite different from Akerman's—Ottinger appears only briefly in the film, for instance—the effects are similar. Ottinger makes her appearance at a crucial moment of transition, near the conclusion of the film. The woman drinker's last appearance in a bar occurs when she and Lutze go to a bar that the woman drinker had visited alone earlier in the film. The bartender repeats his original lines practically word for word during the second visit. The next scene shows Ottinger seated on a street bench at night, drinking from a bottle and reading aloud from a book she holds. The text she reads is from a "sketchbook" by Austrian writer Peter Rosei, a fragment entitled "Drinkers," which alludes to the pleasure and pain of drinking, and to self-destruction and self-hatred:

> In as far as drinkers are known to me, they do not want to drink, but die. What a wondrous plan: To so heighten a pleasure that it leads, by way of tortures, to death. Lately I spoke with a friend about this. He believed: Our addictions are merely the Eumenides in the Theatre of Cruelty. I said: Then we hate ourselves. Yes said the friend, it is not that bad.[19]

Ottinger's recitation of the text is interrupted by a car screeching to a halt, from which a male transvestite is thrown. He screams, crawls toward Ottinger, and drinks from her bottle. Ottinger gets up and walks away, leaving the book on the bench. Thus begins a chain of recitations, as the book is passed from the transvestite to the woman drinker, who passes by accompanied by Lutze, from the woman drinker to a washroom attendant, and from the woman drinker again to a passerby. The fragments of text recited aloud by these passersby all allude to the destruction and ruin of alcoholism, yet the text itself is fragmented and sometimes dreamlike. It has little in common, for example, with the self-serving, sociological discourse of the three ladies, a contrast emphasized by the alternation between the recited fragments from the book introduced by Ottinger and the departing observations of the houndstooth ladies on alcoholism and ritual in today's society.

It is tempting to read Ottinger's intervention as a narrative device that is neither the self-destruction of the woman drinker nor the smug detachment of the three ladies, and thus is a strategy that opens a space for seeing and telling beyond the either/or of narcissistic self-destruction (the woman drinker) or facile judgment (the houndstooth ladies). Yet Ottinger's appearance suggests something of both extremes: Ottinger herself seems to be quite drunk, yet the text she reads assumes a vantage point on alcohol that wavers between clinical observation and passionate consumption. The authorial fiction that Ottinger writes into the film thus situates the woman filmmaker as both subject and object of her text.

What remains a matter of some curiosity, however, is that Ottinger appears in order to recite the text of another author—and a male one, at that. Even in a German context, Peter Rosei hardly has the factor of recognition that other quotations in the film possess—such as those by Gertrude Stein or Oscar Wilde. Nor is there any specific frame to even indicate that what Ottinger reads is a text authored by someone else. There is, however, a fit between Rosei's text and the drinker's itinerary in the film. Portions of the text recited by two passersby in the train station, for instance, are most evocative of the woman drinker's journey:

> Whosoever wakes up in the morning, of sound mind, strong, in good health and says: I am the most superfluous person in the world, is ripe for drinking. He should get dressed, board public transport, travel into town. There he should enter a wine bar, a stand-up beer kiosk or, as I saw lately in a film, beer heaven. Everything else will take care of itself.
> It is above all that certain element of automation, of things-taking-care-of-themselves that is the beauty of drinking. Drinkers are travelers. They are moved without moving themselves. You lift them up, transport them. . . . Do you see the galaxy, I say.[20]

The familiar and somewhat fragmented quality of the text is also in keeping with the tone of the film. Yet Ottinger's quotation of the text also exemplifies the extent to which she is a "mistress of discrepancy," since the personal, individualistic quality of the text is situated in a public sphere where its "I" is assumed by a number of anonymous strangers, and its universe of men assumed by one populated primarily by women. The trope of the liquid-streaked glass, the primary visual means by which a relationship is established between two women in the film, occurs here as well: when the woman drinker goes into the public restroom, the attendant (also a "reader" of the Rosei text) stands behind her in front of a mirror as the woman drinker spits water onto the glass. The strategy is not just one of appropriation of "male" discourse, however, but rather the fantasy of dissolution of the boundaries of gender, if not those of sex.

Ottinger's brief appearance in the film also foregrounds the relationship between her and Tabea Blumenschein. Once lovers, the two women have collaborated on several films, and Blumenschein herself designed the incredible costumes in this and other films directed by Ottinger. Their relationship is not staged in *Ticket of No Return* in quite the same foregrounded way it is in the earlier film *Madame X: An Absolute Ruler* (1977), where Blumenschein plays the title role of the mistress of the ship *Orlando* (as well as the ship's figurehead!), and Ottinger appears in a flashback as Madame X's lost lover, Orlando.[21] If both *Madame X* and *Ticket of No Return* are "monuments" to Ottinger and Blumenschein's relationship, as Sabine Hake suggests, the monument constructed in the later film takes the relationship between female author

Figure 22. Tabea Blumenschein in *Ticket of No Return*
(Museum of Modern Art)

and female character as one of both identification and objectification.[22] It is a relationship, in other words, of female subject and object in which desire is a condition of both connection and separation.

Ottinger's appearance in the film occurs at precisely the moment when the dissolution of boundaries, the crossing of thresholds, cease; the fiction of the film resolves into the oppositions of speaking subjects (the three ladies) and spoken objects (the drinker, Lutze) who are no more than figures in the landscape of social observation. Ottinger's appearance thus opens up another threshold at precisely the moment that the film closes down its own process of display and fascination with otherness. That threshold is, precisely, a threshold of desire, an inscription of authorial investment that absorbs the fascination with differences among women, which defines the cinematic author as another woman drinker whose portrait the film has traced to the extent that Tabea Blumenschein's woman drinker stands as both her mirror self and her desired object.

Ottinger's self-presentation is ironic in that her position of creation is identified simultaneously within the conventions of traditional femininity and outside them; like the transvestite who takes the book from her, that desire is both a mockery of sexual stereotyping and an imitation of it. In dress and appearance, Ottinger is neither the woman drinker nor Lutze nor the houndstooth ladies, yet a connection persists between her and them. Ottinger's appearance in *Ticket of No Return* resembles a "cameo," just long enough to allow her to be recognized as the film director for those familiar with her looks (for those not so familiar, but attentive, Ottinger's appearance matches the Polaroid snapshot of her that appears during the opening credits of the film). While one could cite a venerable history of such cameos, Ottinger's appearance in *Ticket of No Return* is best assessed, I think, in relationship to the fascination with "the other woman" that runs throughout the film.

Ticket of No Return contains a wealth of quotations.[23] There are many quotations of literary sources—Oscar Wilde's influence is particularly strong, given the very title of the film (in German, *Bildnis einer Trinkerin, Portrait of a Woman Drinker,* suggesting *The Picture of Dorian Gray*), the themes of narcissism and social meandering, and most obvious of all, the gay connection. Ottinger also shares with Wilde a fascination with excess and decadence. There are many cinematic quotations as well; a circus scene evokes Fellini, for instance.

Of particular importance is the influence of several films directed by Josef Von Sternberg featuring Marlene Dietrich. The most obvious quotation is of Von Sternberg's 1930 film *Morocco*. The "aller jamais retour" line uttered early in the film, and used as its English title, is drawn from *Morocco*, in which Dietrich plays Amy Jolly, a woman who is described at the beginning of the film, as she makes the ship voyage to Morocco, as a "one way ticket." *Morocco* traces the development of a passionate attachment between Jolly, a club performer, and a soldier played by Gary Cooper. At the conclusion of *Morocco*, Amy Jolly joins the group of women, most of them Moroccan, who follow their men in the French foreign legion from outpost to outpost. Dietrich removes her high-heeled shoes as she walks off into the desert. The concluding scenes of *Ticket of No Return* show somewhat different effects of passion, for Blumenschein's woman drinker stumbles on the stairway of a station and dies. The last image of the film cites *Morocco* once again, and shows Blumenschein's legs as she walks away from the camera in a passageway lined with mirrors. As she walks, her high heels break the mirrors. The final image of the film is detached from the narrative conclusion that occurs with the woman drinker's final demise.[24]

Ticket of No Return explores both women's investment in the pleasures of voyeurism and fetishism and the possibilities of new forms of visual pleasure that take as their point of departure the erotic connections between women. This desire for the reinvention of voyeurism and fetishism inspires a particularly interesting writing of yet another Von Sternberg/Dietrich collaboration into *Ticket of No Return*. I am referring here to *The Blue Angel*, the 1930 film which initiated Dietrich and Von Sternberg's collaboration, and which is the founding myth of Dietrich's persona. *The Blue Angel* is usually read as a film about Dietrich as a femme fatale in her incarnation as Lola Lola, the cabaret performer who inspires fatal passion in the schoolmaster, Herr Rath, who is mesmerized by Lola, and who eventually marries her and is destroyed and humiliated by his love for her. *The Blue Angel* offers a fairly obvious example of the woman who is—according to many feminist film theorists—fetishized so as to assuage the threat that she represents to the male protagonist and, by extension, the male spectator.[25] However, there is another dimension to *The Blue Angel* that has less to do with the relationship between Lola and Herr Rath, and more to do with relations between and among women, particularly as they are dramatized in the different modes of performance that are presented in the film.[26]

When Herr Rath first visits the club, performance is represented as a carnivalesque mode of reversal. A group of women performers sit together on stage, and there is little to set the stage off clearly from the spectators in the nightclub. While Lola is the featured performer, she is not isolated from the other women but rather is a part of a group. Only as the film progresses does Lola become an object of the gaze, and of the male gaze in particular, as the mode of performance associated with her begins to focus on her exclusively, to separate quite clearly the stage from the spectators, and the central object of performance from the background. One of the decisive turning points in this production of spectacle within the film occurs when Lola performs what is undoubtedly the most famous scene in *The Blue Angel*. After Rath has returned to the club, and is seated in a loge as a guest of honor, Lola sings "Falling in Love Again," and the shot–reverse shot alternations between performer and onlooker isolate the man who is falling in love and the woman who is the object of his attraction.

There are some traces of the mode of performance presented earlier in the film—other women are seen on stage with Lola, for instance, and a female statue in the same frame as Herr Rath occasionally draws attention away from his adoring gaze. But for the most part, this scene, as well as the remainder of the film, is marked by the repression and displacement of those carnivalesque elements of performance introduced earlier. In the universe created in Von Sternberg's film, these two distinct modes of performance are opposed in sexual terms—the one, defined by a breaking down of boundaries, is associated with a world of women; the other, defined by a demarcation of a distinct space separating performer and onlooker, is associated with the division of male spectator and female object.

In *Ticket of No Return,* Ottinger rereads these conflicting modes of perfor- mance, and reverses the process that occurs in *The Blue Angel.* For in Ottinger's film, the mode of performance—and, by implication, of identification— associated with the budding relationship between Rath and Lola is bracketed and parodied from the outset. Instead of Rath, we have a midget, who is a projection of the woman drinker, or a group of anonymous male spectators witnessing the mockery of seductive performance in Nina Hagen's act, or yet other anonymous men who fall over themselves at the sight of the woman drinker. *Ticket of No Return* extends the world of performance inhabited by the women at the begin- ning of *The Blue Angel.* The way in which the female body is first represented on stage in *The Blue Angel* suggests a fascination with the differences between women—differences in size (virtually all of the women, aside from Dietrich, are quite large), differences in age, and by extension differences in social class. One of the most interesting aspects of the Marlene Dietrich persona, as it is developed both in *The Blue Angel* and in later films, is its flirtation with differences between women, from the well-dressed and presumably upper-class woman kissed by her in *Morocco* to the grotesque disguise adopted in *Witness for the Prosecution.* In these films, the flirtation is eventually channeled to serve the aims of the heterosexual love story. In *Ticket of No Return,* however, a reversal is affected, so that what is by and large repressed in the Dietrich persona here becomes the very substance of the film.

My case for the importance of *The Blue Angel* as an intertext for *Ticket of No Return* seems thus far to be based on somewhat general thematic evidence. One might argue that the development of a mode of performance in *Ticket of No Return* has only as much relevance to *The Blue Angel* as to several hundred other films in which one finds similar evidence of a repression of female performance. However, what I have identified as a dominant trope in *Ticket of No Return*—the liquid-streaked glass—is drawn precisely from *The Blue Angel*. The woman drinker's encounter with the cleaning woman at the airport, during which the motif of the liquid-streaked window is introduced, cites the first scene in *The Blue Angel*. After the introduction of the small town in which the film begins, we see a cleaning woman throw a bucket of water on a glass window, behind which there is a poster of Lola Lola, her hips thrust forward in the provocative pose for which Dietrich is famous. The woman pauses to briefly imitate the pose, and the film quickly moves on to Herr Rath's apartment and the schoolroom, where photographs of Lola cause a commotion.

From the outset of *The Blue Angel*, a sharp distinction is drawn between the female and the male spectator in relationship to the image of Lola, for the woman spectator imitates Lola's pose, while the male spectator desires Lola. In *The Blue Angel*, there is no question that the male spectator provides the necessary catalyst to tell a story. In comparison to the image of the cleaning woman, which is flat and fairly transparent, the images of the schoolboys admiring Lola's photograph are defined by secrecy and delayed gratification. *Ticket of No Return* suggests, however, that *The Blue Angel* has not had the final word on the significance of the washerwoman and the image, and that there is plenty more to be said not only about female mimicry of the image, but also about the narrative and visual desires that the female look, through a glass streaked with liquid, inspires.

In both *Je tu il elle* and *Ticket of No Return*, the inscription of female authorship is identified within the context of lesbian desire and its relationship to the cinema. As I have suggested, this does not mean that either Akerman's or Ottinger's film is a "lesbian text" in any simple or straightforward sense of the word. Both films demonstrate, rather, the extent to which the pleasures of the cinema draw upon lesbian eroticism.[27] At the same time the films demonstrate a strategy of female authorship in which lesbian desire is foregrounded, and not simply demonstrated as the return of the repressed of the heterosexual codes of dominant cinema. While *Je tu il elle* and *Ticket of No Return* are far removed from Arzner's work, there is a shared preoccupation with disrupting the easy fit in classical cinema between activity and masculinity, passivity and femininity, and with an irony that juxtaposes two different readings of lesbianism—the one foregrounding female friendships and communities of women as connected to yet distant from the institutions of the family and the male-female couple, the other emphasizing, rather, lesbianism as marginal to those institutions, and therefore incompatible with them.

If, however, the evocation of lesbian marginality acquires only the shape of an inflection in Arzner's work, Akerman's and Ottinger's films are concerned precisely to elaborate that marginality into a visual and narrative momentum of its own. In so doing, the films engage with what has been one of the most controversial and confusing arenas in contemporary feminist inquiry. The realm of female activity and desire in both films is that of bodily gesture and orality, and the access to speech and social communication occurs either with great difficulty (in *Je tu il elle*) or virtually not at all (in *Ticket of No Return*). Both films evoke, then, a female world that exists prior to or outside the realm of the symbolic order, an order determined by the regulation of the body and the simultaneous economy of the family and the word. In contemporary feminist theory, particularly psychoanalytic theory and its attendant appropriation by literary critics, this presymbolic realm has been read as a privileged site for the understanding of the specificities of female development in patriarchal culture. For this presymbolic is the pre-oedipal realm to which Freud entertained a most ambiguous relationship, both acknowledging and retreating from the difference that the mother-child (and especially mother-daughter) bond might accentuate, thus threatening the equation of the oedipal scenario (and its subsequent lining up of identifications along the lines of active-male, passive-female) with cultural coherence and significance.

Crucial to both *Je tu il elle* and *Ticket of No Return* is the connection between that so-called pre-oedipal realm and lesbian desire. While both films could be read as evoking some standard homophobic definitions of lesbianism—"arrested development," oral rage, maternal identification, for instance—there is no position of patriarchal or heterosexual authority in the films to ground such definitions. Far more important in this respect is the way both films respond to a common repression of lesbianism in feminist discussions of the pre-oedipal, presymbolic realm. In the American context, Nancy Chodorow, in *The Reproduction of Mothering*, analyzes how female development is more influenced by the pre-oedipal phase than male development, and how that influence accounts to a large extent for the increased relational capacity of women as they are socialized in our culture. Yet there are some disturbing implications in Chodorow's account, for throughout her book one senses that however much the rigid dualities of pre-oedipal, relational, female values versus oedipal, individuational, male values are challenged, there remains a desire to rescue heterosexual symmetry and family life.

Jacqueline Rose has commented of Chodorow's work that the unconsicous is lost amidst assumptions that models of how men and women are "supposed" to act work with great efficiency.[28] Yet as Adrienne Rich has suggested, there is a curious contradictory quality to Chodorow's work, the sense that however great the desire to maintain what Rich calls "heterocentrism," the possibility of strong erotic bonds between women is posed constantly at the edge of the text. In an oft-quoted passage from *The Reproduction of Mothering*, the appeal to majority rule seems weak indeed: "However, deep affective relationships to women are hard to come by on a routine, daily, ongoing basis for many women. Lesbian relationships do tend to recreate mother daughter emotions and connections, but most women are heterosexual."[29] The affirmation of heterosexuality rejoins Rose's point, for in no way is it defined as permeable or contradictory. However, as Rich points out, "on the basis of her own findings, Chodorow leads us implicitly to conclude that heterosexuality is *not* a 'preference' for women, that, for one thing, it fragments the erotic from the emotional in a way that women find impoverishing and painful."[30]

Chodorow's exploration of relational patterns and the pre-oedipal in women simultaneously evokes and dismisses the specter of lesbianism. It is just that specter which informs insistently the representation of the female body and desire in *Je tu il elle* and *Ticket of No Return*. However, the specter thus evoked is a far cry from the idealized view of lesbianism described by Rich, which promises a release and refuge from fragmentation, separation, or pain. If these films tap the realm of the pre-oedipal, it is not in order to confront the institutions of heterosexuality with a utopian and coherent other scene. To the contrary, the narration of "Julie" and the itinerary of the woman drinker insist upon lesbian desire as shaped by the pre-oedipal, certainly, but the pre-oedipal realm thus evoked offers neither the comforting blanket of a realm beyond patriarchy, nor the supposed immature and undifferentiated need of infantile desire.

Chodorow's theory of female development is defined within a sociological framework that has little room for categories of deviance or rupture. Given how extensively Akerman's and Ottinger's films are preoccupied with the complex effects provoked by such deviance or rupture, French theories of representation that engage with a presymbolic realm, particularly those that take their inspiration from Lacan's reading of the imaginary, might offer more useful comparisons. Julia Kristéva's readings of the relationship between the semiotic and the symbolic registers, and of how the semiotic—the realm of the body, of gesture, of rhythm, of sensual experience—exerts a pressure against the symbolic realm, would appear to be particularly relevant. It has been noted many times that Kristéva's work is informed by a rigid sexual duality, whereby male poets have access to the semiotic through their writing, and women through pregnancy. The semiotic is defined simultaneously as the realm of the feminine and the realm of the disruptive. However unalike they may be in almost every other way, Kristéva's semiotic and Chodorow's pre-oedipal share a peculiarly similar preoccupation with an invisible yet implicit lesbianism. In Kristéva's case, the preoccupation with mothering as the privileged realm of female productivity becomes unabashedly literal and essentialist, and the possibility that the pre-oedipal realm might be read, in relation to women's desires, in terms other than maternity hovers constantly at the edges of Kristéva's writing.

Particularly revealing in this context is "Stabat Mater," in which a supposed-ly "new" relationship of women to the maternal is posed as the solution to the problem "posed massively to our culture for over a century," the problem, that is, of "the relationship to the other woman," and of the attendant "necessity to reformulate its [culture's] representations of love and hate. . . ."[31] The relation-ship "to the other woman" is identified by Kristéva as the mother-daughter bond. But one senses on more than one occasion in Kristéva's writing that this relationship to the "other woman" poses a threat; that some relations to the "other woman" (like lesbianism) might threaten the symmetries of the semiotic and the symbolic, the maternal and the paternal, the feminine and the masculine.[32]

As Judith Butler has argued in an extremely lucid critique of Kristéva's work, the "presumption . . . that, for women, heterosexuality and coherent selfhood are indissolubly linked" leads to the relegation of lesbianism to the realms of unintelligibility and psychosis.

> The paternal law which protects [Kristéva] from this radical incoherence is precisely the mechanism that produces the construct of lesbianism as a site of irrationality. Significantly, this description of lesbian experience is effected from the outside, and tells us more about the fantasies that a fearful heteroseuxal culture produces to defend against its own homosexual possibilities than about lesbian experience itself.[33]

It comes as no surprise that Kristéva's occasional forays into the realm of all-female communities pose an undifferentiated mass that can only be a function of psychosis and death:

> Women no doubt reproduce between them the peculiar, forgotten forms of close combat in which they engaged with their mothers. Complicity in the non-said, connivance in the unsayable, the wink of an eye, the tone of voice, the gesture, the color, the smell: we live in such things, escapees from our identity cards and our names, loose in an ocean of detail, a data-bank of the unnameable.[34]

As Teresa de Lauretis has suggested, "The suggestion creeping about discreetly . . . that lesbianism may be *the* contemporary (postmodern and postfeminist) female disease, is raised by Kristéva to the status of a theoretical death sentence."[35]

In most notions of the feminine as "pre-oedipal" or "presymbolic," the desire to maintain the linearity and symmetry of cultural arrangements conflicts with the desire to put such arrangements into question. In both Chodorow's and Kristéva's work, the pre-oedipal and the semiotic are excavated as moments prior to the oedipal symbolic. Regardless of the attempts by both authors to challenge the monolithic quality of the symbolic order, there remains an un-questioned notion of heterosexual norm. The difficulty of any such neat position-ing of the realm of "peculiar, forgotten forms of close combat in which they engaged with their mothers" informs the very structures of *Je tu il elle* and *Ticket of No Return*. The three-part structure of Akerman's film shakes loose any conventional notion of development, for the encounter with the truck driver, more shaped by the codes of the cinematic symbolic than the other sections of the film, and clearly more evocative of heterosexual norms, dangles in the middle of the film, neither the simple other to be rejected in the name of a utopian lesbianism, nor the ostensibly mature symbolic realm to which the woman ascends. In *Ticket of No Return*, the sightseer's itinerary has a built-in refusal of linearity, and even its classic conclusion in death confounds rather than confirms the narrative of passage or initiation.

Any definition of a pre-oedipal "stage" is immediately caught up in the implication that the stage needs to be surpassed. Kaja Silverman has addressed this problem by recasting the question of women's relationship to the pre-oedipal into the terms of the negative Oedipus complex. Silverman notes that Freud conceptualized two versions of the Oedipus complex within which the subject is defined, "one of which is culturally promoted and works to align the subject smoothly with heterosexuality and the dominant values of the symbolic order, and the other of which is culturally disavowed and organizes subjectivity in fundamentally 'perverse' and homosexual ways. . . ."[36] In Freud's writing, this negotiation of two oedipal formulations—the one connecting to identification with the father, the other to identification with mother—would eventually be replaced by the formulation better known today.

In the case of female subjects, the "pre-oedipal" stage of maternal identification relegates to the developmental backwater the possibility of compromising or otherwise problematizing in any active way the woman's paternal identification and the attendant acquisition of heterosexuality. Silverman's insistence, in her rereading of Freud, that maternal identification remain within the realm of the oedipal—that is, within the realm of loss and absence—closes off, as she acknowledges, any simple definition of the pre-oedipal both as "an arena for resistance to the symbolic and as an erotic refuge."[37] However, such an inscription of the maternal within the oedipal, rather than prior to it, makes it possible, in Silverman's words, "to speak for the first time about a genuinely oppositional desire—to speak about a desire which challenges dominance from within representation and meaning, rather than from the place of a mutely resistant biology or sexual 'essence.' "[38]

The negative Oedipus complex in Silverman's analysis casts a wide net, ranging from the explicit choice of a maternal love object in lesbian sexuality to the more diffuse mechanism whereby women take as a primary source of psychic energy their bonds with other women. Put another way, Silverman's reading of the negative Oedipus complex brings to the realm of high theory the feminist notion of "women-identified women" popular in the 1970s. While they could not be more unalike in other ways, Silverman's analysis of the negative Oedipus complex acquires some of the contours of the "lesbian continuum" proposed by Adrienne Rich as informing a wide spectrum of female relationships, from the lesbian who functions primarily within a separate women's sphere at one end, to the heterosexual woman who forms strong friendships with women at the other.[39] Silverman's analysis represents a major contribution to feminist-psychoanalytic thought, since it offers the possibility of challenging and breaking down the rigid and often false barriers that separate lesbian and heterosexual women in many contexts. Yet I fear that such a framework can engender the opposite problem—a lack of attention to the specificity of differing modes on the continuum, to different formulations of the negative Oedipus complex.

The risk of the reconceptualization that Silverman offers of the relationship between women, the maternal body, and oedipal scenarios, is that the lesbian desire so central to the films under discussion in this chapter becomes unraveled in a continuum of desires, so that the challenge of lesbian representation to the institutionalization of heterosexual desire is potentially lost. In a spirit not unlike that which informs Silverman's analysis, Akerman and Ottinger insist upon the lesbian body as it exists within scenarios of desire, within representation, within the cinematic apparatus. However, the lesbian signatures in their films also speak—and write—the marginality of lesbianism. For lesbian desire in these films insists simultaneously on the female body that wallows in inarticulate oral rage and *is* outside symbolic representation as it is conventionally understood, and the female body that informs the difficult connection between the body and language.

Silverman's suspicions about any radical potential of a female body that is relegated to a prelinguistic state are well taken. But the very possibility of narration in Akerman's and Ottinger's films is predicated on the representation of such a female body, not in order to suggest some archaic female mode beyond patriarchy, but to pose lesbianism *both* as the projection of patriarchal—and feminist—fantasies, and as another register of desire altogether. The lesbian subjects in these films both assume the status of lesbianism as cultural "other" to phallocentric and heterosexist norms, and refuse it; indeed, the very possibility of the films is built on that simultaneous acknowledgment and refusal. Akerman's and Ottinger's signatures—the one, a body that is virtually constantly on display, the other, a "cameo" that reiterates the chain of female-to-female desire—embody the ironic juxtaposition of the relationship between lesbian desire and the cinema as both complicit with and radically other than the laws of narrative and visual pleasure.

III.
Early Cinema
and
Women's Films

5. "Primitive" Narration

The period of film history known as the "primitive" era is framed by the first public exhibition of films by the Lumière brothers at the Grand Café in Paris in 1895, and by the development, some ten to fifteen years later, of the codes and conventions of nascent, classical narrative cinema. Although the term *primitive cinema* is used interchangeably with *early cinema* in describing this period of film history, I will nonetheless use it in quotation marks in order to foreground its problematic implications—particularly since the women's films which will be examined in the next chapter are concerned precisely with those implications. For many years, the early cinema was regarded by film theorists and historians, if not as a vast wasteland then at the very least as an uninspiring collection of awkwardly put-together scenes, with little structure and even less art. For most modern spectators, early films are difficult to watch, either because "nothing happens," or because of seemingly endless repetitions of the same events (particularly in chase films), or because of monotonous shots with little or no variation.

The "primitive" style of filmmaking assumes a frontal camera, an unchanging distance in medium long shot, and no camera movement. In other words, the

157

techniques of focusing and centering to which viewers of the classical cinema are accustomed are absent in the early cinema.[1] In what might initially appear as something of a paradox, the "primitive" style also refers to the ways in which early films broke away from these standard characteristics—through a change in camera distance or angle, or through camera movement. When such departures are present, they are virtually always motivated. Early versions of close-ups, for instance, are literally produced in "primitive" films, whether by showing a child gleefully peering through a magnifying lens and closeup, isolated images of the objects of his vision *(Grandma's Reading Glass,* 1900), or by showing a man with a telescope peering eagerly at a woman passerby and a shot of the woman's ankle in close-up *(As Seen through a Telescope,* 1900).

Recent research on the first fifteen years of motion pictures has challenged many assumptions about the evolution of film narrative. Films and filmmakers previously disregarded as mere preludes to the "real" beginnings of cinema—the films of D. W. Griffith—have been reevaluated as providing different formulations of cinematic possibilities.[2] The strangeness or unreadability or many early films has been taken as a sign, not of their irrelevance but of our own conditioning by the apparatus of the classical cinema. Noël Burch locates an "otherness" of the early cinema in what he calls the "acting out, at the level of narrative, of gesture, at the iconographic, scenographic levels, the symbolism of those fundamental strategies which were to develop over the next quarter of a century (ca. 1907 to 1932) and which came to constitute what is still (abusively) called The Language of Cinema."[3] For Burch, early cinema offers bold demonstrations of the appeal of film. In early films a character (usually male) might look through a keyhole at another character (usually female), whereas this voyeuristic relationship would later be incorporated into camera movement, editing, and so on. Study of the early cinema, from this vantage point, is a kind of return of the repressed of the classical cinema.

Tom Gunning pursues the "otherness" of the early cinema in a different direction, arguing that "primitive" films explored areas which would have no place in the classical narrative fiction film—the playfully unique cinematic space of Georges Méliès's films populated by fantastic creatures and disappearing acts, the direct address to the spectator eventually prohibited in the name of a self-enclosed narrative universe, the sheer pleasure of camera movement in early panorama films. These practices were abandoned in the evolution of mainstream film, but they find an echo in the works of avant-garde filmmakers. Gunning acknowledges that the relation between early and avant-garde cinema is not a simple one: "Certainly early filmmakers envisioned no aesthetic project like that of the avant-garde filmmaker. It is dubious that any of these films were thought about aesthetically at all. However, they display quite nakedly new relations to the representation of space that the camera made possible. Some of these possibilities were rediscovered by the avant-garde."[4] However different the approaches of Gunning and Burch may be in other ways, they share a definition of the "otherness" of the "primitive" cinema as something that would be marginalized in the evolution of classical film narrative.

Feminist explorations into the early cinema have followed both of the lines of development suggested in Burch's and Gunning's work. Studies by Linda Williams and Lucy Fischer on the early films of Méliès have demonstrated, from quite different perspectives, fundamental ways in which the emerging forms of cinematic representation affirm the polarity of male subject and female object; hence, Méliès's films offer bold demonstrations of the appeal of the classical cinema, along the lines of Burch's argument.[5] Lynne Kirby has argued, however, that early cinema offers, rather, a spectator who is " 'undone,' uncoded, a subject whose sexual orientation vis-à-vis spectatorship is broken down, put into crisis—hystericized." Kirby's specific point of reference is early train films, and the heterogeneous modes of pleasure and identification she finds there are quite close to Gunning's designation of the alterity of early cinema: "Early train films are as often involved in the undoing of sexual difference, of a set of anchors for sexual identity that floats, comically, in an age of mechanical production."[6] To some extent, of course, the conclusions one draws from early cinema depend upon which films one takes as representative of the era. Williams's and Fischer's analyses of Méliès's films, on the one hand, and Kirby's analyses of train films, on the other, are equally convincing, and their opposing conclusions suggest, most obviously, the need to understand the "primitive" era of filmmaking as composed of different and competing notions of "otherness."

Put another way, much of the attraction of early film lies in its simultaneous evocation of, yet absolute distance from, the classical cinema. Following Gunning's argument, a significant body of work on the early cinema has explored how the films of avant-garde filmmakers, especially but not exclusively male American filmmakers of the late 1960s and early 1970s, may be read in relationship to the early cinema.[7] An equally compelling argument can be made for the works of some women filmmakers. In the next chapter, I will examine a group of films by women directors which revise and redefine the "primitive"; in the process, they unpack the different resonances that the very term *primitive* implies. This chapter will lay the groundwork, as it were, for that analysis. Beginning with an examination of the "primitive" as it applies not just to the early cinema alone but also and especially to how that era has been conceptualized in contemporary film studies, I will move to an examination of how different modes of address in the early cinema are informed by gender dynamics. While some early films offer bold representations of the feminist thesis that the man possesses the authoritative gaze in cinema (therefore adding fuel to the argument that the cinematic apparatus is shaped by one unbroken history of the objectification of the female body), my purpose in this chapter is not to examine how the early cinema set the stage for the classical cinema that was to come, but rather to examine why women filmmakers would be drawn to modes of representation so strongly affiliated with the period.

Many early films, and not just the magic films of Méliès, appear to confirm the widely held claim that the cinematic apparatus, emergent or otherwise, is made to the measure of male desire. Consider, for instance, the representation of the human body, and in particular the fragmentation of the body evident in early versions of close-ups. While the difference is not absolute—men's bodies were fragmented by the camera too—there is little question that the display of a body part is much more characteristic of the representation of the female body.[8] John Hagan has noted the frequency with which women's legs and feet function as fetish objects in the early cinema, citing *It's a Shame to Take the Money* (1905), in which a policeman and a shoeshine boy get to look at a woman's legs; and *Female Crook and Her Victim* (1905), in which a woman falls against a man in order to rob him, and raises her dress to hide the man's wallet. Her victim is duped, but the payoff is the glimpse of leg offered for erotic contemplation.[9] An isolation of feet occurs in *The Gay Shoe Clerk* (1903), in which the shoe clerk's stroking hand motivates a close-up of the foot (although the "woman" in this case is a female impersonator).

In the classical cinema, the close-up is associated, in its most conventional form, with the face; but close-ups of the face in the early cinema—unlike those of legs and feet—tend to be more identified with a mode of enunciation, the direct address to the spectator. In so-called facial films, conscious mugging and contortions are directed at the camera. In *Goo Goo Eyes* (1903), a female impersonator, made up to look stereotypically ugly, grimaces and contorts his/her face. The sexual ambiguity which often is disguised or displaced in the early cinema—the fact that female roles were frequently assumed by men—is here put on display. Another variation on a similar theme occurs in *Wrinkles Removed* (1902), in which a woman's neck and head are being massaged by a man who attempts to turn her head to get a better look at her. Each time he does so, the woman grimaces and contorts her face. These close-ups of "women's" faces are radically different from those of women's feet and legs, and are far more evocative of the alterity of the early cinema of which Gunning speaks. The direct address to the camera would constitute one of many taboos of the classical cinema, and the relative autonomy of the image—that is, the fact that it is not defined completely within the look of another, a designated spectator within the film—suggests an ambiguous status.

A Subject for the Rogue's Gallery (1904) draws on both uses of the close-up. A woman prisoner mugs for the police photographer and for the audience simultaneously, and the camera moves forward to frame her face. The film ends when the woman, now at close range, bursts into tears. Unlike the mugging in *Goo Goo Eyes* or *Wrinkles Removed,* here the woman's face is contained within a structure marked by the separation of subject and object, the climax of which is the conquest of the woman, a conquest marked by the close-up of the face bursting into tears. The production of the close-up here situates the woman's face within the more clearly defined fetishism of *It's a Shame to Take the Money* or *The Gay Shoe Clerk,* but with the important difference that the woman initially resists the act of being photographed, and her resistance suggests a thrill of conquest in the production of the close-up.

Representations of the female body in its entirety in early film tend to have clothing play a central role. In both *Annabelle Butterfly Dance* and *Annabelle Serpentine Dance* (1895), for instance, a woman dances for the camera. She is dressed in billowing fabric which swirls about her, almost engulfing her at times. That the woman is performing for the camera is clear, but the movements of her body and the swirling fabric do not seem to be anchored in a specific context. The film could be taking place on a stage or in a studio. There is an excess in the film, an excess of flowing movement, so that there is little distinction between the movements of the body and the movements of the fabric. The film screen, like the fabric, conceals the female body and displays it simultaneously. The simultaneous display and concealment can be read as one of the fundamental conditions of representation of the female body. A film such as *Trapeze Disrobing Act* (1901) suggests in bold terms that condition. Two men, seated in a theater box, watch a woman, seated on a trapeze, strip. There is little doubt as to the intended audience of this spectacle, and there is little excess in the movements of the woman's body.

Just as *A Subject for the Rogue's Gallery* demonstrates the mechanism of the close-up of the woman's face, *What Happened on 23rd Street, New York City* (1901) suggests, if more subtly, the relationship between concealment and display. The film shows a city street, with people walking toward and away from the camera. As one woman walks toward the camera, her skirt billows upward as she steps onto a subway grate, an action marking the end of the film, and providing a rudimentary narrative structure of exposition and punchline. In this film, a city street is framed in such a way as to suggest that the film screen is located on a boundary line central to many of the pleasures of early film, between a "real" street, bustling with the activity of everyday life, and the voyeur's position suggested in *Trapeze Disrobing Act.* The woman's body, now clad in street clothes, neither dances nor strips; she does nothing more than walk toward

Figure 23. *Annabelle Serpentine Dance* (Museum of Modern Art)

Figure 24. *Trapeze Disrobing Act* (courtesy of the American Federation of
Arts Film/Video Program, from "Before Hollywood" exhibition;
Patrick G. Loughney, photographer)

Figure 25. *What Happend on 23rd Street, New York City*
        (Museum of Modern Art)

the camera. These seemingly natural movements appear restricted when compared to the movements of the woman's body in *Annabelle Butterfly Dance* and
Annabelle Serpentine Dance. Similarly, the billowing fabric which at times
overwhelms the woman's body in the dance films is suggested here as well, but
now in the single, restricted movement of lifting the woman's skirts. The source
of the movement is no longer the body itself but a subway grate. The woman's
body is not just the object of spectacle; it is narrativized, set in place in a chain
of motions not her own. And the onlooker, who is part of the scene in
Trapeze Disrobing Act, here is invisible, contained within the camera and mise-
en-scène.

There is a significant difference between a film such as *Goo Goo Eyes,* on
the one hand, and *A Subject for the Rogue's Gallery,* on the other, or *Trapeze
Disrobing Act* and *What Happened on 23rd Street. Goo Goo Eyes,* with its direct
look at the camera and its designation of a "female" face as a disguise, suggests a
mode of representation that would have no place in what would become the
classical mode of representation of the female face. *A Subject for the Rogue's
Gallery,* however, evokes the classical polarity of man as subject, female as

object. Similarly, the difference between the clothed female bodies in *Annabelle Butterfly Dance* and *What Happened on 23rd Street* indicates how, in the early cinema, the female body acquired a representational function by being placed within a rudimentary narrative structure. *Goo Goo Eyes* and *Butterfly Dance* seem more evocative of the early cinema as embodying a sense of sheer visual discovery (as in Tom Gunning's argument), and *A Subject for the Rogue's Gallery* and *What Happened on 23rd Street* the "acting out" of the pleasures of the classical cinema of which Burch speaks.[10]

I have characterized these different kinds of representation of the female face and the female body as speaking to the increasing narrativization of the woman's body. Many researchers of the early cinema are reluctant, however, to assign narrative functions to the devices of early film, largely because such a search for narrative smacks of the desire to see early film not on its own terms but as the mirror image—even if a negative one—of the classical cinema; to see narrative, that is, as the manifest destiny of cinema, evidenced from the very outset. For some, narrative wish-fulfillment speaks to a larger problem in film studies, the tendency to impose the (verbal and written) categories of narrative and narration imported from literature, to explain filmic narration with which it may, in fact, have little in common.

In response to these potential confusions, André Gaudreault defines narrativity in film as the intertwining of monstration (showing) and narration (telling), with monstration occurring at the level of the shot, and narration at the level of editing.[11] Tom Gunning distinguishes between the cinema of attractions, focusing on visual display and exhibitionism, which dominated early film until 1906–07, and storytelling film, concentrating rather on diegetic absorption, which became dominant later, and which would prefigure the classical cinema of identification and narrative. This is not an absolute distinction, since, as Gunning argues, "the cinema of attraction does not disappear with the dominance of narrative, but rather goes underground, both into certain avant-garde practices and as a component of narrative films, more evident in some genres (e.g., the musical) than in others."

Gunning refers to two of the films discussed previously as examples of the identical phenomenon of "attraction":

> The close-up cut into Porter's *The Gay Shoe Clerk* (1903) may anticipate later continuity techniques, but its principal motive is again pure exhibitionism, as the lady lifts her skirt hem, exposing her ankle for all to see. Biograph films such as *Photographing a Female Crook* (1904) [of which *A Subject for the Rogue's Gallery* is a variation] and *Hooligan in Jail* (1903) consist of a single shot in which the camera is brought close to the main character, until they are in midshot. The enlargement is not a device expressive of narrative tension; it is in itself an attraction and the point of the film.[12]

While *Hooligan in Jail* employs the same camera movement as *Photographing a Female Crook,* the frame of the movement is quite different. The camera movement in *Hooligan in Jail* traces the prisoner's delighted reaction to food that has been brought to him. To be sure, Hooligan and the female crook are both examples of the marginal figures favored in many early films, and in both cases the camera captures a childlike reaction; but there is nonetheless a significant difference between the two films.

If Hooligan "exhibits" a childlike response, what the female crook "exhibits" first and foremost is the fact of her female identity, and of her difference from the men, and the male agency of the camera, that surround her. Both films may be said to be exhibitions, not of the scenes they capture but of the cinema itself, of its capacity to create a closer view; but in this respect, the difference between them is even more striking. For the camera movement in *Photographing a Female Crook* and *A Subject for the Rogue's Gallery* produces a reaction, whereas the camera movement in *Hooligan in Jail* records one. If "exhibitionism" is an appropriate word to use to describe the difference of early cinema—different, that is, from the voyeurism ostensibly dominant in storytelling film—then it needs to account for, rather than obscure, different kinds of display at work.

Gunning himself uses the distinction between early cinema as exhibitionist versus narrative cinema as voyeurist:

> Contrasted to the voyeurist aspect of narrative cinema analyzed by Christian Metz, this is an exhibitionist cinema. [. . .] From comedians smirking at the camera, to the constant bowing and gesturing of the conjurors in magic films, this is a cinema that displays its visibility, willing to rupture a self-enclosed fictional world for a chance to solicit the attention of the spectator.[13]

However, Metz's reading of the classical cinema as voyeurist does not replicate the classic duality of voyeur and exhibitionist, but rather displaces it. The classical cinema does not accentuate voyeurism at the expense of exhibitionism, but puts into place a whole other dialectic:

> cinema manages to be both exhibitionist and secretive. The exchange of seeing and being-seen will be fractured in its centre, and its two disjointed halves allocated to different moments in time: another split. I never see my partner, but only his photograph. This does not make me any less of a voyeur, but it involves a different regime, that of the primal scene and the keyhole. The rectangular screen permits all kinds of fetishisms, all the nearly-but-not-quite effects, since it can decide at exactly what height to place the barrier which cuts us off, which marks the end of the visible and the beginning of the downward tilt into darkness.[14]

The argument that cinema operates according to a scopic economy of voyeurism and fetishism, and not the classic economy of voyeurism/exhibitionism, attains, of course, its most succinct form in Laura Mulvey's classic thesis that cinema "works" precisely by its simultaneous appeal to scopophilia and fetishism.[15]

Even if exhibitionism is not easily placed in opposition to voyeurism insofar as the cinema is concerned, one could still argue that the early cinema is characterized precisely by an acting out of exhibitionist displays which would return in the classical cinema only in the form of spectacular displays subordinated to the dialectic of voyeurism and fetishism. Gunning's argument is based in part on the exhibition context for early motion pictures, where fairgrounds and sideshows would appear to have created a quite literal exhibitionist frame for motion pictures. But one could argue in just the opposite way as well. It could be said that motion pictures marked the erasure of popular entertainment as performance; that the positions of visual identification offered by early films were characterized by the displacement of exhibitionism by fetishism, by the separation of subject and object, and by distance between performer and onlooker.

Although Gunning does not spell this out in detail, the implication in his argument is that gender is not really a category with great signifying authority in early film. Of a 1904 film, *The Bride Retires* (which is cited in Noël Burch's film about the early cinema, *Correction Please),* Gunning notes that it "reveals a fundamental conflict between this exhibitionistic tendency of early film and the creation of fictional diegesis. A woman undresses for bed while her new husband peers at her from behind a screen. However, it is to the camera and the audience that the bride addresses her erotic striptease, winking at us as she faces us, smiling in erotic display."[16] That it was possible in early cinema for a woman to solicit directly the attention of the audience may well be a function of the alterity of the early cinema, but *this* kind of exhibitionism seems to me quite different from other examples of visual display, since it evokes the register of fetishism, of the classic representation of the female body as capable of possessing a look only when that look solicits the attention of a male viewer. To use John Berger's phrase, this seeming "exhibitionist" is more convincingly described as a "surveyed female."

In the context of the present discussion, it is crucial, then, to account for the different ways in which the mode of address of early cinema occurs, and as I have suggested, gender accounts for some rather significant differences between different practices. I would like to move, then, to a discussion of the gendered components in some of the most dominant modes of address, those that employ human figures to embody both the visual fascination and the rudimentary narrative structures of early film. First, however, it is necessary to address another problem common to film studies and particularly relevant to early film: the extent to which one can speak of an actual "narrator" in film. There is a well-founded reluctance in narrative studies to use the term *narrator* except in the most specifically defined instances.[17] The bracketing of the term *narrator* in contemporary discussions of film narrative has evolved in part from the desire to focus on narrative as a process, on narration not as contained in an individual but rather as a structure, a function linking a variety of subject positions. The desire to designate a cinematic "narrator" may appear retrograde at best, whether the product of naive equations between film and categories of literary narrative (which themselves are problematic, since the distinction between "third-person" and "omniscient" is not so clear-cut, for instance), or of an equally naive assumption that the individual human figure is the measure of all narrative authority.

In some studies on the early cinema, this question of the narrator is examined in terms of narrative omniscience. Thus, in his discussion of temporal structures in early cinema, and of the tendency of many early filmmakers to use temporal overlap, André Gaudreault distinguishes two modes. The first relies on a succession of autonomous tableaux, not unlike the narrative mode characteristic of medieval literature. The storyteller, Gaudreault writes, "lacked omniscience, perhaps because he had not sufficiently developed a consciousness of his craft. . . ." The second mode found its most persuasive representative in D. W. Griffith. Here, the "ubiquitous camera" had learned to "go through walls."[18] Gaudreault refers to the power of omniscience associated with the development of narrative techniques such as cross-cutting and camera movement.

Discussion of film narrative in the early years is haunted by omniscience, and the specter virtually always leads, sooner or later, to the figure of D. W. Griffith. Griffith's status has undergone considerable reevaluation in recent years. Griffith may not have "invented" a cinema in which a story "tells itself," but he is nonetheless the single figure most connected to the myth of a self-enclosed narrative universe, understood from the point of view of ideology as well as genius. It is often assumed that Griffith's style represents the dream of classical cinema, but the way in which his presence as narrator was built into the structure of his films was not necessarily successful. As Tom Gunning points out, "This invisible but sensed hand will reach its apogée in Griffith's commercial disaster *Intolerance*. The 'uniter of here and hereafter' will prove an obstacle to much of his audience, a frustration rather than a guide."[19] One of the earliest forms of narration in early cinema was that offered by lecturers who frequently accompanied film programs. They literally demonstrated to spectators the way through film, whether by summarizing the plot of a novel on which a film was based, or by pointing out the central action of a shot. That lecturers disappeared suggests, of course, that their function had become integrated into

Figure 26. *The Living Playing Cards* (Museum of Modern Art)

the developing conventions of film narrative, whether through intertitles or the "invisible hand" guiding the spectator through Griffith's films.[20]

The narrating function fulfilled by the lecturer, by intertitles, and by the "invisible hand" of Griffith's films is primarily one of linear continuity and referential information. Other, more limited kinds of narrating functions are fulfilled by those figures who appear to direct, mediate, or otherwise act out the visual pleasures of the cinematic scene. I will refer to these characters as "primitive narrators," recognizing that they are neither omniscient narrators nor the absolute agents of "primitive" narration—i.e., they are objects of the camera's view at the same time that they act out the emerging visual and narrative capacities of the film medium. The most obvious example of the "primitive narrator" is the figure of the conjuror or magician, most common in the films of Méliès. In *Le Mélomane* (*The Melomaniac* [1903]), Méliès appears as a magical music teacher who repeatedly takes off his head and throws it on a staff to represent musical notes; in *Les Cartes vivantes* (*The Living Playing Cards* [1905]), Méliès portrays a magician who transforms playing cards into living human beings. Here, as in other of his films, Méliès looks directly at the camera, accentuating his role as solicitor of the audience's attention.

Another related category of the "primitive narrator" is the photographer, or image-maker. In *Getting Evidence* (1906), a detective armed with a camera pursues a couple and is frustrated in his repeated attempts to capture them on celluloid; when at last he does manage to photograph them, he discovers he has been following the wrong couple. In *The Story the Biograph Told* (1903), a boy surreptitiously films a man and his secretary kissing in the Biograph office, and the film is screened at a motion-picture show attended by the man and his wife. In one of Méliès's most interesting films, *Une Chute de cinq étages* (*The Photographer* [1906]), Méliès plays a photographer about to take a picture of a young couple in his studio. The background screen falls on them, however, and the camera falls out the window onto a concierge sitting outdoors. As she struggles to remove herself from the camera and dropcloth, a passerby takes her for a bull and attempts some amateur bullfighting.

While films featuring magicians and conjurors persisted alongside those with image-makers, in many ways the role of the image-maker subsumed the role of the magician. The difference between Méliès's *Une Chute de cinq étages* and his many magic films is instructive in this regard. As he adopts the role of image-maker, Méliès's omnipresence and omnipotence as master of ceremonies diminish, giving way to the narrative and spectacular possibilities of the apparatus itself. For in the second shot of *Une Chute de cinq étages,* the camera assumes the role of narrator, which in the previous shot was performed by the photographer.

Other "primitive narrators" function simultaneously as spectators upon whom are bestowed the spectacular and sometimes infantilizing possibilities of the medium. The dream film, popular in particular in the pre-1907 era, offers the dreamer as both the agent and the victim of the power of the dream.[21] In *Let Me Dream Again!* (1900), a man flirts with a young woman who is wearing a mask; he then awakens to find himself embracing his wife in bed. *And the Villain Still Pursued Her, or The Author's Dream* (1906) shows a writer who falls asleep at his desk and imagines himself courting a young woman; the two are pursued by her unwanted suitor. *A Midwinter's Night Dream* (1906) portrays a child who falls asleep in the snow, and a fade depicts a scene in which a girl invites him into a house where holiday festivities occur.

Given the extent to which contemporary analysis of cinema has focused on the power of the gaze, "primitive narrators" in early voyeur or keyhole films offer particularly telling embodiments of the equivalence between cinematic pleasure and voyeuristic fantasies. *Pull Down the Curtains, Suzie* (1903), like the previously mentioned *Trapeze Disrobing Act* (1901), is a single-shot film in which a woman undresses, observed by a male spectator. In other films, the voyeur's gaze motivates more sophisticated structures of the look, alternations between the voyeur and the object of the look.[22] In *Peeping Tom* (1901), a hotel porter looks through the keyholes of a series of rooms, with keyhole masks imitating his vision. A similar structure occurs in *The Inquisitive Boots* (1905), in

Figure 27. *Pull Down the Curtains, Suzie* (courtesy of the American
Federation of Arts Film/Video Program, from "Before Hollywood"
exhibition; Patrick G. Loughney, photographer)

which a bootblack, motivated by nothing more than the desire to look, moves down a hotel corridor looking through keyholes. In both of these films, there is rudimentary punishment of the voyeur: Peeping Tom is chased away by a man who opens a door, and Inquisitive Boots is squirted at through the keyhole.

What serves as punishment in these two films takes on another function in *A Search for Evidence* (1903), where the look through the keyhole is motivated not by mischief but by the ostensibly worthy cause of finding an errant husband. An angry wife and a detective proceed down a hotel corridor in search of her adulterous mate. The woman peers into one room after another, and the camera imitates her look. When she finds her husband, the detective is shown peering through the keyhole, followed by a shot of the interior of the hotel room. The detective in this film acquires a function that is far more "narrative" in the classical sense than any of the other modes of address discussed thus far, since his look authorizes the cut to the final shot of the film, from the hallway to a lateral, interior shot of the room. He crosses the threshold dividing hallway from room interior, the threshold dividing subject and object of the look.[23]

The detective is thus a "primitive narrator," but his function is more complex in that he transcends the role of voyeur and crosses the threshold separating subject and object of the look. His narrative function is one which will be assumed in a variety of ways by the evolution of cinematic technique itself. In *A Subject for the Rogue's Gallery,* the look of the camera and the look of the (invisible) police photographer are joined, and the police officers who restrain the woman become mediators for that conjunction. The integration of the function of a "primitive narrator" like the detective in *A Search for Evidence* into the moving camera in *A Subject for the Rogue's Gallery* is significant in the development of the capacity of film narrative to present itself as pure story, to capture the viewer in the movement of the camera and hence to deaccentuate the marks of discourse.

Put another way, the absorption of the "primitive narrator" into the movement of the camera across the threshold is emblematic of how classical film narration would envelop such bold figures of visual authority and fascination and render them invisible through the apparently seamless narrative of linear, novelistic film narrative. Other early films expand and develop the role of the "primitive narrator" in other ways. *Terrible Ted* (1907) portrays a child who, in the family living room and in the presence of his mother, reads a book. As soon as she leaves the room, he turns his attention to what we assume to be a forbidden text, a volume of the *Wild West Weekly* entitled, appropriately enough, "Terrible Ted." The image on the cover reveals a hold-up, and a close-up of it shows a woman being held captive. Ted reads for a while from the magazine and then folds it up into his back pocket. He takes a gun from a drawer and goes outside, where he begins shooting at policemen on the street. He chases them and begins leading a group of children. Then there is a cut to the countryside, where a hold-up of a stagecoach and a rescue of a damsel in distress recreate the cover of the magazine. Ted suddenly appears on the scene, kills the villains, and begins a series of adventures: he shoots a villain in a saloon, stabs a bear about to kill a Native American woman picking flowers, is captured and tied to a stake, is rescued by the woman, is chased by a group of men who kill the woman, discovers the camp of Native Americans and stabs them all, then scalps them. After a triumphant display of the scalps, we return, suddenly, to the living room, where Ted is asleep. His mother strikes him and the child cries.

Terrible Ted incorporates the figures of both the dreamer and the conjuror. But neither the dream frame nor the enactment of "magic" is clear-cut.[24] The cut to a countryside and the reenactment of a magazine cover are clearly fantasy, but the initial crossing of the threshold clouds the boundary between interior and exterior space, between the real and the imagined, between the dreamer's conciousness and the printed text. With Ted, the viewer crosses a threshold, is located in an ambivalent territory. Only with the return to the living room and the mother's angry gesture—a simple configuration of the oedipal scenario which lurks over the cinema from its outset—is the spectator separated from the dream, given a position of detached observation. In *Terrible Ted* the role of the "primitive narrator" is considerably more complex than the functions of dream and voyeurism, magic and image-making, visible in other films. Here, Ted is located in an ambivalent space between subject and object; he embodies and acts out a narrative desire. In *Terrible Ted,* the child has incorporated the narrative authority of the adult into his own fantasy, in a series of displacements that lead from mother to book to gun to police to various villains.

If *Terrible Ted* is then exemplary of the function of the "primitive narrator" in early film, it would appear that he confirms what has become common wisdom in film theory: that the subject of enunciation in the cinema is male, infantile perhaps, but male nonetheless, emphasized in particular by the parade of "others"—women, Native Americans—as well as the mother's punishing gesture as a reality principle. There are female "primitive narrators," but they appear so rarely as to suggest that they are the proverbial exceptions that prove the rule. Conjurors and magicians are virtually always male, but one curious counterexample discussed by Lucy Fischer is *A Pipe Dream* (1905), in which a woman, smoking a cigarette, conjures a tiny man in her palm. Unlike the conjuror in Méliès's films, this woman is taken aback by her magical powers. A Pathé remake of Méliès's *Le Mélomane* features a woman music teacher and conjuror. Whereas Méliès's magical powers involved putting replicas of his own head on the musical staff as notes, the woman in the 1904 remake removes the heads of men to create her musical notes.

Fischer suggests that such isolated examples of the female conjuror are significant for the more complex view they create of the male-female relationship in early cinema.

> In the cases where women magicians exist, they are figures of awe and dread. This makes clear the fact that woman is not always perceived as powerless—a passive prop. Rather woman's power is often acknowledged, but it is viewed as perilous and perverse. Perhaps, the male magician is not only performing tricks upon the female; he is preventing *her* from performing more dangerous tricks upon *him*.[25]

The way in which women's power is acknowledged, however, is fully consonant with a scenario of male desire. I stress this not in order to return to a feminist vision of film history that has been criticized throughout this book—a vision, that is, that would stress one single, unbroken narrative of male dominance over women—but rather to suggest that for those women filmmakers who have reexamined a "primitive" mode of representation, the issue is not the rediscovery of what would amount to a moment of bliss prior to the imposition of the

Figure 28. *What Happened in the Tunnel* (Courtesy of the American
Federation of Arts Film/Video Program, from "Before Hollywood"
exhibition; Patrick G. Loughney, photographer)

conventions of classical narrative, a moment then to be "excavated" in much the
same way the pre-oedipal has been mined for its possibilities of other modes of
relation and signification.

Some instances where women do function as "primitive narrators" in early
film seem to build upon the resistance of the woman to being filmed in *A Subject
for the Rogue's Gallery,* but "resistance" here should not be read as an alternative
female-centered vision. An instructive example in this context occurs in *What
Happened in the Tunnel* (1903). Two women, a white woman and her black
maid, are riding in a train. When the train passes through a tunnel—a passage
marked by a darkened screen—a male passenger attempts to steal a kiss from the
white woman. Once the train has left the tunnel, he realizes, much to his chagrin,
that he has kissed the black woman. The man looks, and wants to possess what
he sees; but he kisses the "wrong" woman, the inappropriate object of spectacle.
The two women in this film are objects of the male look, but they return the look,
by laughing at the man. This "primitive narrator" crosses a threshold into
potentially dangerous territory, marked by the laughter of the women which is
the punchline to the film. But if that laughter suggests a resistance to the

authority of the male look, it is a resistance that is nonetheless locked into the hierarchy of subject and object, a hierarchy doubly inscribed through sexual and racial difference. The women's laughter is possible only within a firmly established structure of self and other.

Other films which feature female "primitive narrators" continue to define this process of "resistance" as fully part of the emerging scenarios of the classical cinema. In the 1909 film *Choosing a Husband,* a young woman is bewildered by the number of young men who want to marry her. Four men propose to her, and she tells each one that she will make her decision the next day. She then hides behind a screen, and leaves an attractive woman in the drawing room to greet them. Predictably, each suitor arrives, finds the other woman, and makes advances to her. The woman comes out from behind the screen and dismisses the four would-be husbands. At the conclusion of the film, the woman finds true love at last, when another man returns from a trip abroad. The woman in *Choosing a Husband* occupies the position of the husband in *The Bride Retires,* but the direct engagement of the spectator's look in that film is here replaced by an exchange between a man and a woman. The woman does possess an active look, one grounded in her own curiosity, a curiosity based in its turn on a principle of resistance to the authority of the male subject; but her curiosity is stripped of any threat it might represent by being channeled into the conclusion of marriage which would become the classical form of resolution *par excellence.*

A 1913 film, *The Innocent Bridegroom,* traces a plot that evolves from the complications of a woman's curiosity. A widow is suspicious of the man she is about to marry, and hires a private detective to follow him. In the meantime she does some sleuthing of her own, and once she is convinced of her suitor's good faith, they marry. The woman forgets, however, to call off the private detective, who follows them on their honeymoon. Hence the film depicts the clash between two "primitive narrators," the widow and the detective. *How Men Propose* (1913) is a particularly imaginative rendition of the narrative implications of resistance to the equation between woman and image of the male look. We see a young man embrace a photograph depicting a woman's face. A second young man, and then a third, discover that they all are courting the same woman, for each possesses the same photograph. Having distributed identical photographs of herself, the woman sends each man an identical letter. "I'm returning your ring," she writes. "I'm writing an article on how men propose. You can keep the ring." *How Men Propose* offers one of the most interesting forms of female "primitive" narration, since in this film the woman actually responds to her status as image.

One of the most interesting examples of a female "primitive narrator" is in a 1912 film, *The Mind Cure.* Professor Conner, a hypnotist, attempts without success to frighten away the numerous men who court his daughter. Frustrated by the failure of his paternal authority, he writes in his journal that he is going to cure his daughter, a "confirmed flirt," through hypnotic treatment. Unbeknownst to him, daughter Pearl reads his journal, so that when he hypnotizes her ("you will dislike all young men"), she resists. A man enters the professor's office, and Pearl immediately chases him away to convince her father of the success of his treatment. The professor's next patient is Chester, Pearl's suitor, who comes to be treated for bashfulness. He follows Pearl's example, but now embraces Pearl to prove that the treatment has worked. In the concluding shot of the film, Chester and Pearl present their marriage license to the professor.

Professor Conner is a narrator who fails—fails as a principle of paternal authority, fails as a conjuror-hypnotist. A crucial moment in terms of Pearl's own function as narrator occurs when the father attempts to hypnotize his daughter. Pearl faces the camera, her eyes closed in accordance with the taboo against actors' looking directly into the camera.[26] The audience shares in her faking of hypnotic treatment. The conjuror-hypnotist has retreated to the background of the image, with a figure of playful resistance now designated as source of the narration. Pearl's rebellion is limited: Her desire, the audience discovers with the arrival of Chester on the scene, is not to remain a "confirmed flirt" but to marry. While it is the daughter's joke which moves *The Mind Cure* along and gives it a narrative direction, here, as in all of these films which feature a woman's desire, the woman's status within a scopic economy is confirmed.

As I hope is obvious by now, these female "primitive narrators," and their playful resistance to the polarity of male subject/female object, do not constitute a simple position of alterity from which one can imagine other formulations of cinematic desire. Rather, they depend and rely on the classical polarities of (male) subject and (female) object. There are occasional moments where the female narrator acquires a function, not of resistance to be quickly channeled into resolution, but of a playful refusal that seems to offer another possible scenario, like the woman's ironic reduction of marriage to a photograph and a ring in *How Men Propose,* and even in the faking of hypnotic treatment in *The Mind Cure.* But by and large, these designations of female "primitive narrators" continue the narrativization of the female body that one sees in such earlier films as *Subject for the Rogue's Gallery* and *What Happened on 23rd Street.* At the beginning of this chapter, I suggested—following the different feminist arguments that have been made about the early cinema—that the early cinema needs to be seen as simultaneously related to yet radically other than the classical cinema. However, virtually every example I have cited thus far leads to the dismal sense of a master narrative in place from the outset—the master narrative, that is, of a cinematic apparatus seemingly destined to represent the polarity of male subject and female object.

Ironically, the figure of "primitive" narration which seems *less* saturated with the rigid polarity of gender is voyeurism. Given the extent to which *voyeurism* is the shorthand term so frequently used to evoke the specter of cinema as a supremely patriarchal form, such a claim may seem ludicrous. But while voyeurism and fetishism are, in Laura Mulvey's analysis, the two intertwining components of sexual polarity in the classical cinema, in early cinema the one does not necessarily presuppose the other. Some of the films discussed previously, including *A Subject for the Rogue's Gallery* and *What Happened in the Tunnel,* suggest voyeurism and fetishism simultaneously. But the actual and literal representation of voyeurism in early film is not so firmly linked to the emerging structures of Mulvey's definition of visual pleasure. While female voyeurs are in somewhat short supply in early cinema, they do not always function as mere props for the fantasies of the male subject, as is the case in the Pathé remake of the Méliès film mentioned earlier.

This is not to say that insofar as voyeurs are concerned, there is no gender differentiation whatsoever; and I certainly do not want to claim a "progressive" status for female voyeurism in early film! Indeed, it would constitute a kind of regressive utopianism to discover in any single figure of the early cinema a position from which to define an untainted source of female cinematic pleasure. What I am suggesting, rather, is that in early film the interdependence of voyeurism and fetishism, while clearly at work in a nascent way in some cases (such as *A Subject for the Rogue's Gallery*), is not always the condition of visual pleasure that it is in Laura Mulvey's analysis of the classical cinema.

Although the argument could be made that the voyeurs of early cinema are class types more than gender ones, and that voyeurs are so infantilized as to be practically undifferentiated in sexual terms, there are significant differences between female and male voyeurs. Previously I referred to two voyeur films, *Peeping Tom* and *The Inquisitive Boots,* which follow a pattern similar to most films of the type. A man, usually a servant (or, in the case of *The Inquisitive Boots,* a bootblack), moves from one keyhole to another in a corridor, the film thus alternating between a shot of him looking and a shot—frequently through a keyhole mask—of what he is looking at. The voyeur usually mimics what he sees before moving on to the next keyhole, and the conclusion of the film is a rudimentary punishment of the voyeur. In *Peeping Tom,* the voyeur spies on several women (including one female impersonator). When his gaze lands upon an isolated man in a room, the door opens and the voyeur is chased away.

The 1904 film *Un coup d'oeil par étage (Scenes on Every Floor)* offers a somewhat more sophisticated pattern. Here, a male servant delivers mail to each of several flats in a building, and the film alternates between his looking through the keyhole and the scene that he witnesses, although here the scenes are presented without the frame of the keyhole mask. As in *Peeping Tom*, the servant faces the camera and mimics what he has seen on each floor—a businessman making a frantic phone call, three children in a pillow fight, a woman (yet another female impersonator) fondling a cat. On the top floor, the servant discovers a fire, quickly opens the door, and rushes to summon firefighters. In both of these voyeur films, it is not only the relationship between male voyeur and the object of his look that is significant, but also and especially that his look initiates a crossing of the threshold that allows a rudimentary form of resolution. In some voyeur films, the crossing of the threshold actually motivates a reverse angle of the inside of the room, thus prefiguring one of the most standard representations of the look in classical cinema.

In most voyeur films, the individual scenes witnessed by the voyeur are a series of unconnected, often peculiar, fragments.[27] In *A Search for Evidence*, for instance, which differentiates so forcefully between the male and the female look, and inscribes the look of the woman as lacking the authority to cross the threshold, the serial and peculiar character of the scenes witnessed is strong (including a man rocking a baby, and a man who attempts to light a chandelier). A 1905 film, *Die Rache der Frau Schultze (Mrs. Schultze's Revenge)*, is particularly interesting in this respect, since it offers not only a glimpse of a female voyeur but also the production, by the woman, of a scene worthy of the most peculiar vignettes glimpsed through a corridor keyhole. The film portrays a set divided into two rooms that share a wall. On the right is Frau Schultze's bedroom; on the left, the apartment of her neighbor, a musician. Frau Schultze goes to bed, only to be awakened by her neighbor, who returns late to his apartment and begins playing his piano.

When a fly lights on Frau Schultze's nose, she comes up with a plan. She peers through the keyhole of the door that separates her room from her neighbor's, and through a keyhole mask she and we see the musician. Frau Schultze then sends the fly through the keyhole, and it proceeds to torment the musician. He tries to swat it, but misses consistently. He even covers himself and his music with spattered ink (from trying to swat the fly when it is positioned on a bottle of ink), and he wreaks havoc on many objects in his apartment. Finally, a group of men are summoned to put an end to the chaos, and among them is a triumphant Frau Schultze.

In this film, female voyeurism engages not only the pleasure of peering through keyholes, but also and especially the desire to manipulate the scene. In *La Fille de bain indiscrète (The Indiscreet Bathroom Maid* [1902]), a female bath attendant moves down a hallway, peeking through transoms in much the same fashion as Peeping Tom. She too mimics the gestures of her clients in various stages of undress—first a woman, then a man, and finally a man with his servant. While the alternating structure is identical to that of other voyeur films, the resolution is not. When the man in the last "scene" pushes his servant into the bathtub, this voyeur dissolves in laughter, allowing neither the punishment, the climax, nor the reverse angles to room interiors motivated by other scenarios of male spectatorial desire. In this film, female voyeurism does not inspire a crossing of the line separating subject and object of the look.

Although it is impossible, with such limited examples drawn from only two early films, to draw anything resembling a firm conclusion, it is nonetheless notable that in both cases, female voyeurism does not require the punishment or scolding of the voyeur. To be sure, a film such as *A Search for Evidence* suggests that a female voyeur can peek, but does not possess the authority necessary to penetrate the room—a privilege reserved for the detective. But perhaps what the female voyeur does possess is, precisely, a desire that would have no place in the emerging codes of narrative cinema laid out so neatly in *A Search for Evidence*. Neither of the female voyeur films contains prescient paradigms of the classical cinema. But *exhibitionism* does not seem to be the right term to describe the activities of the female voyeurs, either.

I have expressed some reservations about Tom Gunning's designation of what he calls the cinema of attractions as "exhibitionist," as opposed to the presumably "voyeurist" pleasures of classical narrative, particularly insofar as the term *exhibitionist* can mask a series of effects that are more properly described as fetishistic, and which are more connected to the gender polarity of the classical cinema than the word *exhibitionist* would suggest. In the case of female voyeurism, however, I think early cinema does offer a suggestion of another kind of pleasure in the cinema which would "go underground," as Gunning puts it, only to emerge in some films by women directors.

Although most researchers into the early cinema are careful to avoid any simple idealization of the radical difference that early films represent, there is a perhaps inevitable tendency, if not to idealize the early cinema then to simplify and monolithize the classical cinema to which it contrasts. The tendency is perhaps most apparent in Burch's work, as the very phrase "Institutional Mode of Representation" suggests. One of the most common assumptions in contemporary film theory of the last fifteen years has been that the classical Hollywood cinema is, in Raymond Bellour's words, a "machine of great homogeneity," a system which serves to affirm white, patriarchal, Western values through a self-enclosed narrative universe of crisis and resolution.[28] It is beyond the scope of the present chapter to engage in the long-standing debate in film studies on the homogeneity of classical film narrative.[29] But given the extent to which so much feminist film theory supports the monolithic view of classical film narrative, it is important to specify that neither the "primitive" narration I am describing in this chapter nor the figures of the "primitive" in women's films to which I will turn in the next chapter can be read as rigidly distinct or absolutely excluded from the realm of classical film narrative. Many studies of early film, while attentive to the dangers of overromanticizing the "primitive" era, seem nonetheless to regard the classical cinema as completely saturated with the laws of continuity, fictional coherence, and diegetic illusion.

Tom Gunning is extremely attentive to how the "cinema of attraction" dominated the early cinema and acquired other forms with the advent of classical narrative cinema. But in his discussion of point of view and early voyeur films, Gunning differentiates between early and classical film by appropriating both Metz's and Mulvey's descriptions of the latter. Early keyhole films, says Gunning, "find their heir in Cocteau's Hôtel des Folies-Dramatiques sequence from *Blood of a Poet* with its dream-like discontinuities and sense of wonder, rather than in the highly narrativized *Rear Window*." Continuing the distinction, Gunning writes:

> While these films [early keyhole films] involve voyeurism, the spectator they address is still far from the voyeur spectator of classical narrative film, that invisible witness who watches unobserved by any of the inhabitants of the film's world, secure in his isolation in the dark. The classical spectator is constructed within a fantasy of a powerful invisible gaze able to insinuate itself into the most private of dramas.[30]

I assume that *Rear Window* exemplifies for Gunning, as it did for Laura Mulvey, the construction of the "classical spectator." Tania Modleski's rereading of *Rear Window* is intended primarily as a revision of the widely held view that this film, like most of Hitchcock's works, exemplifies the polarity of male subject and female object that most theories of the classical spectator take as a given. Hence Modleski demonstrates that the film, far from positing an unquestioned authority of the male gaze, both problematizes male voyeurism and investigates the components of female spectatorship.[31] Equally interesting in the present context is the way Modleski, borrowing from Susan Stewart's analysis of "miniatures," describes the scene of voyeurism in *Rear Window*—the apartment building across the courtyard—as a dollhouse, a miniature which in Stewart's words "tends toward tableau rather than narrative."[32] Although the contexts are obviously quite different, there is nonetheless a strong connection between this "tableau" and the figures of display which Gunning demonstrates as so central to the "other" visual pleasure of early film. The point I want to stress, then, is that figures of "primitive" narration may be far more influential and reverberate more strongly than most notions of classical narrative or the classical spectator would lead us to believe.

I am thinking, in this context, less of how dominant figures of narrative authority may be seen—following Burch's argument—in relationship to their infantile counterparts, and more of how different kinds of narrative and visual agency may coexist in a single film. In Josef von Sternberg's 1932 film *Blonde Venus*, for example, Helen Faraday's (Marlene Dietrich) son, Johnny (Dickie Moore), acts as a "primitive narrator" and recalls Terrible Ted's entry into the cinematic. The various male protagonists of *Blonde Venus* desire Dietrich but cannot possess her. Their desire finds a constant echo in the child's desire to possess the woman. It has often been said that *Blonde Venus* never manages to portray convincingly the dual role of Dietrich—as mother and as performer.[33] In narrative terms, however, the function of the child as "primitive narrator" is to make visible the fragile connection between the two roles. There is a scene in the film where Johnny's function occasions a very peculiar mise-en-scène. He and his mother are framed and theatricalized by the gauzy curtains in an archway of their apartment, and their discussion is quite literally decentered by the grotesque mask which Johnny wears perched sideways on the top of his head, suggesting just as literally another scene of representation.[34]

In William Wyler's 1940 film *The Letter*, two worlds are depicted, one "Western" and one "Asian," with the character of Leslie Crosbie (portrayed by Bette Davis) located in a transgressive space between the two. The lawyer who defends Mrs. Crosbie at her trial for having murdered her lover functions as the most obvious principle of narrative authority in the film. But in the Asian sphere of the film, there is another controlling figure, the Chinese wife of Leslie Crosbie's victim. The Asian woman is a "primitive narrator" in that she quite literally does not speak the language of the film, and embodies a mysterious power akin to that of a conjuror. She exercises an authority which the forces of Western civilization are never quite successful in dispelling. She may not play a joke on the lawyer, as Pearl does on her father in *The Mind Cure*, but she does function to question the neat hierarchy drawn in the film between East and West.

The function of the Asian woman in *The Letter* suggests, of course, that the notion of a "primitive narrator" has to do with Western constructions of the so-called primitive that extend much further than the early history of motion pictures, into the realm of cultural and racial difference. This could be the result of mere coincidence—the term *primitive* having "stuck," where any one of a number of other words might have done as well. Not all historians of the period are happy with the word *primitive*, but it has become the most common short-hand phrase to refer to a variety of aspects of the early cinema.[35] This is not to say, however, that ideological reverberations of the "primitive" have been completely ignored by scholars of early film. But like most convenient shorthand terms, the word *primitive* is sometimes used without further attention to its implications.

Tom Gunning has observed that "the term *primitive* persists . . . partly out of inertia, but also because it cradles a number of connotations that stand in need of further examination and critique." Gunning notes two such connotations, a "childish mastery of form in contrast to a later complexity," and a "period of *lack* in relation to later evolution," particularly insofar as the absence of editing is concerned. While the former, simplistic view of the primitive cinema is on the wane, the latter, more sophisticated view, Gunning says, presents its own series of problems: "Even those who maintain the uniqueness and value of early film within a nonlinear view of film history have a hard time avoiding a description of early cinema as a sort of degree zero in the evolution of montage."[36] Indeed, whatever the degrees of difference between "childish mastery" and "lack," both take as their point of reference and return the classical cinema, and the assumption that the early years of filmmaking both departed from and laid groundwork for the codes of linear continuity, narrative identification, and patterns of opposition and closure characteristic of the classical Hollywood cinema. As Gunning puts it, early cinema is "simultaneously different from later practices—an alternate cinema—and yet profoundly related to the cinema that followed it."[37] To a considerable extent, then, how one defines the "primitive" in the early years of film history will rely on assumptions, both implicit and explicit, about the classical Hollywood cinema.

Still, one wonders about the extent to which a definition of the "primitive" cinema is inflected by the cultural meanings associated with the word *primitive*. Kristin Thompson, analyzing the relationship between the "primitive" and classical cinema, and alluding to the problems that inhere in the term *primitive*, writes:

> The term "primitive" is in many ways an unfortunate one, for it may imply that these films were crude attempts at what would later become classical filmmaking. While I use the word because of its widespread acceptance, I would prefer to think of primitive films more in the sense that one speaks of primitive art, either produced by native cultures (e.g., Eskimo ivory carving) or untrained individuals (e.g., Henri Rousseau). That is, such primitive art is a system apart, whose simplicity can be of a value equal to more formal aesthetic traditions.[38]

Thompson's validation of the "primitive" cinema, as different from but not necessarily inferior to the classical cinema, draws explicitly on the modernist appropriation in visual arts of so-called primitive cultures as a source of inspiration and challenge to Western traditions.[39] The frame of reference here is stylistic, and Thompson does not really pursue the analogy in any depth. But again, one wonders if the "primitive" in "primitive" cinema has persisted, not only in terms of history and style but in terms of cultural preoccupations as well.

The "scene" of "primitive" cinema is informed by a fascination with otherness, with the exotic, with all that is seemingly alien to Western culture and subjectivity. It has been an observation of long standing that the early cinema borrowed extensively, both in form and in subject matter, from popular arts of the time—vaudeville, magic shows, cartoons, stereoscope cards, dime fiction.

A popular theme in these arts was the encounter, both between the West and its colonized other, and between whites and blacks. It is no surprise that early film would replicate such encounters. The popularity of the Lumiére brothers' scenes of village life in Africa suggests that film was particularly well suited to the circulation of racist stereotypes where the native "other" is portrayed as the object of a view. The relationship between the white woman and the black woman in *What Happened in the Tunnel* taps the construction of racial, and racist, difference as well. The cinematic representation of people of color as "primitives"—whether through the pernicious racial stereotypes of early films or the tourist's view of "native life"—suggests, of course, that the frame of cinematic fantasy served to perpetuate and rationalize the distinction between a white Western self and its other.

But the "primitives" of early cinema include servants peeking through keyholes as well as black youths stealing watermelons; naive spectators such as Uncle Josh as well as Native Americans of comic-strip proportions. One common denominator to all of these representations of class, racial, and ethnic difference is childlike naiveté. That some film historians have focused on modes of spectatorship in their revision of the early cinema suggests that here, too, an implicit assumption has been made that early film viewers brought with them only a "primitive" capacity to distinguish between illusion and reality. The supposedly terrified reaction of early viewers to the Lumière film of a train arriving in a station has remained a persistent anecdote of early cinema, suggesting that some film historians have understood not only early films but early viewers as captured within a naive, childlike state of reception.[40]

The infantilism that inheres in the word *primitive* has a particularly strong psychoanalytic resonance in French, where "scène primitive" translates as the "primal scene." While Noël Burch frequently refers to the early cinema as so many "primal scenes" of the cinema, his psychoanalytic terminology functions in a more general metaphoric sense, whereby the early cinema is a kind of "id" to the "ego" of classical cinema. For some psychoanalytic critics in France, however, the early cinema functions very literally to stage the primal scene.

For instance, Michel Marie takes as his point of departure Metz's assertion that the cinema is made to the measure of reactivations of the primal scene. Marie refers to characters in early films, such as the voyeurs in *Un coup d'oeil par étage* and *The Inquisitive Boots,* as "metaphoric expressions of the infantile spectator, of the regressive adult, a perverse scopophiliac who escapes the universe of 'normal' sexuality . . . he is apparently not I, a lucid and conscious spectator, but the Other, the eccentric and repressed aspect that every adult rediscovers in going to the cinema."[41] It *is* true that early film offers some bold representations of classic psychoanalytic scenarios. Uncle Josh tears down the material of the screen (typical primal scene material) only once the parental couple have appeared on screen; Georges Méliès's control of the female body speaks quite obviously to the threat of femininity. However, the possibility of an equivalence between film and the primal scene is based on an originary moment of cinematic identification, an assumption most prevalent in Metz's work, which has been criticized strongly within psychoanalytic film theory.[42]

Gunning's analysis of the early cinema as a cinema of attraction establishes a context for a discussion, not only of the alterity of the early cinema but also of the project of those avant-garde filmmakers whose work is inspired by the thrill of visual discovery evident in early film. If the notion of exhibitionism is central to Gunning's distinction between early and classical film, it also informs his reading of avant-garde practice. Drawing on Sergei Eisenstein's concept of a "cinema of attractions," based on principles of visual shock and confrontation, Gunning suggests that like early cinema, the avant-garde film inspired by it develops a relationship to the spectator grounded in "exhibitionist confrontation rather than diegetic absorption."[43]

The preoccupation with the "primitive"—understood in several senses—in the works of some women filmmakers seems to me related to what Gunning suggests, but different at the same time. Related, to the extent that women filmmakers have been drawn to the sense of visual discovery evident in early film; but different, to the extent that the reverberations of the "primitive" in the films I will discuss are not purely formal, and can in no way be described as an "exhibitionism" that downplays "voyeurism," or a direct confrontation that circumscribes narrative. Rather, the inquiry into "primitivism" is very much connected, not to the dismantling or bracketing of narrative but to its reconceptualization. A number of women filmmakers have taken up the interrogation of the "primitive" on several different levels. In the next chapter I turn to an examination of the ways in which the "primitive" has been explored, revised, and recontextualized in different ways in women's films.

6. Revising the "Primitive"

In this chapter, I will discuss three different contexts of women's filmmaking where explorations of the "primitive" both cite the example of early film and examine relationships between different meanings of the term *primitive*. The first context includes two films, Maya Deren's *Meshes of the Afternoon* (codirected with Alexander Hammid, 1943) and Suzan Pitt's *Asparagus* (1974), in which the style of "primitive" filmmaking is appropriated. While these two films are closest to the kind of avant-garde filmmaking influenced by early film that Tom Gunning discusses, they take as their primary point of departure not just the "primitive" style of filmmaking, but also and especially the "primitive" representation of the female body and its relationship to other definitions of the so-called primitive. While both of these films excavate "primitive" narration—and the "primitive" narrator, in Pitt's film—the second group of films is more specifically concerned with the *narrative* implications of the "primitive" in terms of early cinema, of gender, and—in the case of Akerman's film—of psychoanalysis.

In Germaine Dulac's *The Smiling Madame Beudet* (*La Souriante Madame Beudet* [1922]), Agnès Varda's *Cleo from 5 to 7* (*Cléo de 5 à 7* [1962]), and

184

Chantal Akerman's *Jeanne Dielman, 23 Quai du Commerce, 1080 Bruxelles* (1975), a form of "primitive" narration is associated specifically with a female character, and the narration of the films both incorporates and distances itself from it. In each case, "primitive" narration evokes simultaneously the realm of early filmmaking and the realm of traditional female activities. That all three of these films are in the French language is suggestive, as well, of a shared tradition, one split between their connections with the movements with which they are associated (impressionism in the case of Dulac, the New Wave in the case of Varda; less specifically defined, in the case of Akerman, is the contemporary European narrative film) and with each other.

Finally, the third context involves the relationship between women, a "primitive" mode of representation, and the cultural meanings of "primitivism" in an anthropological sense. Trinh T. Minh-ha's *Reassemblage* (1982) and Laleen Jayamanne's *A Song of Ceylon* (1985) are meditations upon the construction of otherness, and their evocations of the "primitive" range across documentary cinema and anthropology, as well as the modernist appropriation of primitivism and the cinematic avant-garde. Both of these films were made by women who quite literally have crossed thresholds separating "West" and "East"; Trinh T. Minh-ha is a Vietnamese woman who works in the U.S., and Jayamanne, born in Sri Lanka, now works in Australia.

Tom Gunning's discussion of the relationship between early cinema and the avant-garde does not focus exclusively on male filmmakers; Maya Deren is mentioned as one filmmaker influenced by Méliès, and a scene in *Meshes of the Afternoon,* where a group of Maya Derens sit around a dining table, is cited as influenced by Méliès's preoccupation with multiplications of his own body.[1] The reverberations of the "primitive" in Deren's work provide an excellent example of the relationship between early cinema and the context of gender and female identity. Deren's relationship to different configurations of the "primitive" involves, at one point at least, an inquiry into exhibitionism which, while quite different from the context in which Gunning uses the term, nonetheless suggests a similar preoccupation with alterity.

In the 1947 notebooks describing her most ambitious and never-realized project, a film which would compare the rituals and gestures of various non-Western cultures, Deren described the sense of "otherness" she encountered in examining footage of Balinese dance made available to her by the anthropologists Gregory Bateson and Margaret Mead. Noting the "complete lack of identification between audience and performer" in Balinese dance, Deren writes: "In our culture the tension between exhibitionist and spectator is one of identification: the spectator either would like to be capable of the acts of the performer or identifies himself temporarily, and this enviable and envied 'model' role is the incentive for the performer." Deren goes on to question whether the polarities of exhibitionist and onlooker are even pertinent to Balinese dance: "A condition of exhibitionism is an acute consciousness of exhibiting oneself, and this the little girls in amnesic trance certainly are not. Nor do they have 'memories' of their moments of glory, so to speak—trunks of souvenirs, or the dress they performed in the night the Prince of Wales sat in the right box. No—*exhibitionism* is the wrong word."[2]

Deren's fascination with Balinese dance, like her well-known interest in Haitian culture, is characterized by a questioning of some of the oppositions which form the very basis of Western identity, and a preoccupation with the logocentric dualities of Western consciousness runs throughout her work. The relationship between performer and spectator is one such opposition, and much of Deren's attraction to non-Western cultures had to do with the possibilities of other formulations of difference. She notes with glee that "Freud wouldn't do so well in Bali. Hooray for the Balinese."[3] That Freud has done fairly well within feminist film theory suggests, perhaps, at least one of the reasons why Maya Deren's film work has not received the sustained critical attention one might expect within feminist film studies, particularly given her status in the history of the American avant-garde.[4] Deren's work is informed by a utopian sensibility, a desire not just to rethink the categories of opposition but to discard and surpass them, and in this sense her work has much in common with those films that have been central in feminist writing on film. Yet her rethinking of opposition focused more explicitly on cultural differences and less on sexual ones. Thus, Deren explored so-called primitive cultures. Her film project on comparative rituals was never completed. Perhaps Western dualities are so integral to the cinema that the radical otherness which Deren hoped to capture and explore was virtually unrepresentable on film. However, that desire does inform virtually all of the films that Deren did complete, as well as many of her writings on film.

Indeed, it is in the category of the "primitive," and particularly in the cross-referencing between different meanings of the "primitive," that Deren's work occupies a difficult and challenging area of inquiry for feminist film theory. For the notion of the "primitive" foregrounds the often unacknowledged connections between the feminine and the culturally exotic, and unless those connections are explored, feminist film theory risks perpetuating a female subject fully consonant with white, Western notions of the self. Now the immediate temptation, in Deren's case, is to characterize her outright celebration of the "primitive," her distrust of Western rationality, and her attention to the spiritual side of creation as "essentialist." Such a categorization and implicit dismissal obscure, however, the extent to which her work involves a significant inquiry into cultural and historical difference. Although Deren herself does not often refer specifically to a female (or much less feminist) investment in such an inquiry, such connections are suggested in some of her writing and certainly in her films.

Deren's interest in "primitive" cultures is charcterized by a criticism of those who have adopted "primitivism" as a way of describing art work that in fact shares little with the cultures in question, as well as a frustration with the lack of attention to the larger cultural context that shapes "primitive" art and rituals. A section of her 1946 pamphlet *An Anagram of Ideas on Art, Form, and Film,* for instance, is devoted to just such a criticism:

> I am certain that thoughtful critics do not use the term "primitive" without definition and modification. But its general usage, and as a category title for exhibits, reveals a comparative ideal based on the superficial similarity between the *skilled simplicity* of artists whose culture was limited in information and crude in equipment; and the *crude simplifications* of artists whose culture is rich in information and refined in its equipment."[5]

In an earlier essay, Deren compares the trance state characteristic of ritual dance in "primitive" cultures with hysteria.[6] Noting that both are motivated by "psychic conflicts and insults" and characterized by "suggestibility and hypnotism, and hypnoid trances," she observes as well that "hysteria, as possession also, occurs only within social context, when there are one or more witnesses to the scene. In other words, the role of the community as a necessary frame of reference may include an audience function similar to that of the audience in cases of hysteria." This comparison between possession and hysteria should not be read as a simple equation, since Deren is again careful to stress the radical difference in social context, and the fact that they are "parallel, rather than identical phenomena."[7] What Deren does not foreground is the common association between women and hysteria, and the therefore implicit assumption that the cultural conditions for the production of hysteria and the subsequent parallelism with possession and trance states are particularly relevant to women.

Given the extent to which Deren's films focus on the dreams and anxieties and perceptions of women, however, one might extend the comparison she makes in more gender-specific terms. Some of Deren's film work—like the never-completed film on Balinese dance referred to above—explores quite literally the affiliation with "primitive" cultures. In her better-known films, including *Meshes of the Afternoon,* another, quite different affiliation with the "primitive" emerges, one more along the lines of the relationship Gunning explores between early film and the avant-garde. *Meshes of the Afternoon* is structured by the repetition of a series of scenes. A woman, played by Deren herself, sees a figure go around the bend of a street, as she is heading toward a flight of stairs to her

Figure 29. Maya Deren in *Meshes of the Afternoon* (Museum of Modern Art)

home. As she is about to unlock the door to her house, she drops the key. When at last she enters the house, she sees a table with two chairs, a loaf of bread with a knife, a telephone with its receiver off the hook. The woman goes up a flight of stairs to a bedroom, returns downstairs, and sits in a chair. She strokes herself gently, and as her eye appears in extreme close-up, the film begins to tell the same story again. Each retelling of the pursuit of the unknown figure and entry into the house—there are three such retellings in all—is initiated by Deren's gaze through the window. In each of the three repetitions, different elements are foregrounded. In one version, for instance, the mysterious figure on the road enters the house, and reveals a mirror in the place of a face; in another, the passage from the first floor to the upstairs of the house is made only with great turbulence and difficulty.

Narration itself is foregrounded in *Meshes of the Afternoon*, particularly insofar as the film turns further and further inward with each recasting of the story's "meshes," until there are four Maya Derens. In addition, the two most central repeated elements in the film are the quintessential narrative components of pursuing an other (the androgynous figure which disappears down the road) and crossing a threshold. Narration is also fragmented in the film, most obvious-

ly in the way Deren is presented initially. At the very beginning of the film, the
only parts of her body visible are her feet and her hands, with the sense of her
presence connoted rather by the shadows she casts as she moves down the road,
and up the stairway to the house. There is a split vision from the outset, between
what Deren sees and what we see of Deren. With the repetition of the initial
event of *Meshes of the Afternoon,* Deren is designated simultaneously as narrator
and as enigma, as subject and object of narration, but the elusive figure walking
down the road remains unnamed, unidentified—specifically, remains unsexed.
The objects foregrounded in the film, like the knife and the key, signal passage,
the crossing of a threshold, whether the space separating inside and outside or the
boundary between self and other.

The trajectory of the woman in *Meshes of the Afternoon* evokes a wide range
of complex psychic questions, and the shape of the trajectory evokes much of the
spirit and style of the "primitive" era of filmmaking. Deren herself is identified
as both a dreamer and conjuror in a way that recalls two of the most common
frames of the early cinema—the dreamer who awakens only to be confronted
with a reality that contrasts brutally with the dream, and the conjuror who makes
objects, including his own body, appear and disappear at will. The use of double
exposure in the film to represent the multiplied personae of Maya Deren is also
evocative, as Gunning suggests, of "primitive" filmmaking, and captures a sense
of awe and wonder in the very representability of the woman's interior life. This
evocation of the early cinema in *Meshes of the Afternoon* acquires a very specific
gendered component, for the dream/fantasy frame of the film is interrupted twice
by the man, played by Hammid. When the third Maya Deren approaches the
sleeping woman, about to stab her, the woman awakens to find Hammid awaking
her. Hence the appearance of the man seems to redraw the line separating dream
and waking. If the pursuit of the ambiguous figure, as well as the constant
folding of the event, suggests a threshold space, then the appearance of Hammid
seems to mark the closing down of that threshold, and the attendant emergence of
duality.

His appearance also signals a return to order, a designation of the space of
the house as a dream space. That very polarity is again thrown into question
when Deren reaches for the knife—now transformed from the flower, the object
initially associated with the "other" in the first place—and stabs him. But "he"
now is a mirror image, and the shattering of the mirror into fragments, dispersed
on a beach, suggests the persistence of the narrative vision embodied by the
woman—a narrative vision in which the polarities of self and other, of female
and male, of dream and waking are fragile. The second ending of *Meshes of the
Afternoon* tells another story. Now Hammid enacts the role of narrator, repeating
the itinerary of Deren at the beginning of the film. His discovery of Deren in the

house, with her throat slit and her body covered with seaweed, suggests the impossibility of that threshold space. As female and male, as the two sides of duality, then, Deren and Hammid enact, in these two endings to the film, two radically opposed narrative itineraries: the one which poses an endless movement between opposing poles, which opens up a threshold space between the dualities of self and other, and the other, certainly more "conventional," which asserts those dualities.

In other films by Deren, the realm of the "primitive" is evoked in ways that evoke the intersection between the feminine, the archaic, and the cinematic. As the female subject of *At Land* (1944), for instance, Deren emerges from the sea at the beginning of the film, and eventually discovers a meeting in progress inside a mansion, at which she gazes with all of the wonder of an Uncle Josh discovering the cinema for the first time, or an indiscreet bathroom maid peeking at forbidden scenes. *Ritual in Transfigured Time* (1945–46) begins with two open doorways in a corridor, with Deren, now situated on the other side of the threshold, observed with awe by a woman in a scene that is quite evocative of "primitive" journeys down hotel corridors.[8] The realm of the "primitive" is given a particularly strong inflection of traditional femininity here. Once the woman crosses the threshold, she holds a skein of yarn while Deren winds it into a ball, and the rhythm of their motions creates a pattern of connection between them.

That the woman is black suggests, perhaps, the desire to rewrite the racist stereotypes of a film such as *What Happened in the Tunnel;* but it can suggest— much more problematically—the assumption of a patronizing desire for "racial harmony" or the appropriation of image of "exotic" femininity on Deren's part. While I do not think Deren's fascination with racial difference, as evidenced in this and other films, as well as in her writings, can be equated with the disturbing appearance of racist clichés of performance in Arzner's *Dance, Girl, Dance,* this does not mean her explorations of racial boundaries are not problematic in their own way.

Like most of Deren's films, *Ritual in Transfigured Time* suggests the trancelike state which so fascinated her in the dances of "primitive" culture. She herself made the connection between "primitive" dance and hypnoid states. Here, the representation of the winding of the yarn suggests—despite Deren's suspicions about Freud—another psychoanalytic association of the "primitive," recalling Freud and Breuer's assertion that "hypnoid states" often "grow out of the day-dreams which are so common even in healthy people and to which needlework and similar occupations render women especially prone."[9]

Undoubtedly the most persistent figure of the "primitive" in these films is the threshold—between dream and waking and man and woman in *Meshes of the Afternoon,* between nature and culture in *At Land,* between white woman and

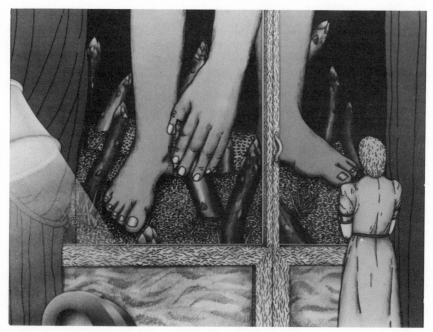

Figure 30. Suzan Pitt's *Asparagus* (Museum of Modern Art)

black woman in *Ritual in Transfigured Time*. The representation of the threshold taps the "primitive" in several senses of the word—as a mode of filmmaking, as a dream world apart from the reality of waking and spatial stability, and—most controversially in feminist terms—as a cultural realm to which women, it would appear, have privileged access. The female narrator in these films embodies a desire, a fantasy of narrative as a persistent movement, the creation of a threshold space.

Asparagus evokes those early films in which "primitive" narrators act out the pleasures of the cinema. Pitt's animated film depicts different stages of a woman's relation to a series of images, stages which take us from the interior of a house, to a city street, to a theater. The animation of the film creates a universe that is at once dreamlike, painterly, and childlike. The woman's imaginary world is most graphically portrayed in the tableaulike garden panorama that unrolls at the window in her house early in the film. Lush floral imagery is juxtaposed with a barren and somewhat dismal-looking asparagus patch. It does not require too much imagination to see here a rather brutal juxtaposition of female and male imagery, a juxtaposition that becomes a kind of running joke in the film. The female narrator's relationship to a world of dream, magic, and image-making suggests a reincarnation of the "primitive" narrator.

The psychoanalytic reference point is quite strong, since the process of narration in *Asparagus* draws upon the creation of dream images. The encounter of the female narrator of the film with a luscious world of imagery is like the transformation of dream thoughts into dream images in the dreamer, a process for which Freud used the term *primitive* ("All the linguistic instruments by which we express the subtler relations of thought—the conjunctions and prepositions, the changes in declension and conjugation—are dropped, because there are no means of representing them; just as in a 'primitive' language without any grammar, only the raw material of thought is expressed and abstract terms are taken back to the concrete ones that are at their basis").[10] In Deren's films, there is also an evocation of the state of dreaming. But in *Asparagus,* the specific relationship of women to the activation of dreams and imagination does not rely on the "feminine" defined in terms of traditional domestic activities—for instance, the winding of yarn in *Ritual in Transfigured Time*—but rather in terms of traditional sexual ones.

In the second section of the film, the woman narrator journeys to a theater where a claymation audience watches a spectacle of amazing special effects. The woman goes backstage, where she opens up a Pandora's box of images and sets them loose. The images float into the midst of the amazed audience; thus the woman transgresses the boundary line separating audience from spectacle. The world outside the theater is depicted as obsessed with sexual polarity, whether through phallic imagery (a gun shop, a sex store) or the storefront with two baby dolls, one on a pink blanket, the other on a blue one. The space of the theater thus becomes an other space, where the illusion of oscillation and fluidity is operative. In the concluding section of the film, the woman returns to the house, and the formerly resistant asparagus now not only yields to her caress but undergoes a series of fanciful transformations, from waterfall to colored sprinkles to stars. The images recall those images set loose in the theater. The narrator is certainly no longer an observer but an active participant, and a participant no longer concealed backstage, as in the theater.

The connection between the woman and the asparagus is overtly sexual, becoming a fanciful rendition of a blow job. Throughout most of the film, the woman has been portrayed either as faceless or as the impression left in a mask which she dons to enter into the world at large. But in this final section of the film, the woman acquires at least one facial attribute: extremely red lips. At the very beginning of the film, the first asparagus motif occurs when the woman defecates into a toilet bowl. In one of many of a series of magical transformations in the film, the turds become asparagus stalks. Given the mouth and the sexual act as the film's conclusion, it would appear that one of the film's many fantasies is the rereading of the very notion of a psychic or sexual stage, since the conclusion of the film could be read simultaneously as "regression" (to an oral stage) or "development" to something of a "phallic" stage. While I suppose the film could be read as informed by penis envy, the fantasy of incorporation evidenced at the conclusion suggests a refusal of the very divisions, the "stages," that would make such a reading possible. The incorporation is quite literal, of course, but it is figurative as well, the sexual act becoming an exchange of the polarities of male and female imagery.

In other words, a fantasy of a threshold space informs *Asparagus,* and this fantasy of the threshold shares some similarities with the woman's journey in *Meshes of the Afternoon.* The three sections of *Asparagus* can be seen as a progression toward the fantasy of the incorporation of male into female at the film's conclusion, but the last two sections can also be read, along the lines of *Meshes of the Afternoon,* as a double ending. In other words, like *Meshes of the Afternoon, Asparagus* juxtaposes two narrative modes. The two endings of *Meshes of the Afternoon* suggest two different encounters between man and woman, as well as a juxtaposition of a conventional narrative resolution (the separation of dream and waking, male and female), with the persistence of narrative understood as a threshold space between opposing terms. In *Asparagus,* the two narrative modes are defined explicitly in terms of the position of the woman—in the one case a masked figure backstage who creates a different kind of spectacle, and in the other, a sexual being who becomes both active and passive, creator and recipient of sexual imagery.

The female narrator embodies a fantasy of movement, of transformation, whereby the imagery of "male" and "female" is interchangeable; thus it is a narration located in a hypothetical moment anterior to narration as a conquest of the other, evidenced in early films such as *A Subject for the Rogue's Gallery* and *What Happened on 23rd Street. Asparagus* appropriates, then, the metaphoric figure of the female voyeur in films such as *The Indiscreet Bathroom Maid.* If a condition of female voyeurism in early film is the pleasure of crossing the threshold, but in ways fundamentally different from the imposition of the law (in *A Search for Evidence*) or the conquest of the female body (in *A Subject for the Rogue's Gallery*), then the female narrator in *Asparagus* extends the possible fantasies of the threshold.

I turn now to three films in which it is not so much the representation of the female body per se that is central, but rather the narrative modes associated with traditional femininity. That these films are part of the history of French cinema (Akerman's film is Belgian, but is read largely within the context of French cinema defined in the broader terms of "French-speaking") situates differently their inquiries into "primitive" representation. The distinction between dominant and avant-garde cinema does not hold quite the same currency in a French context as it has in the American context, particularly since the rejection of narrative so central to the American avant-garde has not been a defining characteristic of French film. To be sure, it has been a recurring characteristic of French cinema to reject or revise considerably the narrative conventions of the American cinema. But this search for alternative cinematic forms has not entailed the dismissal of narrative, but rather its reconceptualization. Throughout the history of French cinema, and particularly at moments of crisis and transition, filmmakers have paid homage to, probed, and explored the "primitive" era. At certain moments within French film history, women filmmakers have appropriated forms of "primitive" narration, and have explored the links between the "primitive" and the feminine by staging tensions between different narrative modes.

Like many other films associated with the development of impressionism in France in the 1920s, Germaine Dulac's 1922 film *The Smiling Madame Beudet* attempts to convey inner, subjective states, in this case the inner frustration of a sensitive, musically inclined provincial woman who is trapped in a conventional marriage to a boorish husband.[11] From the outset, Mme Beudet's conflict with her husband is staged as a conflict of differing points of view: when they are invited to the opera, Monsieur Beudet conjures up an image of a group of happy singers, while Mme Beudet can only imagine an overbearing man bellowing to a woman crouched beneath him. While Dulac's film is technically more sophisticated than many films of the 1920s, it is characterized by a selective, foregrounded use of "primitive" narration.[12] For Mme Beudet fantasizes in a "primitive" mode. She is like the dreamers in early films who imagine fictional characters coming to life as they nod over a book, or like the conjuror in a Méliès film who makes threatening objects disappear—usually women, in Méliès's case; her husband, in the case of Mme Beudet.

As a dreamer, a fantasizer, Mme Beudet is portrayed in a far more complex way than are her fantasies.[13] In other words, a distance is created in the film between how the woman's fantasy life is represented and how she is portrayed in relationship to it. The depiction of Mme Beudet taps a wide variety of angles, camera distances, and lighting effects. The style of her fantasies and dreams tends, however, to be quite similar: she reads a magazine and imagines a character coming to life, drawing upon the kinds of superimpositions quite common in early cinema. She reads a poem and imagines one image after another—each shot in the straightforward, frontal style characteristic of early film—with no connection between them.

In Dulac's film, different narrative modes are juxtaposed with ironic effect.[14] The most obvious irony results from the juxtaposition of Mme Beudet's fantasy life with the equally "primitive," but even more limited, fantasy life of her husband. More significant is the interplay between two different narratives that constitute the overall structure of the film. On one level is the "primitive" narration that characterizes the points of view of the characters, and especially Mme Beudet. On another level is the narration of the film in a larger sense, involving crisis and resolution around the film's central event. Monsieur Beudet plays a "suicide game" in which he pulls an unloaded gun from his desk drawer and threatens to kill himself at moments of conflict and frustration. The turning point of the film is Mme Beudet's decision to load the gun.[15] Her plan misfires in more ways than one, however. For when Monsieur Beudet next pulls the gun from his drawer, he points it at her; and when he shoots it (harming no one), and discovers it was loaded, he foolishly assumes that his wife wanted to kill herself, and not him.

In a film so concerned with making visible the inner states of its characters, and of its heroine in particular, the absence of a shot actually showing Mme Beudet loading the gun—initiating some kind of narrative action—is particularly significant. The absence of such an image suggests a collision, within Mme Beudet, of two differing narrative modes—the "primitive" mode I have already described, and a more properly classical one, in the sense that the surreptitious "murder" of her husband requires the planning of just the kind of cause-and-effect actions that are central to the evolution of the classical mode of narration. The nonrepresentation of the significant action of loading the gun suggests the impossibility of Mme Beudet's position within that classical narrative mode.

However, this is not to say that *The Smiling Madame Beudet* brackets classical narrative altogether. Rather, the film represents the conventions of narrative resolution in order to problematize them. In the final image, we see the couple in the street, and Monsieur Beudet nods to a priest who passes. The representation of the outdoors, of the public sphere of the town, indicates a division between Mme Beudet's inner existence and the social universe that surrounds her. The film begins with standard "establishing shots" of the village in which the couple lives, although it becomes clear that there is no seamless fit between that social context and the inner world of Mme Beudet. Indeed, this is another dimension of Dulac's ironic narrative style, for the few shots of the outside world that occur suggest all the more forcefully the increasing distance between Mme Beudet and her surroundings.[16]

The final image of the film is the first time that Mme Beudet is actually seen outdoors, and she is framed by two men, their exchange occurring across her body. The image "cites" the conventions of the classical cinema—husband and wife reunited, order restored—in what is undoubtedly the most far-reaching irony of the film. For the supposed integration of Mme Beudet into the in-

Figure 31. Germaine Dulac's *The Smiling Madame Beudet*
(Museum of Modern Art)

stitutions of provincial life requires the failure of any narrative of her own. Like the narrators of the early cinema, Mme Beudet can conjure and dream isolated images, but she cannot construct a narrative. But Dulac, of course, can.[17] *The Smiling Madame Beudet* brings together a historical moment of the cinema with a particular mode of female consciousness, creating an encounter between the "primitive" cinema and the classical cinema, between a female imagination unable to break out of the duality of home versus public world, of isolated images versus complex narrative, and a more properly classical narrative which offers only the position of the obedient wife.[18] It is in the ironic juxtaposition of these modes that female narration takes shape.

Somewhat like filmmakers of the 1920s, the directors of the New Wave were interested in stretching the boundaries of narrative filmmaking, and they too entertained an ambiguous relationship to the conventions of the classical American cinema. Perhaps the most striking feature in the films of the directors associated with the New Wave was the consciousness of the history and theory of the medium that influenced their styles of filmmaking. Anecdotes of childhoods and adolescences spent at the Cinémathèque Française have become part of the standard histories of the period, and as is well known, the central group of filmmakers who formed the "core" of the Nouvelle Vague—Jean-Luc Godard, François Truffaut, Claude Chabrol, Eric Rohmer, and Jacques Rivette—all began their cinematic careers as writers and critics at *Cahiers du cinéma*.[19] Virtually all of the films of the New Wave—and especially those of Jean-Luc Godard—are films about film, about the particular nature of cinema as a form of representation. In keeping with the ambiguous relationship with American cinema that has informed so much French film practice, New Wave films that reflect upon the classical American cinema have received the most attention. But an equally important dimension of the films of these and other filmmakers of the period involves citations of, and inquiries into, the early years of film history.

Jean-Luc Godard's 1963 film *Les Carabiniers,* for instance, depicts two naive men whose departure to do battle for their king initiates them into a world where image and referent are split. When the two men return from the war, they display a series of "title deeds"—postcards depicting a wide range of department stores, women, and tourist attractions. The film features a first visit to the movies by one of its protagonists that recalls *Uncle Josh at the Moving Picture Show.* The program which Michel-ange watches shows a train, a family meal, and a woman bathing, all with exaggerated sound effects. Like Uncle Josh, Michel-ange is tantalized by the image of woman on the screen. After his efforts at peeking around the sides of the screen to get a better look at the woman bathing are unsuccessful, he then proceeds to tear down the screen. There is no rear-projectionist to confront Michel-ange, but rather an exposed brick wall and the continued projection of the film images over his astonished face and body.

In a different yet related way, François Truffaut's 1970 film *The Wild Child* (*L'enfant sauvage)* also cites the early cinema.[20] Based on Jean Itard's *Mémoire et rapport sur Victor de l'Aveyron* (1806), the film tells the story of the famous "wild child" found in the forest—his difficult access to the culture and civilization of France, and the role of his mentor, Itard, played by Truffaut himself. Throughout the film, Truffaut uses devices associated with the early cinema, such as iris shots, and eschews the use of techniques uncommon in the "primitive" era, such as close-ups; and he cites several "primitive" films, most notably the famous *Repas de bébé,* an early Lumière film showing Auguste Lumière and his wife feeding their child. Most notably, Truffaut draws an analogy between two kinds of relationships—his own relationship to the early cinema, and Itard's relationship to the zero degree of culture represented by Victor. Thus Victor is identified as "primitive" in both a cinematic and a cultural sense.

In both of these examples, the evocation of the early cinema serves to mark the passage of the individual—more specifically, the male individual—into realms of paternal authority, whether the comically defined (and never seen) "king" who distributes postcards as title deeds in *Les Carabiniers,* or the paternalistic figure of the physician who takes charge of Victor in *The Wild*

Figure 32. Agnès Varda's *Cleo from 5 to 7* (Corinth)

Child. Agnès Varda's 1962 film *Cleo from 5 to 7* also "cites" the early cinema, in what appears—initially, at least—to be a gesture similarly engaged with "maturation," but now of a female figure. The protagonist of Varda's film is a mediocre but successful pop singer who embodies virtually all of the clichés of the stereotypical woman-as-object—she is narcissistic, childlike, and dependent on the reassuring images of those who surround her. The "5 to 7" of the film's title refers to the temporal trajectory of the film (actually more like 5:00 to 6:30 P.M.), the time spent waiting for the results of a medical examination which will show whether Cléo has cancer or not. Indeed, there is an obsession with time in the film. Cléo is extremely conscious of the passage of time until the test results will be ready, and the film marks off time in a series of thirteen segments, ranging from three to fifteen minutes long, each identified in titles flashed onto the screen with the name of a character or groups of characters attached.

It is tempting to describe the film in terms of Cléo's transformation from object to subject. Sandy Flitterman-Lewis, noting that in the film "relations of power are associated with vision," reads Cléo in these terms: "In assuming a vision of her own, Cléo assumes the power to direct her life, and the power to construct her own image as well."[21] There is no question that Cléo's passage in the film involves a literal discarding of many of the fictions of feminine identity—her blonde wig, her doll's house of an apartment, the substitute family within which she is forever the child. However, the scenario to which Cléo accedes is that of classical film narrative. At the conclusion of the film, Cléo strikes up a friendship with a young solider about to leave for Algeria. While this is not exactly a typical Hollywood ending, it is nonetheless a girl-meets-boy, walk-off-into-the-horizon conclusion full of hope and optimism.

The threat of cancer is still real, but the fear has diminished; and the final segment of the film in which these changes occur offers the longest stretch of uninterrupted time. To be sure, it could be argued that the classical scenario is reproduced and defamiliarized simultaneously, through the representation of and insistence upon the woman's relationship to it. But if *Cleo from 5 to 7* develops a critical reading of the relationship between women and classical film narrative, it is a reading that has as much to do with the narration of the film as with Cléo's transformation from female object into female subject. For underlying the apparently radical change in Cléo is a far more complex and contradictory process of narration, whereby two different kinds of narrating authorities intersect.

Like Dulac, Varda associates "primitive" narration with the traditionally female. It is not primarily Cléo who is designated a "primitive narrator," however, but rather a woman fortune-teller in whose apartment the film begins. In the film's "prologue," the woman card reader lays out a series of cards and interprets them. The entire cast of characters of the film, as well as its central events, is displayed in a series of still, static images. The card reader brings to mind the early Méliès film *Les cartes vivantes (The Living Playing Cards)*, in which a (male) conjuror brings a series of playing cards to magical life. In Varda's film, however, the woman's presence is identified as wavering between the narrative authority of the conjuror and a superstitious belief in a fatalistic narrative agency beyond her powers of interpretation. The universe she inhabits is enclosed and claustrophobic, reminiscent of the Beudet apartment in Dulac's film (here, however, the husband is quite literally banished to the closet).

Given that Cléo's superstitiousness seems to be part of the feminine identity that is shed in the course of the film, it is tempting to regard this unnamed (and untimed) narrator as a presence that the film disavows. Cléo's superstitious nature is also revealed during a taxi ride later in the film, when another association of the "primitive" appears: a shop window reveals African masks, and a group of students—including one prominently displayed black man—surround the cab, terrifying Cléo. If the female fortune-teller is associated with "primitive" narration, the racial and racist stereotype here on display is an image with no narrative authority of its own. While it is tempting to assume that the stereotype emerges in order to indicate the limited state of Cléo's consciousness, it is equally possible that the "Africa" thus evoked is an exotic other for the film as well as for its protagonist.

A more direct citation of the early cinema occurs later in the film when Cléo goes to the movies. Raoul, the character with whom this segment is identified in the subtitles, is a projectionist who shows a short silent film comedy. A young man (played by Jean-Luc Godard) watches his loved one (played by Anna Karina) depart down the steps of a quay. When he turns to put on sunglasses, his gaze shifts to the opposite stairway where, unbeknownst to him, a different young woman—but who he thinks is his lover—follows the same trajectory in a reverse field. A series of comic-tragic mishaps arrives, and the young man runs down the steps only to arrive too late to save his beloved. Back at the position at which the film began, he removes his sunglasses to wipe away a tear, and turns his head to discover that he had made a mistake, that because of his shift in position he had identified another woman's actions as those of his girlfriend. His "real" beloved is continuing to walk down the opposite stairway. He runs after her, and they embrace in the requisite "happy ending."

This re-created silent film is modern in very conspicuous ways, since it employs techniques of cutting, matching, and alternation of medium shots and close-ups that were quite alien to early filmmakers. That it is shown at sound speed increases the sense of "citation." However, the film's punchline relies on a use of time that is quite distinctly "primitive." Sequential events are repeated with a disregard for what have been, since the 1910s, "rules" of linear temporality. When the young man turns to wipe a tear, a temporal "mistake" has occurred, for he watches his lover depart as if the other intervening events had not occurred, as if no time had elapsed since she first began walking down the stairs.

The most frequently cited example of temporal overlap in the early cinema occurs in Edwin S. Porter's *Life of an American Fireman* (1903). From the interior of a room in which a woman and her child have collapsed from the effects of a fire, we see a fireman rescue the woman, and then return to rescue the child. The same action is shown again, but from the exterior of the house. As André Gaudreault has suggested, the repetition of the action of rescue from outside the house allows the representation of a climax: "on reaching ground, the woman implores the fireman to rescue her child still trapped in the room. Perhaps Porter added the last shot with the intention of showing us the mother's request." The motivation for this temporal repetition is the possibility of representing multiple perspectives. As Gaudreault says, "the simple copresence of two different points of view toward one single event justifies their successive presentation, which produces a repetition of the action and finally a temporal overlap that today can only astonish."[22]

In Varda's scene, there does not initially appear to be a real change of point of view, since Godard's young man is the focal point for both descents. The mistake in his perception occurs when he puts on dark glasses. The entire scene is filmed, it seems, as if shot through his dark glasses—the woman who departs down the stairs is black, for instance. But the filter of the dark glasses does not really determine the tint of the scene, since it is more properly described as an attempt to replicate a negative image—literally with costume and skin colors reversed, and figuratively with the heroine's sudden death replacing the couple's previous bliss. That race again emerges in the context of another kind of so-called primitivism, now one associated specifically with the history of cinema, makes it clear that race is central to the evocation of the "primitive" in the film.

But as with the racist stereotypes in Arzner's *Dance, Girl, Dance,* there is little to suggest that race is evoked in order to explore its construction in a critical way. The temporal repetition that would be motivated by a change in point of view in the early cinema is here motivated, rather, by the dualities of white and black, happiness and misery. As Claudia Gorbman has said, the silent film "works as a metaphor for Cléo's own dilemma of perception. Put dark glasses on (pessimism, superstition, anxiety) and you will see death, darkness, sadness; look by the light of day and you will find life, love, happiness."[23] But the allusion to early cinema provides a metaphor not just for Cléo's own development, but for the narrative of the film as well. For this evocation of the "otherness" of the "primitive" cinema suggests a pull toward another mode of representation, an affinity between Varda's own unorthodox use of temporality and the supposed "mistakes" of the "primitive" era. That pull, that affinity, complicate somewhat the seemingly smooth movement in *Cleo from 5 to 7* toward self-knowledge and subjecthood.

In the concluding segment of the film, Cléo and her new friend Antoine encounter the doctor, who confirms that Cléo does indeed have cancer. The prediction of the fortune-teller at the beginning of the film is confirmed, but it seems as though the doctor, a narrative authority associated with science, reason, and, need I add, masculinity, has replaced the superstitious female "primitive" narrator of the film's prologue. The diametrically opposed responses of Cléo appear to confirm this change: terrified and childlike at the beginning of the film, stoic and adult at the conclusion. However, there is a subtle irony in this apparent transformation, a suggestion that the enclosed, feminine world of superstition and "primitive" narration is not so easily separable from the bright light of science and the confident resolutions of classical narration.[24]

The force of the "primitive" narrator echoes not only in the actualization of her prediction, but also in a small gesture performed by the doctor. As he turns from Cléo and Antoine, he puts on his dark glasses in movements that echo very precisely Godard's movements in the short film that we have seen with Cléo in the movie theater. *Cleo from 5 to 7* is characterized by a considerably ironic narrative. The condition of Cléo's transformation would appear to be entry into a cinematic order from which any vestiges of the "primitive" are banished, whether in the form of narrative structures or female narrators who create cinematic equivalents of "living playing cards." However, the narrative of the film insists, rather, on the fold of the "primitive" into the classical, and the attendant impossibility of neatly separating the female object from the female subject. Yet while the film connects female subject and female object, the overlapping itineraries of the "scientific" (the doctor) and the "primitive" (the fortune-teller) suggest, just as forcefully, a distinctly unproblematized relation between black and white; indeed, the black remains as the unexamined projection of the white man's sunglasses, or the spectacle of a "primitive" mask.

In contrast to the contexts for Dulac's and Varda's films, there is no "movement," no "new Belgian cinema," no shared alternative tradition, of which Chantal Akerman's 1975 film *Jeanne Dielman, 23 Quai du Commerce, 1080 Bruxelles* is a part. No shared *cinematic* tradition, that is. Rather, one of the most important contexts for *Jeanne Dielman* is contemporary feminism. Akerman herself has said, "*Jeanne Dielman,* for instance, I wouldn't have . . . made the film in that manner, the idea wouldn't have been so clear, were it not for the women's movement."[25] Akerman's film responds more directly to a feminist context, one in which the notion of the "primitive" has surfaced in fairly controversial ways. From the resurrection of the pre-oedipal and the attendant child-mother bond in feminist psychoanalytic writing, to the insistence on the body in discourse in *l'écriture féminine,* to the conceptualization of a female aesthetic defined in so-called pre-aesthetic terms, contemporary feminism has been obsessed with the excavation of a space, an area, somehow prior to and therefore potentially resistant to the realm of the patriarchal symbolic. In *Jeanne Dielman,* Akerman taps this feminist preoccupation with the "presymbolic" and creates a dialogue between it and the supposedly "presymbolic" phase of the cinema, a dialogue that refuses any relegation of the feminine or of female desire to the status of the "pre-." In feminist terms, then, the "primitive" surfaces in *Jeanne Dielman* through the preoccupation with the mother-child bond, as well as with the rituals of everyday life.

Jeanne Dielman, like *Cleo from 5 to 7,* is preoccupied with time, and in particular with duration, repetition, and ritual. Although it makes no effort to represent Jeanne Dielman's states of consciousness and perception, as Dulac does with Mme Beudet, there is nonetheless a strong sense of lived duration in the film, an attempt to draw the spectator into the temporal framework of the protagonist. *Jeanne Dielman* is best known for its length—three hours and eighteen minutes—and its slow pace. For while the film does condense and elide time, it devotes extensive "real" time to the rituals of housework and everyday life. Most viewers watch *Jeanne Dielman* waiting for "something to happen." And while a climax eventually does occur—in the last fifteen minutes of the film—*Jeanne Dielman* demands nothing less than a revision of what is meant by "something happening." The film follows three days in the everyday routine of a Belgian widow in Brussels, played by Delphine Seyrig. Her routine includes prostitution, daily visits from regular male clients which are totally, obsessively integrated into the pattern of household chores. While documenting the gestures and rituals that make up Jeanne Dielman's everyday life, the film spends more time in the kitchen and the living room than in the bedroom, and it is not until the conclusion that we see Jeanne Dielman in the bedroom with one of her clients. The scene revealed is not just a scene of sex, but one of death: after Jeanne experiences what appears to be sexual orgasm, she kills her client.[26]

It should not be surprising that given its obvious affiliations with feminism, this film has become—as much as any other film made in the last twenty years—a feminist classic. Two issues in particular have emerged in the considerably extensive feminist commentary available on *Jeanne Dielman*. First, the film develops an aesthetic form equal to the task of the examination of women and the cinema undertaken by feminist film theorists. B. Ruby Rich describes the "filming degree zero" of Akerman's style, and Marsha Kinder emphasizes how Akerman "cultivates the unseen" and the "unheard."[27] That *Jeanne Dielman* can be read as a meditation on the very nature of the cinema has been noted by many critics, and of particular importance is the absence of the "reverse shot," the refusal to construct a fictional space along the conventional lines of seer/seen.[28] Hence, as Claire Johnston has argued, there is in *Jeanne Dielman* an "opening up of what suture attempts to fill."[29]

This is not to say that *Jeanne Dielman* can be read, in feminist terms, uniquely through its formal structure; indeed, most feminists who have written about this film foreground consistently the challenge it represents to any purely formal notion of alternative cinema. Second, feminist critics have drawn attention to the strong ambivalence in the film, the sense throughout of competing levels of agency, identification, and pleasure. The most obvious embodiment of ambivalence is Jeanne herself. Jayne Loader is quite critical of the film precisely for the reason that Jeanne's final action, the murder of the client, is presented so ambiguously.[30]

Others have found the ambiguous representation of Jeanne to be one of the greatest challenges of the film. Brenda Longfellow puts it this way: "Is she a hysteric or feminist revolutionary? Perhaps the only answer is both, and simulta-

Figure 33. Delphine Seyrig in Chantal Akerman's *Jeanne Dielman, 23
          Quai du Commerce, 1080 Bruxelles* (Babette Mangolte, cinema-
          tographer) (New Yorker Films)

neously so."[31] Laleen Jayamanne speaks in similar terms of the representation of
housework in the film; noting Akerman's self-described "loving acknowledge-
ment" of women's household tasks, Jayamanne says that those tasks are "loving-
ly viewed at a distance because they also signify woman's absence; they are
beautiful and lethal because they help her transcend her situation."[32] The
ambivalence of *Jeanne Dielman* works in terms of its narrative structure as well.
Janet Bergstrom has noted the split in the film between character and director,
between two definitions of the feminine: "the feminine *manquée,* acculturated
under patriarchy, and the feminist who is actively looking at the objective
conditions of her oppression—her place in the family."[33] And Danièle Dubroux
reads *Jeanne Dielman* in terms of the Freudian uncanny, with the film's sense of
women's place rendered as both extremely familiar and extremely strange.[34]

This sense of ambivalence, of the uncanny, of the "beautiful and the lethal,"
reverberates throughout the film. Virtually every gesture and event represented is
composed of a complex itinerary of pleasure and control, desire and repression.
The orgasm is particularly significant in this context, but it is one instance in a
long series of losses of control. It becomes clear that something has gone wrong
in Jeanne's routine when, on the second day of the film, she leaves the cover off
the soup tureen after putting the client's fee in, leaves her hair uncombed, burns
the potatoes. So much has the film created a rhythm around the precise order of

Jeanne Dielman's routine that these seemingly small disruptions are quite significant.

But what remains unspecified in the film is the exact source of the disruption. Perhaps the client on day two of the film stayed too long—but given the elliptical way in which the sexual encounters are shown, this is impossible to say with certainty. While day one of the film would appear to be the stable routine only disrupted on the following day, the letter from her sister Fernande in Canada seems to provoke disruption, particularly with Fernande's suggestion that Jeanne should think of remarriage. The letter ends with mention of a birthday present for Jeanne, and after Jeanne reads the letter aloud to her son, she wonders what the present might be. Jeanne is unwrapping the belated birthday package from Fernande when the doorbell rings on the third day, announcing her client. As a result, the scissors are left in the bedroom where they don't belong, soon to be grabbed as the murder weapon.

On the second day of the film, a neighbor of Jeanne's drops off her baby, whom Jeanne tends to for a short while. The neighbor—played by Akerman herself—is never seen, but when she returns to pick up the baby, we hear her voice as she asks Jeanne what she is making for dinner. She then proceeds to tell a humorous story about her own inability to decide what to buy at the butcher's. She decided to listen to what other women were ordering, but was uninspired, so when her own turn came she ordered what the woman before her had ordered. As a result, she was burdened with an expensive cut of veal, which her family doesn't even like. She continues to talk of her husband and her children. A sense of randomness dominates the woman's conversation, as she moves from one topic to another, and a sense below the surface of what she says of the enormous frustration of caring for her children and pleasing her husband.

Significantly, Jeanne stands at the door with her arm protecting the passage during the encounter, as if to ward off not only the possible intrusion of the neighbor but also the threat of randomness. When the neighbor asks Jeanne what she is making for dinner, Jeanne replies that on Wednesdays, she makes veal cutlets with peas and carrots. But later in the day, when the afternoon client leaves, he says he will see Jeanne next Thursday. One assumes that Jeanne regulates her clients with the same precision with which she regulates her choice of meals, so the mistake—if indeed it is a mistake—reads as one more possible cause for disruption. There may not be an exact and identifiable cause for the murder of Jeanne's client, but the threat of randomness, of an interruption which is not immediately regulated and defined within cycles of repetition and ritual, looms over the film from the outset.

Jeanne Dielman begins in the kitchen in the middle of the first day. Jeanne's routine is a model of synchronization: as the film begins, we see her preparing potatoes. The doorbell rings, and she greets a male client. Jeanne times her encounters precisely so that the potatoes that she and her teenage son will eat for dinner cook while she and her client are in the bedroom. After Jeanne shows her client out, she quickly and efficiently erases the traces of his presence. Here, as throughout the film, the camera occupies a stationary position, at approximately the same distance from Jeanne, in a medium-long shot. While the angles of the camera may change within each room, the shots are always paragons of symmetry, with Jeanne framed and defined very precisely by the objects that surround her.

There is little dialogue in the film, and what there is is usually conveyed in a stilted, stiff manner. Rather, it is the sounds of everyday life—water in the sink, heels clicking across the floor—which are exaggerated and which form the sonoric texture. While there are quite obviously cuts in the film, the individual shots are of long duration. Only the shots in the bedroom are significantly briefer than those of other rooms, thus emphasizing the somewhat forbidden quality of the room, even when it is a place to be cleaned up rather than occupied by sexual contact. Throughout *Jeanne Dielman,* virtually every shot focuses not only on how Jeanne is contained by her surroundings, but also on the passageways connecting and/or obstructing movements elsewhere—windows (through which only darkness is visible), archways, doors, curtains.

Put another way, the space of *Jeanne Dielman* is simultaneously claustrophobic and "open," or at least defined by the possibility of passage. The representation of space continues, then, the ambivalent quality characteristic of the film as a whole. So, too, is the representation of control that dominates the film from the outset marked by ambivalence. Jeanne's most obvious expression of control is the constant attention to switching lights on and off. Yet throughout the film, a neon light from the street outside flashes into the living room, its blue color and rhythmic flickering an intrusive presence in the space of Jeanne's home. If the style of the film appears to be as controlled and controlling as Jeanne's rituals, that style is disrupted as well.

Rooms are by and large represented with unchanging camera angles and distances, so as to create in the viewer a sense of the familiar not unlike that which characterizes Jeanne's routine. But sometimes angles change, just enough to make a room appear slightly different in one shot than in another. Most significantly, there is a change in mise-en-scène in the kitchen. Sometimes there is one chair at the kitchen table, and sometimes two, with no motivation or explanation as to why the change has occurred.[35] One is tempted to see in these "faux raccords," or mismatches, an homage to Godard, for whom such mismatches and refusals of continuity were deliberate subversions of classical technique. In *Jeanne Dielman,* however, the joke remains subtle, never called attention to in the way that Godard, for instance, in *Weekend,* inserts a written title announcing "Faux raccord" into the fabric of the mismatch.

The ambivalence which characterizes the representation of space and of control in the film characterizes the representation of Jeanne Dielman as well. Certainly, the film traces the restrictive conditions of housework, the dehumanizing effects of continuous labor and servitude, while it portrays Jeanne as an unmistakable compulsive. Yet it also produces an equally unmistakable sense of pleasure in the rituals of everyday life. Jeanne Dielman is observed, in other words, as both a symptom and a gesture, as an object to be studied at a distance and as a subject engaged in the pleasure of process. Given the extent to which the character of Jeanne occupies screen time in the film, it is perhaps tempting to read the narration in terms uniquely of her activities. But as the game of the disappearing chairs indicates quite emphatically, the representation of Jeanne's activities is only one part of the larger narrative of the film. The ambivalence of the narration acquires particular contours through the appropriation of "primitive" narration.

To be sure, the staging of "primitive" narration in *Jeanne Dielman* occurs, on one level, in the person of Jeanne Dielman herself. Silvia Bovenschen has used the term *pre-aesthetic* to describe the ways in which women's aesthetic impulses have traditionally taken shape in the forms of domestic arts, such as quilting; or personal decoration, such as make-up and costume.[36] In *Jeanne Dielman,* there is no object, pre-aesthetic or aesthetic, associated with Jeanne Dielman, but rather the gesture itself, constantly repeated and signifying both drudgery and a kind of meditative beauty. What is perhaps most strikingly "primitive" about the representation of the feminine in the film is that, like those gestures represented in the early cinema, they attach themselves to the devices of narrative closure only with great awkwardness and difficulty. In *Jeanne Dielman,* female narration is built precisely on that "difficulty," understood not as a lack but as a difference.

On a second level, the narration of *Jeanne Dielman,* however controlled and precise, evokes the early cinema by virtue of the absence of camera movement, the duration of the shots, and the camera distance. Noël Burch has categorized Akerman's rediscovery of the "primitive" mode of representation along the lines of contemporary film studies' attention to the exploration of early cinema in works of the avant-garde. But Burch draws here on Peter Wollen's well-known distinction between the two avant-gardes, one largely "formal" and resolutely antinarrative in orientation, and the other more directed toward political understandings of language and representation. As Burch puts it, the former is "outside" the institution, the latter on its "fringes." Most avant-garde films for which an affiliation with the early cinema has been claimed belong to the first category, but Burch suggests that the "other avant-garde, mainly European, has incorporated into its critical arsenal strategies which clearly hark back to the Primitive era."[37]

Jeanne Dielman exemplifies what Burch describes as the "Primitive camera stare," in which the camera "typically remains staring into space, unable or unwilling to move, when a character goes out of shot . . . and finally returns only after a long absence. . . ."[38] Noting that *Jeanne Dielman* incorporates the medium long shot and the front medium close-up central to the "primitive stare," Burch describes the film as

> one of the most distanced narrative films of recent years, recreating to a large extent the conditions of exteriority of the Primitive Mode (the sparseness of speech seems to be a further contributing factor here), positioning the spectator once again in his or her seat, hardly able because hardly enabled to embark upon that imaginary journey through diegetic space-time to which we are so accustomed, obliged ultimately to reflect on what is seen rather than merely experience it.[39]

Many critics have agreed with Burch's assessment of *Jeanne Dielman,* if not because of the specific affiliation of the "primitive," then at least because of the film's documentation of the woman's alienation. As I have suggested, however, I think that there is considerably more ambivalence in this film than claims to distance or alienation would suggest. The point is crucial not just in terms of the female narration of the film, but also in terms of the specific appropriation of the "primitive" that is performed. While I certainly agree that the film encourages one to "reflect on what is seen," I do not think reflection is opposed to experience, as Burch suggests. Rather, the appropriation of "primitive" narration engages a rethinking of the opposition between distance and identification.

Part of what distinguishes the appropriation of the "primitive" in *Jeanne Dielman* is not just the simultaneous inquiry into the "primitive" as it applies to both a mode of filmmaking and a mode of traditional femininity, but also the reverberations of the "scène primitive," the primal scene, in the film.[40] In *Jeanne Dielman* the components of the primal scene are quite obviously (and almost parodically) in evidence—the forbidden space of the mother's bedroom, and the accouterments of classical primal scene material, including drapes and thresholds. But there is a disjuncture between the visual components of the primal scene and its customary association with the male child. For Jeanne Dielman's son speaks the language of oedipal and primal desire in terms that are flat, obvious, and completely detached from any signs of narrative fascination.

Near the conclusion of the first day of the film, when Sylvain is in bed reading, he asks his mother about her first meeting with his father. Like virtually all extended "stories" told by the characters within the film, Jeanne rapidly and in monotone recounts her meeting with her future husband after the end of World War II, his loss of money, her aunts' (with whom she lived) initial enthusiasm and then opposition to their marriage. The questions which Sylvain poses suggest his own identification with his mother. He wonders how, if his father was ugly (as Jeanne's aunts insisted), she could make love with him; whether she would marry again if she were to fall in love; and finally—in one of the most curious exchanges between mother and son in the film—he says that, if he were a woman, he could not make love with someone with whom he was not truly in love. Jeanne's reply is one of many in the film that suggest repressed hostility: "How could you know? You are *not* a woman."

On the second day of the film, the possibility that Sylvain's emerging adolescence might be yet another source of disruption in Jeanne's routine is suggested more strongly, but once again, Sylvain's seeming identification with a woman's point of view is apparent. In a replay of the earlier scene—Sylvain again in bed, and Jeanne bidding him goodnight—he tells his mother that his friend Yan is becoming interested in women. It is clear that Yan's growing maturity (or Sylvain's perception of it) is putting a strain on their friendship. In a condensed narrative of a number of clichés of male oedipal development, Sylvain describes Yan as the source of his knowledge about a variety of sexual topics, from the equivalence between a penis and a sword (to which Sylvian protested that swords cause pain), to the sexual activities of parents, both for pleasure and for procreation.

Sylvain tells his mother that once he knew about sex, he called his mother in the night so that his father couldn't hurt her. Jeanne responds, in her typically laconic fashion, that he needn't have worried. The tangled web of the primal scene is picked up again on the third day of the film, but now it is Jeanne who tells a shopkeeper some details about her family past. Many years before, her sister Fernande—who seems, on each successive day of the film, to be an ever-increasing source of anxiety—spent three months in Belgium with her son John, who was younger than Sylvain but still bigger and stronger. While Fernande and John slept on the couch—presumably the same one that now serves as Sylvain's bed—Sylvain slept in the same bedroom as Jeanne and her husband.

Now it is crucial to remember that in the overall scheme of *Jeanne Dielman*, words and stories such as these are not given the foregrounded importance, as means of access to a privileged past, that they might be accorded in more classical films. Indeed, the process of flattening out speech and sound in the film stresses that the significance of everyday gestures is as great as if not greater than that of spoken language. Nonetheless, however downplayed the function of these lengthy narratives within the film, they are present, and are significant by virtue of their unconventional placement. Much of what is spoken in the film suggests a conventional psychoanalytic reading of the primal scene as an event, as a privileged cause, as the truth of a past. But there is something of a tease in this respect as well—significant details begin to be patched together, but never in a way that allows for a coherent scene to emerge. While Jeanne's son is certainly coddled, his every physical need attended to, his presence in the film never quite achieves the centrality one might expect, particularly given the evocations of primal scene material. Alongside the mother-son relationship, and frequently displacing it from center stage, are suggestions of another kind of primal scene, one informed by the tangled web of connections that inform the family, desire, and identification. In this rendition of the primal scene, in other words, the son's desire is displaced not only by the mother's—as the increasing significance of Aunt Fernande in the various "narratives" would suggest—but by the daughter's.

That *Jeanne Dielman* is a film made from the daughter's point of view has been suggested many times, both by Akerman's own comments and in critical readings of the film.[41] Akerman's literal signature (in the credits) to *Jeanne Dielman* is interesting in this respect. In *Je tu il elle*, Akerman's fictional name, Julie, is not given until the final credits, and the name inscribes the differing pronouns that constitute the text and address of the film. In *Jeanne Dielman*, Akerman signs her name "Chantal Anne Akerman." While there is no absolute rule for the use of middle names, they tend to signify—especially when they are not frequently used—family affiliation. But more obviously, the "Anne" is part of "Jeanne," a quite literal writing of the authorship of *Jeanne Dielman* as connected to the figure of Jeanne herself.

In the context of the present discussion, it is particularly significant that the daughter's perspective is not only a reversal—e.g., the daughter's primal scene in place of the son's—but also and especially a vantage point from which to revise substantially just what the primal scene is, both psychically and cinematically, for women. The most significant components of the primal scene that emerge in this context are, first, that the daughter's vision is necessarily intertwined with that of the mother, that there is no moment of pure distance or separation. Second, there is nothing autonomous about the tableau of the primal scene; rather, the bits and pieces of primal scene material, visual as well as verbal, lead to an ever-expanding narrative and visual scene, rather than the shock of a single spectacular crisis.

Jeanne Dielman recuperates "primitive" narration on three distinct levels— the feminine, the cinematic, the psychoanalytic—and maintains them in unwavering tension. Never, in other words, does one register totally subsume the others. The final representation of this tension is the seven-minute shot at the film's conclusion, during which Jeanne Dielman sits at the table in the living room, while the blue neon light continues to flash. During most of the film, and in keeping with the ambivalence that characterizes virtually every level, Jeanne wears a facial expression that sometimes seems to express compulsion and repression, and sometimes serenity and pleasure. The intrusion of randomness and the breakdown of her routine tilt the facial expression toward the former. But in the last shot of the film, more of the serenity has been recaptured.

It is impossible to draw a neat feminist conclusion, if by "conclusion" one means either a triumph over victimization or a condemnation of such an irrational solution as murder. To be sure, there is something in the way several threads are drawn together in the murder scene to suggest a resolution—the scissors, fetched to open the birthday present, are the female equivalent of the sword metaphoriz-ed as the penis by Sylvain and his friend; and if Sylvain imagines his father hurting his mother during sex, then Jeanne's attack is a brutal reversal of the son's imaginary scene. But the lengthy still shot at the film's conclusion deflates any such consolidation of narrative elements. One is left, rather, with the overarching sense of things unresolved, of levels of tension that cannot and will not resolve into coherent ends, of an ironic juxtaposition of narrative modes.

In all three of the French films just discussed, differences among women are central to the construction of female narration. The women whose names provide the titles of the films are symptoms, stereotypical products of patriarchally defined womanhood (the housewife in *The Smiling Madame Beudet,* the sex object in *Cleo from 5 to 7,* and a somewhat peculiar combination of the two in *Jeanne Dielman*), and female narration is the simultaneous investment in and distance from these women's activities. In other words, female narration in these films is a reexamination of the traditionally and stereotypically feminine, and an exploration of the position from which such a reexamination can take place without resurrecting the patriarchal dualities of repudiation or glorifi-cation.

In each of these films, the equation between "primitive" narration and female identity is largely a function of class: both Madame Beudet and Jeanne Dielman are bound by the rituals of domesticity as shaped by the expectations of a middle-class ethos, and Cléo's encounter with a "primitive" narrator, the female card reader, is the first of several cross-class encounters—culminating in her relationship with the soldier, Antoine—which shape her change in conscious-ness. The last two films to which I turn explore differences among women in a larger, cultural sense, and draw upon the associations of the "primitive" as they apply to the feminine, certainly, but more specifically as those associations intersect with anthropological definitions of the so-called primitive other. Too often, the phrase "differences among women" assumes a logocentric relationship between "West" and "East," or between "white" and "black," where the first term remains the norm. These films do not simply reverse the duality, but challenge its very foundations.

Trinh T. Minh-ha's *Reassemblage* is an examination and critique of the anthropologist's view of village life in Senegal. While the image track of the film "documents" the patterns and rituals of everyday life (with particular attention to the activities of women), there is no consistent or coherent narrative to emerge from the series of images. Rather, the filmmaker questions the very possibility of seizing the reality of Senegal through such a visual documentation. Hence, many of the images of the film are difficult to read. Close-ups of a human face, for instance, are placed in a discombobulating relationship to long, presumably "establishing" shots; other close-ups focus on a single body part—part of a face, or a breast—so that it is difficult to read the whole out of the part. Some images are deliberately out of focus; others are intercut with each other in such a way that any sense of continuity is disrupted. Documentary sound is also manipulated, with sound track and image track in a contrapuntal rather than synchronous relation. When rhythmic clapping sounds are heard, for instance, over an image of women pounding, they seem initially to be "natural," direct sounds; quickly, however, the image and the sound tracks are revealed to be separate and nonsynchronous.

The most obvious way in which *Reassemblage* critiques the tradition of anthropological filmmaking is in the use of the voice-over, spoken by Trinh herself. In much documentary filmmaking, of course, the voice-over is the primary means by which a coherent and supposedly objective perspective is assumed. From the outset, Trinh's voice functions as a self-conscious voice, one that questions constantly its own relationship to what is being shown and heard. Indeed, most of her comments are explorations of the significance of filming Senegalese life. It is an unexamined assumption of much anthropological filmmaking that the camera serves to document the "primitive" customs of "primitive peoples," and the voice-over is perhaps the most obvious embodiment of that desire. In *Reassemblage*, however, the voice-over becomes an embodiment of another desire, not just to critique the conventions of anthropological filmmaking, but to explore the possible connections between the filmmaker and the patterns that emerge from her observations of Senegal.

In other words, *Reassemblage* does not just critique the anthropological construction of the "other," for beyond that critique—or "near by," to use Trinh's words in the film ("I do not intend to speak about/Just speak near by")—is a renarrativization of the relationship between she who speaks and she who is spoken about, between she who looks and she who is looked at, one that draws upon another appropriation of the "primitive."[42] If *Reassemblage* critiques the appropriation of the "primitive," particularly insofar as the control of the "primitive" body relies on mechanisms similar to those used to represent the female body, it attempts simultaneously to read the "primitive" in a different, more complex way, resistant to the lure of an archaic femininity, a tribal past, or a one-dimensional "Third World" identity.

What I have described of the film thus far suggests that its "primitive" style has far more to do with a documentary tradition than with the early years of motion-picture history. For in documentary cinema, "primitive" technique can function as a marker of authenticity. As Trinh herself puts it, "It is, perhaps, precisely the claim to catch life in its motion and show it 'as it is' that has led a great number of 'documentarians' not only to present 'bad shots,' but also to make us believe that life is as dull as the images they project on the screen."[43] Much of the style of *Reassemblage* stretches the limits of anthropological observation, particularly through the relationship between the images and sounds of Senegal and the narrator's voice. Images which in another context might be signs of "authentic" observation—sights captured on the sly, or on the run, as it were—here are presented rather as markers of the difficulty and impossibility of ever capturing another on film. A frequently used technique in the film is the jump cut, and as Trinh herself has commented, "Recurrent jump cuts within a single event may indicate a hesitation in selecting the 'best' framing. They may also serve as rhythmical devices that disrupt spatial and temporal continuity, and suggest a grasping of things in their instantaneousness, in their fragility."[44]

Yet the technique of *Reassemblage* does evoke the "primitive" style in its historic as well as its generic dimension, particularly insofar as another recurrent technique is concerned—the use of stop motion, whereby a human or animal figure will suddenly disappear from the frame. This use of stop motion is far more evocative of the early trick film than of the authentic sloppiness of documentary cinema. A much-contested commonplace of film history is that the difference between documentary and fictional traditions can be traced back to the two lines of development suggested in France by the films of the Lumière brothers on the one hand, and those of Georges Méliès on the other.[45] The Lumière films were documentations of scenes of everyday life, while Méliès's films used the manipulative effects of the camera to create fantastic and supernatural effects. In *Reassemblage,* the sudden disappearance of human figures from the Senegalese landscape suggests an affinity between the magician in Méliès's films and the narrator of *Reassemblage*—suggests, that is, a resurrection of the "primitive" style of early filmmaking in order to question and extend the accepted primitivism of documentary technique. Put another way, Trinh juxtaposes two kinds of "primitive" style, one which is readable within the tradition of documentary authenticity and one which is not. The "primitive" narration of the film seeks, then, not only to critique the conventions of the anthropological documentary, but also to reinvent another kind of narration, one which reconceptualizes the "magical" properties of the film medium.

Like most dualisms, the opposition between the "real life" subjects of the Lumières' films and the manipulated, fantastic subjects of Méliès's films masks a number of assumptions, particularly insofar as the truth-telling capacity of the cinema is concerned. *Reassemblage* does not assume the simple opposition of the Lumières and Méliès, of documentary and fiction, but rather seeks to inflect one notion of "primitive" filmmaking—"artless," capturing life "unawares"—with its presumed opposite—manipulative, magical—thereby putting the very opposition itself into question. Now in the appearances and disappearances so central to Méliès's magic films, it is a male magician who exercises his control and mastery over a world in which women tend more frequently than not to be the disappearing objects. If it is appropriate to describe Trinh's voice as the primary narrative perspective of the film, and if that voice acquires—by virtue of the various visual strategies associated with it—the function of a magical "primitive" narrator as well as a deconstructed anthropological one, then how are we to assess the gendered dynamics of the film?

At several points in the film, the female narrator tells anecdotes about the compulsions of whites to assign meanings to the observed experiences of Africans, meanings which are, of course, determined by white, Western notions of coherence and order. The narrator tells of a man and child who are dismissed by a "catholic white sister" for coming to the dispensary on Sunday, the day it is closed according to Catholic religion and therefore when its potential clientele should not presume to be in need of medical attention. Still another anecdote tells of an ethnologist who does not bother to actually listen to the music and stories of the people he has come to observe, since his tape recorder is on. If these examples serve to stress the extent to which colonial narratives impose their own framework on the experiences of others, they also function—somewhat ironically—as the most immediately readable and accessible "stories" within the film—that is, for a viewer trained and conditioned by classical film narrative.

But this is not to say that *Reassemblage* opposes these stories of Western "logic" with randomly selected images and words, for there is a very obvious process of selection that takes place in the film. Most of the film focuses, for instance, on the women of Senegal, with men most obviously present only at the beginning and the end. And the images which are repeated, as leitmotifs, are virtually all associated with women. Near the beginning of the film, the narrator says, "A film about what? my friends ask. A film about Senegal; but what in Senegal?" As she speaks, we see an image of a fire, an image that reappears several shots later. After these images of fire, the narrator tells of the association between women and fire: "In numerous tales/Woman is depicted as the one who

Figure 34. Trinh T. Minh-ha's *Reassemblage* (Women Make Movies)

possessed the fire/Only she knew how to make fire/She kept it in diverse places/At the end of the stick she used to dig the ground with for example/In her nails or in her fingers."[46] As she speaks, the accompanying image track shows men for the most part. But several images and lines of commentary later, the narrator repeats several lines ("She kept it in diverse places/At the end of the stick she used to dig the ground with for example"), and we see a woman holding a stick, shooing away a chicken. Such examples of apparent and immediate unity between image and sound are unusual in the film, and for a brief moment, one might perhaps read the impossible into the image—that is, see fire instead of a chicken, see the magical myth alluded to by the narrator instead of the documented reality before one's eyes.

A frequently repeated image in *Reassemblage* depicts women with sticks, whether digging, cleaning, or preparing food. Also repeated frequently are images of women's breasts, sometimes with babies nearby and sometimes not, but still suggestive of women's nourishing powers. The female body that emerges so centrally in *Reassemblage* is privileged to the extent that the entire film attempts simultaneously to question and to assume the maternal and nourishing properties of the female body. The film also examines the narrative modes irreducible to the traditions of either documentary or classical narrative filmmaking, modes which are associated with the rhythms and patterns of women's everyday lives. But there is little in *Reassemblage* to suggest that such a search for alternative ways of storytelling is the same as romanticizing the female body as an originary plenitude, as a wholeness to substitute for the fragmentation of "Western" experience.

One of the anecdotes told by the narrator describes a "man attending a slide show on Africa [who] turns to his wife and says with guilt in his voice: 'I have seen some pornography tonight.' " The images accompanying the voice show bare-breasted young women, and recall an earlier comment by the narrator: "Filming in Africa means for many of us/Colorful images, naked breast women, exotic dances and fearful rites."[47] But in both instances, something slips in the relationship between image and voice; the narrator uses the awkward phrase "naked breast women" (rather than "naked-breasted" or "women with naked breasts") and pronounces "pornography" with the accent on the wrong syllable (por-no-graph'-y, rather than por-no'-graph-y). Similarly, the narrator's voice assumes an affinity with those female voices whose words are repeated in the film in a kind of looping effect, thus assuming a rhythmic cadence. For Trinh's voice is too inflected with an accent to function as the transparent, overarching, "neutral" voice of documentary. The accent is not one typically associated with African speakers of English; thus, throughout the film, the female voice speaks as one who is not a part of Senegalese or African culture, but who is not a part of the tradition of white anthropological filmmaking either. Any presumed unity of the "Third World" disintegrates in the film, but at the same time the very division between the voice and the image suggests the possibility of another kind of observation, one resistant to the dualities of "West" versus "Third World."

The final section of Trinh's book-length study of feminism and postcolonialism, *Woman, Native, Other,* is entitled "Grandma's Story," and explores the significance of oral traditions of storytelling for women writers of color. "She who works at un-learning the dominant language of 'civilized' missionaries also has to learn how to un-write and write anew," she writes.[48] *Reassemblage* is a stunning demonstration of that process of "un-writing" whereby colonial notions of the "primitive" are demystified, certainly, but also where the very notion of a "primitive" mode of storytelling is reexamined in another light. *Reassemblage* is subtitled *From the Firelight to the Screen.* One could read in this subtitle the desire for a connection between the fire (which signifies a variety of aspects of women's lives in the film) and the cinema—for a cinema, that is, illuminated by the light of another experience. This is not to say that *Reassemblage* replicates the anthropological tradition it criticizes, but that it attempts another inflection, another pronunciation, whereby the "primitive" emerges not as the rigid duality of self and other but as the exploration of other modes of storytelling.

Like *Reassemblage,* Laleen Jayamanne's *A Song of Ceylon* critiques anthropological views of the "primitive," and takes the representation of the female body as its primary point of inquiry. But whereas *Reassemblage* refers to an entire tradition of anthropological filmmaking, *A Song of Ceylon* is much more specific in its reference to ethnographic definitions of the "primitive." The title of the film cites Basil Wright's 1935 British film *The Song of Ceylon,* which Jayamanne has described as "not pure ethnography [but] it has elements in common with an ethnographic enterprise, of rendering an 'ancient culture' visible as it enters the rapid transformations wrought by the colonial process of a plantation economy and international trade."[49] If Wright's film romanticizes Ceylon, the citation of the title in Jayamanne's film is an ironic displacement, both of a "name erased from the map of the world" and of the cinematic conventions which create the illusion of possession, whether of a culture, an experience, or a body.[50] And possession, in many senses of the term, is central to *A Song of Ceylon*. *A Song of Ceylon* is a rereading, or more precisely a performance, of a case study of Gananath Obeyesekere of a Sri Lankan woman, called Somavati in the text, who is possessed by demon spirits. The case study is a "psychocultural exegesis" of the woman's possession and subsequent exorcism. Obeyesekere's text is an exploration of "primitivism" understood in an anthropological as well as a psychoanalytic sense—anthropological insofar as the possession exemplifies ostensibly "primitive" beliefs in the relationship between the human and the spiritual world, and psychoanalytic insofar as Somavati's possession is also a function of her inability, or refusal, to contain infantile rage within the confines of "appropriate" female behavior.

Somavati's exorcism ritual is performed most literally in the spoken sound track to the film, which consists almost exclusively of citations from the case study. The inflection of the voice sets the components of the case study in a different relation to each other than is possible in the written text. To be sure, Obeyesekere includes in the case study lengthy quotations from the exorcism ritual, but these are always framed by his commentary. In the film, the different voices—and in particular the voice of Somavati, performed by Jayamanne herself—acquire more autonomy, and processes which remain subtle in the written text are more dramatically represented in the film. For instance, the first words spoken in the film are Somavati's description of her "spirit attacks": "My hands and feet grow cold; it is as if I don't possess them. Then my body shivers—shivers, and the inside of my body seems to shake. . . . This goes on and on . . . and if I hear someone talk I get angry. My rage is such that I could even hit my father and mother . . . this is how the illness starts."[51]

Somavati's voice acts out the words *shiver* and *rage,* so that one can practically feel a chill in the former word and anger in latter. But this performance of the text is no simple attribution of agency or authority to Somavati, for her voice is also quite literally "possessed" from the outset—a male voice accompanies hers, sometimes echoing what she says, sometimes completing a phrase that she begins. An example of this strategy occurs later in the film, when one of the more memorable utterances of the exorcism ritual is spoken: "Do you think I am a woman, ha! Do you?"[52] The female voice begins the phrase ("Do you think I am . . ."), but a male voice completes it (" . . . a woman?"). Put another way, then, the voices of the film perform the contradictions of Obeyesekere's case study, on the one hand by identifying Somavati as a far more palpable, dynamic presence than she is in print, and on the other hand by embedding her speech within the speech of men.

If the spoken track to *A Song of Ceylon* performs and cites a specific ritual of possession, the image and music tracks explore other permutations of possession, and the film plays on "possession" in the collision of cultural meanings. More specifically, the Sri Lankan context of "possession" (i.e., spirit possession) finds its most striking "Western" echo in a series of poses, borrowed from film stills, denoting romantic possession. As Jayamanne explains, "the image track of the film is based on tableaux vivants constructed not from films but from looking at *film stills* of a selection of films. The film has tried to recreate certain classic postures and gestures of Western erotic and romantic possession taken from film stills."[53] These include poses of men and women in a series of romantic embraces, with an element of defamiliarization occurring through the stiff, tableaulike representations, or the casting of a transvestite in a woman's role; and a black-and-white sequence of fragmented body parts and frozen poses which cites Jean-Luc Godard's *Une Femme Mariée (A Married Woman)*.

However, *A Song of Ceylon* does not set up a simple opposition between the visual and the aural, or between "Western" and "Asian" possession. The final performance within the film is a recital, where Schubert's "Litany for All Souls Day"—heard only in fragments previously in the film—is sung, in an example of what Jayamanne has described as "cultural hybridization."[54] For the participants in the recital, musicians as well as onlookers, are a combination of Western and Asian "types," and even the music itself is at times performed in such a way that the boundaries between Western and Asian music become tenuous. Similarly, *A Song of Ceylon* probes and stretches the gender polarities of possession. Somavati's desire to "play"—as uttered on the sound track—acquires a number of visual forms, particularly concerning various possibilities of rearranging the sexual hierarchy of male agent and female object. One of the most common motifs in the film is the "posing" sequence, in which the limbs of actors are manipulated by other actors (with often just an isolated arm visible), only to fall away in a kind of passive resistance to the gesture of control. The interchangeability of

Figure 35. Laleen Jayamanne's *A Song of Ceylon* (Women Make Movies)

gendered roles here both amplifies and contradicts the play of voices on the sound track.

A Song of Ceylon is shot almost exclusively in the static, tableaulike images characteristic of the early cinema, and in the rare instances that camera movement does appear, it is—again, as in the early cinema—quite visibly motivated. But if Trinh's film critiques the way in which the "primitive" is captured on film in order to explore other possible formulations of "primitive" narration, *A Song of Ceylon* seems, rather, to eschew any such reappropriation. Put another way, one might argue that the "primitive" style of *A Song of Ceylon* has more to do with a postmodern mode of performance than with an exploration of the intersection between different associations of the "primitive." However, both *Reassemblage* and *A Song of Ceylon* embody a desire, not to repossess what Jayamanne has called "pristine cultural identities," but rather to redefine "primitive" narration as simultaneous connection with and distance from the female body.[55]

In *A Song of Ceylon*, the realm of the "primitive" is evoked by the disembodied voices which speak the tale of Sri Lankan possession, and by the visible bodies which may occasionally sing but which do not speak. The tale of possession collapses, in other words, into the tale of hysteria; "primitive" culture overlaps with the "primitive" body language of the hysteric. Indeed, Obeyesekere's case study is quite evocative of Freud's case history of Dora. Obeyesekere assumes, for instance, that if Somavati remained with her apparently sadistic husband, it is because she herself fits the profile of a masochist; in other words, if she is beaten by her husband she must like it—just as Dora, in Freud's view, must have welcomed the sexual advances of Herr K.[56] And like Dora, Somavati's body acts out what it cannot or will not speak.

While an impressive body of feminist psychoanalytic criticism has read Freud, Dora, and hysteria symptomatically, Jayamanne's approach is different, precisely to the extent that *A Song of Ceylon* performs the two registers of spirit possession and hysteria by insisting upon both their common denominator and their difference. This simultaneous connection and difference takes theatricalization, performance, and public spectacle as its central terms. Jayamanne describes part of her fascination with the case study as "the way in which 'my culture' dealt with hysteria in the form of a theatrical ritual, that is to say a public ceremony."[57] This is not to say, of course, that theatrical metaphors are alien to the description of hysteria; to the contrary. Josef Breuer's famous patient, Anna O., described one of her hysterical symptoms as her "private theatre": "While everyone thought she was attending, she was living through fairy tales in her imagination; but she was always on the spot when she was spoken to, so that no one was aware of it."[58]

Central to *A Song of Ceylon* in this context are the competing roles of private and public spheres in defining possession and hysteria. The film addresses how notions of the private and the public shape the cinema, particularly insofar as spectatorship is concerned. Catherine Clément has described the cinema as the "institutionalization of hysteria." In the context of the relationship between the cinema and the spheres of private and public life, this suggests a public spectacle far removed from the kind of public ritual Jayamanne describes, a spectacle—as Clément puts it—"without possible contagion."[59] But the relationship established in *A Song of Ceylon* between possession and hysteria inflects—and infects—one notion of a public sphere with the other.

In the different modes of performance in the film, the common denominator is virtually always the female body as "possessed," as "hysterical." When the elderly woman completes her song in the above-mentioned chamber-music scene, she collapses; the condition of performance is the inextricable connection between body and voice. "Primitive" narration in *A Song of Ceylon* is where possession and hysteria cross in the representation of the female body. If it is implied in Obeyesekere's case study that hysteria is cross-cultural, that the price of social interdiction is the division of the woman, then how are we to read Jayamanne's film, which itself returns constantly to the scene of possession as the scene of hysteria, and vice versa? In other words, is "cultural hybridization" just another name for psychocultural homogeneity? One of the key moments in the exorcism ritual as described by Obeyesekere is the chair episode. After Somavati and the two men performing the exorcism dance around a chair, one man "grabs Somavati by the hair and forces her down in front of the chair. He has a cane in his hand and with it directs the woman to crawl under the chair. She crawls under the chair on all fours. 'Get up—get to the other side,' says David. She crawls under the chair in the opposite direction. This is repeated several times." Obeyesekere explains the significance of the chair episode as simultaneously the capitulation of the demons inhabiting Somavati to the superior gods represented by the men, and "Somavati's self-abnegation; she literally grovels in the dust at the feet of the priests, and later of the deities. She is broken, humiliated, made abject, and made pliable psychologically."[60]

The performance of this scene in the film displaces the resolution offered by the humiliation of Somavati. Instead, we see a body, dressed in a sari, wearing Cuban dancing shoes, dance atop the seat of a chair. The face and chest are invisible, and eventually the hands become a frenetic part of the dance. The dance itself begins as a rather mundane cha cha, but evolves into a most peculiar and disturbing sight, a frenzy of bodily gestures impossible to read—to "possess"—absolutely in cultural or psychoanalytic terms. At the same time, the dancer's body is difficult to read in terms of gender—is this another man impersonating a woman? Or a woman caught up in the frenzy of bodily excess? The desire of the film is precisely there—to imagine a body, not so much "free" of gender as absolutely unreadable in either/or terms. The film does not rescue the "primitive" body of possession and/or hysteria, nor does it collapse the one kind of "primitivism" into the other. Rather, the film *performs* the "primitive," sets the public and private verions of the body in tension with each other, and in so doing deinstitutionalizes cinematic possession and hysteria.

I began this chapter with two films which parallel the appropriation of early cinema by (male) avant-garde filmmakers, moved to three films which are more specifically narrative in their focus, and concluded with two films in which the very distinction between avant-garde and narrative is suspect, but more specifically which explore the cultural connotations of the "primitive" as what is repressed not only in patriarchal but also in some feminist notions of the subject. In other words, I have situated Trinh's and Jayamanne's films, if not as "last words" then at least as appropriate conclusions to the exploration of the "primitive" in the works of white, Western women filmmakers.

To regard *Reassemblage* and *A Song of Ceylon* as "continuations" of the projects central to the other films risks the flattening out of difference in the name of a "women's cinema" that assumes too quickly a universal, shared set of concerns. But to separate these two films from the rest involves another kind of risk, by placing the burden of the demonstration of cultural and racial difference on those women filmmakers to whom the descriptions "women of color" or "Third World" apply. In other words, a discussion of the cultural connotations of the "primitive" in films such as *Reassemblage* and *A Song of Ceylon* can evolve—however unconsciously or unthinkingly—from the assumption that these ramifications of the "primitive" apply only to *them*, to the "other woman" of white, Western feminism. But as the fascination with cultural "otherness" in Maya Deren's work or, even more problematically, the invocation of racial stereotypes in the context of "primitive" narration in *Cleo from 5 to 7* demonstrates, the lure of the "primitive" in women's cinema is also the lure of cultural constructions of the "other," and there is no guarantee that the displacement of the male subject simultaneously displaces his white skin or his Western assumptions.

Afterword

As I stated in the introduction, one of my aims in writing
this book was to explore issues in women's cinema that have not been widely
addressed. While I realize that the subtitle of my book—*Feminism and Women's
Cinema*—indicates a preoccupation with the concerns shared by women's films
with other films and with feminist theory, I nevertheless approached this project
with the assumption that global definitions of women's cinema, no matter how
many qualifiers and disclaimers they provide, are usually quite limiting. Thus, I
wanted to discuss very specific contexts for women's cinema, with the understanding that these are not in any way exclusive categories. Certainly, I
wanted to look at common ground—at how, say, Helke Sander's representation
of a women's political community in *Redupers* would read in relation to Julie
Dash's exploration of a black feminist response to filmmaking, or how two
filmmakers (Akerman and Ottinger) whose works are otherwise quite different
nonetheless read authorship in relationship to lesbian desire, or how the appropriation of the "primitive" style of filmmaking can provide a point of departure to reread the relationship between three women filmmakers working in
the French language. But I wanted to explore these connections in a way that
would be more attentive to the interesting and compelling details that some-

times get lost when one is attempting to construct a panoptic survey of women's cinema.

My interest in the screen as the ambivalent site of projection, for instance, began some years ago when I saw *The Big Sleep* as both a confirmation of and a challenge to feminist insights about the classical cinema. While Hawks's film offered textbook-like demonstrations of the separation between the man who looks and the woman who is looked at, I kept returning to the scene where Harry Jones is killed and to the peculiar relationship between the two sisters, elements which did not seem so immediately readable or obvious. At about the same time, I saw Helke Sander's *Redupers,* and I began to see a connection between the way the Berlin Wall and the billboards functioned in that film and the screen surface and its narrative implications in *The Big Sleep.* Put another way, what was beginning to coalesce in my mind was a relationship between women's filmmaking and the classical Hollywood cinema based not so much on the dominant features of the latter but on its stubborn features, its own points of ambivalence.

Ambivalence is a term that appears frequently in this book to describe what is—despite my claims of nonuniversality—a feature of virtually all of the films discussed. While I am obviously drawn to ambivalent representations which encourage conversation and dialogue, I am aware too—as I have suggested in previous chapters—that ambivalence can become an easy abstraction, a value to be celebrated in its own right rather than examined and explored. There has been in recent years a tendency in film studies—in part as a response to the groundbreaking work of Laura Mulvey and others—to emphasize conflict and contradiction rather than hegemony and authority, particularly insofar as the classical Hollywood cinema is concerned. The desire to challenge monolithic constructions has sometimes led to a reading of every tension as a contradiction, every conflict as a symptom of patriarchy's weak links. At the same time, the very terms for such critical oppositions (either you see Hollywood as a monolith or you don't) can speak to a rigid dualism.

Such dualism is much harder to shake than one might think. In the discussion of the "primitive" in women's films (chapter six), for example, I found myself on more than one occasion wanting to find proof, incontrovertible evidence, that the white, Western filmmakers discussed either do or do not replicate the colonial appropriation of "primitive" cultures. And when I began writing on Trinh's and Jayamanne's films, I hoped initially for reformulations which would make clear and visible the dividing line between what is complicit with white, patriarchal definitions of the subject and what is not. Their films are reformulations, certainly, but ones that refuse such secure positions of knowledge and authority. Indeed, resistance to easy categorization inspires all the women's films discussed in this book, but that does not mean that an engagement with the ambivalence in theoretical terms is any easier than it is in visual or narrative ones.

In any case, my own desire for a "local" analysis of films by women notwithstanding, it has come as something of a relief to discover, during the writing of this book, that the cinematic topics at hand are not so local—or narrow, depending upon your point of view—after all. I knew there were plenty of lesbian films (however one wishes to define the term) which had been discussed rarely, if at all, in feminist writing; but the particular contours of lesbian authorship in Akerman's and Ottinger's films initially seemed to me nonetheless to constitute a fairly limited category of films. But in the course of writing the book, I discovered other films—such as Sheila McLaughlin's *She Must Be Seeing Things* (1987) or Léa Pool's *La Femme de l'Hôtel* (*A Woman in Transit* [1984]) and *Anne Trister* (1986)—in which lesbian authorship was central in ways quite compatible with *Je tu il elle* and *Ticket of No Return*. My point is that reading what initially appears to be an "atypical" or "unusual" strategy can often lead to questioning the very categories that made you define the strategy as atypical in the first place.

By way of conclusion, then, I would like to turn to a film which is an appropriate epilogue to this book, since as felicitous coincidence would have it, it is preoccupied with the three areas of inquiry—the screen, lesbian authorship, and "primitive" narration—that give this book its structure. Midi Onodera's *Ten Cents a Dance (Parallax)* (1985) is a short (30 minutes) film, divided into three sections, each concerned with a different configuration of sexual desire and language. A split screen is used throughout, so that the two players in every scene are divided from each other. In the first section, two women, while waiting for (or just having finished) dinner in a Japanese restaurant, discuss whether or not they will have a sexual relationship. In the second section, shot from a high angle, two men have sex with each other in a public restroom. And in the final section, a man and a woman engage in phone sex. The use of the split screen creates a wide-angle effect, since the top and bottom of the frame are masked, and the two screens appear "projected" against a black background, with a dividing line between them.

The relationship between the two screens in each section acquires the contours of simultaneous connection and separation. In this way, Onodera's use of the screen is quite close to how the screen functions in *Redupers, Illusions, I've Heard the Mermaids Singing,* and *The Man Who Envied Women*, evoking, as in those films, a figure of permeability and division at the same time. In each of those films, the screen becomes a site of tension, and this occurs in Onodera's film by the doubling of the screens, and by the relationship between the two

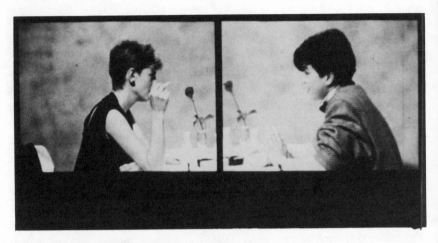

Figure 36. Midi Onodera's *Ten Cents a Dance (Parallax)*
(Women Make Movies)

edges that never quite touch. In the first section of the film, one of the two women is portrayed by Onodera herself. She is both the "experienced" lesbian discussing the possibility of an intimate relationship with a woman she had considered "essentially straight," and an Asian-Canadian having dinner in one of the most popularized Western clichés of Asia, a restaurant. In other words, she appears to occupy a position of some authority, but like Akerman in *Je tu il elle* and Ottinger in *Ticket of No Return,* Onodera defines authorship so as to expose its fictions as well as its desires.

For the position that Onodera occupies, on the right side of the screen, is taken up by a gay man engaging in anonymous sex in the next section, and a woman offering phone sex (for sale, one assumes) in the last part of the film. Given the extent to which anonymity and sex for sale are defined, in much lesbian writing, as symptomatic of either male sexuality or heterosexuality, the affiliation between Onodera's position and those of the man and the woman in the subsequent scenes brackets any simple notion of lesbian desire as isolated from other forms of sexual desire. At the same time, of course, the lesbian scene *is* different from the other two, with more emphasis on conversation and the erotics of the look. Onodera's ambiguous role in the film, as both author and actor, and as both like and unlike gay men and heterosexuals, thus evokes the lesbian irony central to Akerman's and Ottinger's films, with the lesbian author defined as both complicit in and resistant to the sexual fictions of patriarchal culture.

Ten Cents a Dance, like the films discussed in the previous chapter, cites the frontality and the immobile camera of the early cinema. The use of real time in each of the individual segments is somewhat evocative of Akerman's use of the "primitive" film style in *Jeanne Dielman,* in the sense that each scene in Onodera's film captures a sense both of pleasurable duration and of occasionally uncomfortable pauses. Whereas all of the films discussed in chapter six cite "primitive" style as it relates to the earliest years of motion picture history, *Ten Cents a Dance* goes even further back in cinema history by citing one of the visual "predecessors" of the moving pictures—the stereoscope. The stereoscope card is a doubled image which, when viewed at the proper distance, creates the illusion of depth. In Onodera's film, however, the two views are juxtaposed to disrupt the seamless fit between the participants in sexual dramas.

I have spoken throughout this book of the threshold, of the attention drawn to relations between women on either side of the keyhole, as both subjects and objects of the look. The visual and narrative structure of Onodera's film articulates beautifully the stubborn dualities to which I just referred, acknowledging the lure of symmetrical halves, yet refusing to ground itself in any easy oppositions. The two women in the first section of *Ten Cents a Dance* look at each other, but they also avoid each other's gaze; they talk, but they experience long periods of awkward silence, too. Like the films discussed in this book, *Ten Cents a Dance* dramatizes both the possibilities and the difficulties of the cinema in relationship to women's conversations, both with each other and with the "other"—however that other is construed.

The "screen tests" performed in *Redupers, Illusions, I've Heard the Mermaids Singing,* and *The Man Who Envied Women* affirm and question simultaneously the possibilities for communities of women. The communities thus examined are diverse—in *Illusions,* it is a community of women based on a common exclusion from white, male culture, certainly, but it is also the shared community and spectatorship possible amongst black women; in *I've Heard the Mermaids Singing* it is a community where art is celebrated as self-expression, and sexual marginality defined as a position of simultaneous investment and distance. In *Redupers* and *The Man Who Envied Women,* artistic communities make possible a critical dialogue about alternatives and the risks of recuperation.

Lesbian authorship, as defined in Arzner's films, as well as in *Je tu il elle* and *Ticket of No Return,* explores relations between women in erotic terms and—to paraphrase the title of Akerman's film—the possibility of a "je/tu" relationship from which "il" has not exactly been banished, but certainly has been displaced from center stage. The reconceptualization of the "primitive" in films ranging from Maya Deren's *Meshes of the Afternoon* to Trinh T. Minh-ha's *Reassemblage* and Laleen Jayamanne's *A Song of Ceylon* engages with the definitions of "woman" and "women" (to again borrow Teresa de Lauretis's formulation) insofar as they determine, and are shaped in their turn by, cultural definitions of the "other." In the films discussed in this book, thresholds of representation are defined in various ways, and the kinds of relationships established between women are both complex and complicated. Yet all of these films affirm the necessity and the vitality of conversations between women—conversations where impossible ideals of "simple" communication and impermeable boundaries of rigid isolation are both put to the test, overlapping yet separate like the edges of the screens that both divide and connect the two women in *Ten Cents a Dance*.

NOTES

INTRODUCTION

1. "Re-vision—the act of looking back, of seeing with fresh eyes, of entering an old text from a new critical direction—is for women more than a chapter in cultural history: it is an act of survival. Until we understand the assumptions in which we are drenched we cannot know ourselves." Adrienne Rich, *On Lies, Secrets, and Silence* (New York: Norton, 1979), p. 35.

2. Molly Haskell, *From Reverence to Rape* (New York: Penguin, 1973), p. 155.

3. Mary Ann Doane, *The Desire to Desire* (Bloomington: Indiana University Press, 1987), chapter 3.

4. For discussions of *Stella Dallas* which raise crucial issues concerning feminism and the woman's film, see Doane, *The Desire to Desire*, pp. 74–78; E. Ann Kaplan, "The Case of the Missing Mother: Maternal Issues in Vidor's *Stella Dallas*," *Heresies*, no. 16 (1983), 81–85; and Linda Williams, " 'Something Else besides a Mother': *Stella Dallas* and the Maternal Melodrama," *Cinema Journal* 24, no. 1 (Fall 1984), 2–27.

5. Doane, *The Desire to Desire*, chapter 2.

6. Ibid., p. 13.

7. The first section of Irigaray's *Speculum of the Other Woman* (Ithaca: Cornell University Press, 1985), trans. Gillian C. Gill, is entitled "The Blind Spot of an Old Dream of Symmetry."

8. Tania Modleski, *The Women Who Knew Too Much: Hitchcock and Feminist Theory* (New York: Methuen, 1988); Lucy Fischer, *Shot/Countershot: Film Tradition and Women's Cinema* (Princeton: Princeton University Press, 1989).

9. Doane, *The Desire to Desire*, p. 13.

10. Haskell, *From Reverence to Rape*, p. 155.

11. Kaja Silverman, "Lost Objects and Mistaken Subjects: Film Theory's Structuring Lack," *Wide Angle* 7, no. 1–2 (1985), 25.

229

12. Joan DeJean, "Female Voyeurism: Sappho and Lafayette," *Rivista di Lettera-ture moderne e comparate* XL, no. 3 (August–September 1987), 201–205; Nancy K. Miller, *Subject to Change: Reading Feminist Writing* (New York: Columbia University Press, 1988), chapter 7; Naomi Schor, "Female Fetishism: The Case of George Sand," in Susan Suleiman, ed., *The Female Body in Western Culture* (Cambridge: Harvard University Press, 1986), 363–72.

13. Teresa de Lauretis, *Alice Doesn't: Feminism, Semiotics, Cinema* (Bloomington: Indiana University Press, 1984), p. 15.

14. "It is wrong to conclude, as some have, that because there may be no objective truth possible, there are not objective lies." See Linda Gordon, "What's New in Women's History?" in Teresa de Lauretis, ed., *Feminist Studies/Critical Studies* (Bloomington: Indiana University Press, 1986), p. 22.

15. See Trinh T. Minh-ha, *Woman, Native, Other* (Bloomington: Indiana University Press, 1989), pp. 64–65, 123–25.

1. SPECTACLE, NARRATIVE, AND SCREEN

1. Guy Debord, *La Société du spectacle* (1967; rpt. Paris: Editions champ libre, 1971), p. 9.

2. Charles Eckert, "The Carole Lombard in Macy's Window," *Quarterly Review of Film Studies* 3, no. 1 (Winter 1978), 21. For an excellent case study of tie-ins which extends the parallel between film screen and display window, see Jane Gaines, "The Queen Christina Tie-ups: Convergence of Show Window and Screen," *Quarterly Review of Film and Video* 11, no. 1 (1989), 35–60.

3. Jean Baudrillard, *La société de consommation: Ses mythes, ses structures* (Paris: Denoël, 1970), pp. 309–310.

4. Dana Polan, " 'Above all else to make you see': Cinema and the Ideology of Spectacle," *boundary 2* 11, no. 1–2 (Fall–Winter 1982–83), 133–34.

5. See André Bazin, "The Myth of Total Cinema," in Hugh Gray, ed. and trans., *What is Cinema?* (Berkeley: University of California Press, 1967), pp. 17–22; Jean-Louis Baudry, "The Apparatus," *Camera Obscura*, no. 1 (Fall 1976), 104–126.

6. See Jane Feuer, *The Hollywood Musical* (Bloomington: Indiana University Press, 1982), especially chapter 2 ("Spectators and Spectacles").

7. For discussions and analyses of suture in film, see Stephen Heath, *Questions of Cinema* (Bloomington: Indiana University Press, 1981), pp. 76–112; Kaja Silverman, *The Subject of Semiotics* (New York: Oxford University Press, 1983), pp. 194–236.

8. Laura Mulvey, "Visual Pleasure and Narrative Cinema," *Screen* 16 (1975), 6–18.

9. John Berger, *Ways of Seeing* (1972; rpt. New York: Viking Press, 1973), pp. 47, 64.

10. For feminist critiques of Baudry, see Constance Penley, "Feminism, Film Theory, and the Bachelor Machines," *m/f*, no. 10 (1985), 39–59; Joan Copjec, "The Anxiety of the Influencing Machine," *October*, no. 23 (Winter 1982), 43–59; and Jacqueline Rose, "The Cinematic Apparatus: Problems in Current Theory," in Teresa de Lauretis and Stephen Heath, eds., *The Cinematic Apparatus* (New York: St. Martin's Press, 1980), pp. 172–86.

11. ". . . feminism is not a new ghetto where women are confined to concerning ourselves about only a select list of topics separated from the overall social and economic context of our lives. Similarly, feminism is not just 'add women and stir' into existing institutions, ideologies, or political parties." See Charlotte Bunch, "Prospects for Global Feminism" (1981), in *Passionate Politics: Feminist Theory in Action, Essays, 1968–1986* (New York: St. Martin's Press, 1987), p. 302.

12. Mary Ann Doane, *The Desire to Desire* (Bloomington: Indiana University Press, 1987), p. 23.

13. E. Ann Kaplan, *Women and Film: Both Sides of the Camera* (New York: Methuen, 1983), pp. 23–35.

14. See, for example, David Rodowick, "The Difficulty of Difference," *Wide Angle* 5, no. 1 (1982), 4–15; Teresa de Lauretis, *Alice Doesn't: Feminism, Semiotics, Cinema* (Bloomington: Indiana University Press, 1984), chapter 5; Miriam Hansen, "Pleasure, Ambivalence, Identification: Valentino and Female Spectatorship," *Cinema Journal* 25, no. 4 (Summer 1986), 6–32.

15. Laura Mulvey, "Afterthoughts on 'Visual Pleasure and Narrative Cinema' Inspired by *Duel in the Sun* (King Vidor, 1946)," *Framework*, no. 15–16–17 (1981), 12–15; Mary Ann Doane, "Film and the Masquerade: Theorising the Female Spectator," *Screen* 23, no. 3–4 (September–October 1982), 74–87.

16. De Lauretis, *Alice Doesn't*, pp. 143, 144.

17. The journal *Camera Obscura* has been the most important source for translations of Bellour's work and positive assessments of its importance; for a lucid critique of Bellour's assumptions, see Tania Modleski, *The Women Who Knew Too Much: Hitchcock and Feminist Theory* (New York: Methuen, 1988).

18. Raymond Bellour, "The Obvious and the Code," *Screen* 15 (1974), 15.

19. Cited in Roger Shatzkin, "Who Cares Who Killed Owen Taylor?" in Gerald Peary and Roger Shatzkin, ed., *The Modern American Novel and the Movies* (New York: Frederick Ungar, 1978), p. 81. But Annette Kuhn has observed that while virtually all critics cite the same anecdote concerning the difficulty of the plot of *The Big Sleep*, the plot is not really *that* hard to follow. "Close study," writes Kuhn, "suggests that at the level of narrative, the film's renowned confusion is more apparent than real." See "*The Big Sleep*: Censorship, Film Text, and Sexuality," in *The Power of the Image: Essays on Representation and Sexuality* (London and Boston: Routledge and Kegan Paul, 1985), p. 77.

20. For a discussion of the significance of Shaun Regan's role in the film (in the novel his name is Rusty Regan), see Shatzkin, "Who Cares Who Killed Owen Taylor?" pp. 80–94.

21. Mulvey, "Visual Pleasure," p. 11.

22. In this respect, the film recalls Pam Cook's discussion of *Mildred Pierce* (1945) in terms of its articulation of a women's sphere which in the course of the film will be demolished; "the project of the film is to re-present the violent overthrow of mother-right in favour of father-right through the symbolic use of film lighting and the organisation of its narrative structure." See "Duplicity in *Mildred Pierce*." in E. Ann Kaplan, ed., *Women in Film Noir* (London: British Film Institute, 1978), pp. 68–82.

23. Jean-Louis Comolli and Jean Narboni, "Cinema/Ideology/Criticism," *Screen Reader*, no. 1 (London: Society for Education in Film and Television, 1977), 7.

24. Ibid.

25. For a lucid reevaluation of the notion of the "progressive text," specifically in relationship to genre, see Barbara Klinger, " 'Cinema/Ideology/Criticism' Revisited: The Progressive Text," *Screen* 25, no. 1 (January–February 1984), 30–44.

26. Lucy Fischer, *Shot/Countershot: Film Tradition and Women's Cinema* (Princeton: Princeton University Press, 1989), p. 9.

27. See, for example, Constance Penley: "And when someone like Raymond Bellour says 'all Hollywood film is about marriage,' I think he is saying that the problem of Hollywood film is how by the end of the film the narrative system gives you a definition of femininity and of masculinity such that they are utterly complementary. We know from numerous studies of films, from textual analysis, that it is a highly perfected system, it works, it is homogeneous, there is closure or at least there is the sensation of homogeneity and closure. The feminists are not trying to discount that. But, on the other hand, what

232 Notes for pages 25–37

they want to try to say is that there is always something amiss, there is always something that isn't quite sealed over at the end. The problem is how do you talk about that without once again falling back into saying that femininity is always already a rupture." See "Discussion," recorded from the 1984 *m/f* conference presentation of her paper "Feminism, Film Theory, and the Bachelor Machines," p. 59. See also Janet Bergstrom, "Enunciation and Sexual Difference (Part I)," *Camera Obscura,* no. 3–4 (1979), 32–65.

28. ". . . this is an organized system whose meaning is regulated by paradigms and units of value that are in turn determined by male subjects. Therefore, the feminine must be deciphered as inter-dict: within the signs or between them, between the realized meanings, between the lines . . . and as a function of the (re)productive necessities of an intentionally phallic currency, which, for lack of the collaboration of a (potentially female) other, can immediately be assumed to need *its* other, a sort of inverted or negative alter ego—'black' too, like a photographic negative." See Luce Irigaray, *Speculum of the Other Woman,* trans. Gillian C. Gill (1974; Ithaca: Cornell University Press, 1985), p. 22.

29. Kuhn, *"The Big Sleep:* Censorship, Film Text, and Sexuality," pp. 91, 95.

30. Ibid., p. 90.

31. What I am calling "homotextual" is what Eve Kosofsky Sedgwick would describe as "homosocial." Although Sedgwick makes a convincing case for the difference between "homosocial" and "homosexual," the case of *The Big Sleep,* with male homosexuality rendered "invisible" in such a striking way in the movement from novel to film, calls for a term that suggests both the sexual and its erasure. See the introduction to Sedgwick's *Between Men* (New York: Columbia University Press, 1985), esp. pp. 1–5.

32. Describing Jones as Marlowe's double, who represents "the passive, 'female' side of the protagonist's nature," Christopher Orr argues that Marlowe is complicitous in Jones's murder: "Marlowe's loss of his position as the film's perceptual center, its enunciator, further establishes his ambiguity and complicity. He is unable to intervene because he desires the murder of his double—the ultimate repression." See "The Trouble with Harry: On the Hawks Version of *The Big Sleep,*" *Wide Angle* 5, no. 2 (1982), 70.

33. Annette Kuhn points out that most of the rewrites of the film's screenplay, as well as the eventual reshooting of some scenes and addition of others, were "devoted to the further enhancement of the Marlowe-Vivian romance. . . ." Before the final revisions of the film were completed, Bogart and Bacall were married; thus "the film became something of a celebration of their real-life romance." See *"The Big Sleep:* Censorship, Film Text, and Sexuality," p. 83.

34. See Noël Burch, pamphlet accompanying his film *Correction Please, or How We Got into Pictures* (London: Arts Council of Great Britain, 1979).

35. For a discussion of how *Uncle Josh at the Moving Picture Show* and other films of the primitive era articulate a relationship between private and public spheres, see my *Private Novels, Public Films* (Athens: University of Georgia Press, 1988), chapter 3.

36. Noël Burch writes of the pre-1906 cinema: "in many ways and on many levels these films seem to be acting out, at the level of narrative, of gesture, at the iconographic, scenographic levels, the symbolism of those fundamental strategies which were to develop over the next quarter of a century. . . ." See *Correction Please,* p. 14.

37. That Mulvey's analysis is overly categorical insofar as relationships between men and the function of the male look are concerned has been suggested by several critics; see, in particular, Steve Neale, "Masculinity as Spectacle: Reflections on Men and Mainstream Cinema," *Screen* 24, no. 6 (November–December 1983), 2–16.

38. De Lauretis, *Alice Doesn't,* pp. 134–35.

39. Melanie Klein, "Infant Analysis" (1923), in *Contributions to Psychoanalysis* (London: Hogarth Press, 1950), pp. 87–116; cited in Daniel Dervin, *Through a Freudian*

Lens Deeply: A Psychoanalysis of Cinema (Hillsdale, N.J.: The Analytic Press, 1985), p. 10.

40. Ibid., p. 18.

41. Christian Metz, *The Imaginary Signifier,* trans. Ben Brewster (Bloomington: Indiana University Press, 1982), p. 64.

42. For criticisms of Metz in just these terms, see Mary Ann Doane, "Misrecognition and Identity," *Ciné-tracts* 3, no. 3 (Fall 1980), 25–32; and "The Film's Time and the Spectator's Space," in Stephen Heath and Patricia Mellencamp, eds., *Cinema and Language,* American Film Institute Monograph Series, vol. 1 (Frederick, Md.: University Publications of America, Inc., 1983), pp. 35–49.

43. Jean-Louis Baudry, "The Apparatus," in Theresa Hak Kyung Cha, ed., *Apparatus* (New York: Tanam Press, 1980), trans. Jean Andrews and Bertrand Augst, p. 56.

44. See Bertram Lewin, "Sleep, the Mouth, and the Dream Screen," *Psychoanalytic Quarterly* 15 (1946), 419–43, and "Inferences from the Dream Screen," *The Yearbook of Psychoanalysis* 6 (1950), 104–117.

45. Robert T. Eberwein, *Film and the Dream Screen: A Sleep and a Forgetting* (Princeton: Princeton University Press, 1984), p. 34.

46. For criticisms of Metz and Baudry's models of the cinematic apparatus, see Penley, "Feminism, Film Theory, and the Bachelor Machines"; Copjec, "The Anxiety of the Influencing Machine"; Rose, "The Cinematic Apparatus: Problems in Current Theory"; Doane, "Misrecognition and Identity"; de Lauretis, *Alice Doesn't,* chapter 5; Kaja Silverman, *The Acoustic Mirror: The Female Voice in Psychoanalysis and Cinema* (Bloomington: Indiana University Press, 1988), chapter 1.

47. Stephen Heath, *Questions of Cinema* (Bloomington: Indiana University Press, 1981), pp. 37–38. In another essay, Heath observes: "It is also noteworthy in this respect that the very term itself is fixed from the start, with neither challenge nor fluctuation: the first official cinematographic usage of the word *écran* occurs in the Lumière programme-prospectus for the Grand Café shows ('the apparatus permits the subsequent reproduction of the movements by projecting their images, life size, on a screen in front of a whole audience')." See "Screen Images, Film Memory," in Phil Hardy, Claire Johnston, and Paul Willemen, eds., *Edinburgh Magazine: Psychoanalysis/Cinema/Avant-Garde* (London: British Film Institute, 1976), pp. 33–42.

48. De Lauretis, *Alice Doesn't,* p. 143.

49. See Silverman, *The Subject of Semiotics,* pp. 185–89; and *The Acoustic Mirror,* chapter 1.

50. Jacques Lacan, *The Four Fundamental Concepts of Psychoanalysis,* ed. Jacques-Alain Miller, trans. Alan Sheridan (1973; New York: Norton, 1981), pp. 107–108, 96.

51. Heath, *Questions of Cinema,* p. 15.

52. Jacques Lacan, *Television* (1973), trans. Denis Hollier, Rosalind Krauss, and Annette Michelson, *October,* no. 40 (Spring 1987); Shoshana Felman, "Lacan's Psychoanalysis, or The Figure in the Screen," *October,* no. 45 (Summer 1988), 97.

53. Felman, "The Figure in the Screen," p. 103.

54. Raymond Bellour, "Cine-Repetitions," *Screen* 20, no. 2 (Summer 1979), 71.

55. In relationship specifically to this function of the screen, but also to the entire preceding discussion of the screen in Lacan, see Kaja Silverman, "Fassbinder and Lacan: A Reconsideration of Gaze, Look, and Image," *Camera Obscura,* no. 19 (January 1989), 55–84. Reading Lacan on the screen, Silverman suggests (p. 75) that while the screen has a structuring role, "it might be possible for a subject who knows his or her necessary specularity to put 'quotes' around the screen through an Irigarayan mimicry, or even to hold out before him or herself a different screen. . . ."

56. Doane, *The Desire to Desire*, p. 169.

57. Of Mark's "identification" with the images of his victims, Kaja Silverman says: "Far from maintaining the requisite distance from the image of woman-as-lack, Mark recognizes himself in that image, and tips over into it." See *The Acoustic Mirror*, p. 35.

58. Kaja Silverman (ibid., p. 37) writes, "Due to the irony of Mrs. Stephens' blindness, Mark is unable even to deploy his mirror, and is thus thrown back upon his own lack."

59. Linda Williams, "When the Woman Looks," in Mary Ann Doane, Patricia Mellencamp, and Linda Williams, ed., *Revisions* (Frederick, Md.: University Publications of America, Inc., and the American Film Institute, 1984), p. 91.

60. Luce Irigaray, "Commodities among Themselves," in *This Sex Which Is Not One*, trans. Catherine Porter (1977; Ithaca: Cornell University Press, 1985), p. 193.

61. Alice Jardine, *Gynesis: Configurations of Woman and Modernity* (Ithaca: Cornell University Press, 1985).

62. Stéphane Mallarmé, "Mimique," cited in Jacques Derrida, *Dissemination*, trans. Barbara Johnson (1972; Chicago: University of Chicago Press, 1981), p. 175.

63. Derrida, *Dissemination*, p. 224. In an analysis of a text by Robert Desnos, *Pénalités de l'enfer ou Nouvelles Hébrides*, in which a white screen figures prominently in a scene "at the movies," David Wills suggests the relationship between the hymen and the film screen: "The screen is noted for its diaphanous effect, and when the curtain is opened it reveals yet another veil, as if ready to give way in turn to the real which supposedly exists behind it. If a form of stage is still in use, this does not serve the needs of optics, since projection would be possible on any part of a fourth wall; it seems rather to serve as a form of that paradoxical desire to venerate what is about to be disavowed. Whether this amounts then to a form of fetishization or to a material manifestation of *différance*, the function of the cinematic screen seems comparable to the hymen as discussed by Derrida." See "Slit Screen," *Dada/Surrealism*, no. 15 (1986), 92. The relationship between film screen and hymen is also suggested briefly in Pascal Bonitzer and Serge Daney, "L'écran du fantasme," *Cahiers du cinéma*, no. 236–37 (March–April 1972), 33.

64. For lucid assessments of the difficult relationship between feminism and deconstruction, particularly in relationship to Derrida's writing, see Alice Jardine, *Gynesis*, esp. chapter 9; and Gayatri Spivak, "Displacement and the Discourse of Woman," in Mark Krupnick, ed., *Displacement: Derrida and After* (Bloomington: Indiana University Press, 1987), pp. 169–95; "Love Me, Love My Ombre, Elle," *Diacritics* 14, no. 4 (Winter 1984), 19–36.

65. Jardine, *Gynesis*, p. 191. Irigaray has developed something of a conceptual alternative to Derrida's hymen in her postulation of the placenta as a more appropriate representation for the veil that both unites and separates mother and child. See "La Croyance même," in *Sexes et Parentés* (Paris: Minuit, 1987), pp. 35–65.

2. SCREEN TESTS

1. See in particular Kaja Silverman, *The Acoustic Mirror: The Female Voice in Psychoanalysis and Cinema* (Bloomington: Indiana University Press, 1988).

2. In her discussion of the film, Mary Gentile suggest that this scene embodies the preoccupation evidenced throughout *Redupers* with multiple and shifting perspectives: "it is impossible to capture all the versions of reality, all the separate narratives that exist around any one event or at any one moment for all the individuals who experience it. . . . in this scene, we are offered pieces of experience in the films and in Aunt Kate's letter that

in themselves suggest several political and personal critiques; together, at any moment, these images and words also offer an interlocking sort of analysis. They reflect upon one another. And finally, even as we develop an analysis of the relation between a certain set of images and words, these images and words have slid past us and changed." See *Film Feminisms: Theory and Practice* (Westport, Conn.: Greenwood Press, 1985), pp. 128–29.

3. Sandra Gilbert and Susan Gubar use the term *affiliation complex* to describe how women writers of the twentieth century engage with and identify themselves within the complicated web of familial metaphors for the creative process. "The idea of affiliation, as we propose to use it," they write, "suggests an evasion of the inexorable lineage of the biological family even while it also implies a power of decision in two historical directions. One may imagine oneself as having been adopted, and thus legitimized, as a literary heiress, but one may also adopt, and thus sanction, others to carry on the tradition one has established. Unlike 'influence,' then, which connotes an influx or pouring-in of external power, and 'authorship,' which stands for an originatory primacy, the concept of affiliation carries with it possibilities of both choice and continuity. Choice: one may consciously or not decide with whom to affiliate—align or join—oneself. Continuity: one is thereby linked into a constructed genealogical order which has its own quasi-familial inevitability." See *No Man's Land: The Place of the Woman Writer in the Twentieth Century,* vol. 1 *(The War of the Words)* (New Haven: Yale University Press, 1988), chapter 4. As Helke Sander's frequent citation of Christa Wolf indicates, the "affiliation complex" for the woman filmmaker involves not only the designation of allies within the field of filmmaking, but cross-disciplinary affiliations as well.

4. Christa Wolf, "The Reader and the Writer" (1968), in *The Reader and the Writer: Essays, Sketches, Memories* (New York: International Publishers, 1977), trans. Joan Becker, pp. 190–93.

5. Christa Wolf, "The Diary: An Aid to Work and Memory," in *The Reader and the Writer,* p. 75.

6. Ibid., p. 70.

7. In an essay which contains an earlier version of much of what is said here about Sander's film, I read the poster in relationship to the poster for Jean-Luc Godard's film *Two or Three Things I Know about Her.* See Judith Mayne, "Female Narration, Women's Cinema: Helke Sander's *The All-Round Reduced Personality/Redupers,*" *New German Critique,* no. 24–25 (Fall–Winter 1981–82), 155–71.

8. See Thomas Cripps, "Historical Overview," in *Black Images in Films, Stereotyping, and Self-perception as Viewed by Black Actresses,* Proceedings of a conference sponsored by Afro-American Studies and American Studies (Boston: Boston University, 1974), p. 14. Virtually all of the examples of increased black visibility that Cripps mentions resulting from the convention are male.

9. Teresa de Lauretis, "Feminist Studies/Critical Studies: Issues, Terms, and Contexts," in Teresa de Lauretis, ed., *Feminist Studies/Critical Studies* (Bloomington: Indiana University Press, 1986), p. 9.

10. Kwasi Harris, "New Images: An Interview with Julie Dash and Alile Sharon Larkin," *The Independent* 9, no. 10 (December 1986), 18.

11. Ibid. The mulatto character has a long history in literature that predates and coexists with the cinema: see, for example, Judith R. Berzon, *Neither White nor Black: The Mulatto Character in American Fiction* (New York: New York University Press, 1978). For discussions of the figure of the mulatto in the writings of black women, see Hazel Carby, *Reconstructing Womanhood: The Emergence of the Afro-American Woman Novelist* (New York: Oxford University Press, 1987), esp. pp. 88–91; and Barbara Christian, *Black Women Novelists: The Development of a Tradition, 1892–1976)* (Westport, Conn.: Greenwood Press, 1980).

12. Hortense J. Spillers, "Notes on an Alternative Model—Neither/Nor," in Elizabeth Meese and Alice Parker, eds., *The Difference Within: Feminism and Critical Theory* (Amsterdam and Philadelphia: John Benjamins Publishing Co., 1989), p. 167.

13. For an excellent discussion of *The Bluest Eye* and the significance of vision, see Madonne M. Miner, "Lady No Longer Sings the Blues: Rape, Madness, and Silence in *The Bluest Eye*," in Marjorie Pryse and Hortense J. Spillers, eds., *Conjuring: Black Women, Fiction, and Literary Tradition* (Bloomington: Indiana University Press, 1985), pp. 176–91.

14. For an analysis of cinema as a form of Platonic realism and its relationship to the novel, see Thomas H. Fick, "Toni Morrison's 'Allegory of the Cave': Movies, Consumption, and Platonic Realism in *The Bluest Eye*," *Journal of the Midwest Modern Language Association* 22, no. 1 (Spring 1989), 10–22.

15. Toni Morrison, *The Bluest Eye* (1970; rpt. New York: Pocket Books, 1972), p. 97.

16. Toni Morrison, *Sula* (1973; rpt. New York: Bantam, 1975), pp. 43, 44.

17. Ibid., p. 44.

18. In his devastating critique of contemporary film theory, Noël Carroll makes an observation about Jean-Louis Baudry's postulation of the film screen as breast/dream screen that is extremely relevant in this context: "Maybe some white people envision breasts as white and then go on to associate the latter with white screens. But not everyone is white." See *Mystifying Movies* (New York: Columbia University Press, 1988), p. 29. Carroll may confuse the realm of conscious and unconscious desire in his criticism, but the point is nonetheless well taken, especially in relation to Dash's film.

19. Mulvey says: "As the spectator identifies with the main male protagonist, he projects his look on to that of his like, his screen surrogate, so that the power of the male protagonist as he controls events coincides with the active power of the erotic look, both giving a satisfying sense of omnipotence. A male movie star's glamorous characteristics are thus not those of the erotic object of the gaze, but those of the more perfect, more complete, more powerful ideal ego conceived in the original moment of recognition in front of the mirror." See "Visual Pleasure and Narrative Cinema," p. 12.

20. Monique Wittig, "The Straight Mind," *Feminist Issues* 1, no. 1 (Summer 1980), 110.

21. Cindy Fuchs reads *I've Heard the Mermaids Singing* in terms of the progression from "'safety' of anonymous spectatorship" to "a risky activity that brings with it consequences and responsibilities." Of the "final" conclusion to the film, when Polly opens the door for Mary and Gabrielle onto the lush, golden forest, Fuchs writes that "Polly's transgression of her observer status leads not to a conclusion but to a beginning. . . ." Fuchs's review of the film appears in *Cinéaste* 16, no. 3 (1988), 54–55.

22. Kay Armatage, " 'All That Lovin' Stuff': Sexuality and Sexual Representation in Some Recent Films by Women," *CineAction!*, no. 10 (Fall 1987), 37.

23. Asked why she chose the line from T. S. Eliot's poem "The Love Song of J. Alfred Prufrock" ("I have heard the mermaids singing, each to each. / I do not think that they will sing to me") for the title of her film, Patricia Rozema replied: "Ever since I became caught by that line, I have been aware of the feeling—as is my character Polly, modeled on Prufrock—that there is something out there beautiful beyond belief and ethereal, and I will never be able to capture it or recreate it." See Karen Jaehne, *"I've Heard the Mermaids Singing:* An Interview with Patricia Rozema," *Cinéaste* 16, no. 3 (1988), 22. When Polly first sees the painting at the Curator's house, after a birthday party, there is in her reaction to it a sense of awe, close to what Rozema describes. But in other ways, the sentiment Rozema expresses here actually seems much closer to the character of Gabrielle, particularly when Gabrielle expresses her frustration to Polly about her own desires for artistic greatness, just before the fiction of the paintings is introduced.

Polly may, as a spectator, embody a sense of the "beautiful beyond belief," but insofar as artistic creation is concerned, she seems to create, as I have suggested, for the pure joy of it.

24. See Bruce F. Kawin, *Mindscreen: Bergman, Godard, and First-Person Film* (Princeton: Princeton University Press, 1978).

25. Yvonne Rainer, "Thoughts on Women's Cinema: Eating Words, Voicing Struggles," *The Independent* 10, no. 3 (April 1978), 16.

26. Lucy Fischer, *Shot/Countershot* (Princeton: Princeton University Press, 1989), p. 327.

27. On *The Man Who Envied Women* and female spectatorship, see Teresa de Lauretis, "Strategies of Coherence: Narrative Cinema, Feminist Poetics, and Yvonne Rainer," in *Technologies of Gender* (Bloomington: Indiana University Press, 1987), pp. 107–126; on feminist dialogic discourse in the film, see Fischer, *Shot/Countershot*, pp. 301–329; on space, see Peggy Phelan, "Spatial Envy: Yvonne Rainer's *The Man Who Envied Women*." *Motion Picture* 1, no. 3 (Winter–Spring 1987), 16–19; on the impossibility of heterosexual relations, see Bérénice Reynaud, "Impossible Projections," *Screen* 28, no. 4 (Autumn 1987), 40–52; on language and the gaze, see Patricia Mellencamp. "Images of Languages and Indiscreet Dialogue: *The Man Who Envied Women*," *Screen* 28, no. 2 (Spring 1987).

28. There is a somewhat uncanny resemblance between *The Man Who Envied Woman* and *I've Heard the Mermaids Singing* in this regard. Polly's position vis-à-vis the video camera, in the first-person narration segments of the film, is almost identical to that of Jack Deller. In both cases the character does not address the audience directly but looks at a slight angle screen left. The white wall of Polly's apartment in the background of the images of her is covered with her photographs, and while these are in no way identical to the screened film clips in the "therapy sessions" in *The Man Who Envied Women*, they evoke the similar problematics of the surface and the threshold in both films.

29. Lucy Fischer suggests that Jack "turns his back on the films, as though they were irrelevant to his concerns—just so much 'feminine' popular culture." See *Shot/Countershot*, pp. 310–11.

30. This double sense of the "screen test" is a striking instance of Teresa de Lauretis's thesis that *The Man Who Envied Women* "constructs the filmic terms, the filmic conditions of possibility, for women spectators to be asking the question, even as it denies the certainty of an answer." See *Technologies of Gender*, p. 124.

31. Much of what Deller says in the "therapy sessions" is drawn from the writings of Raymond Chandler, and while the effect of citation runs throughout the film, in this context it is particularly striking, creating the sense that Deller quotes from an already written patriarchal text about women.

32. Rainer, "Thoughts on Woman's Cinema," pp. 14, 15.

33. I believe that this attention to threshold surfaces, to simultaneous separation and connection, is quite close to what Peggy Phelan calls Rainer's "filmic architecture," which "takes flexibility and flow as defining principles, and film's inevitable failure to meet the desire to fix or possess space itself as its philosophic spine." See "Spatial Envy," p. 19.

34. Lucy Fischer, for instance, writes that "Trisha's tableau is a microcosm of Rainer's filmic style, which places disparate texts in radical juxtaposition." See *Shot/Countershot*, p. 322.

35. Unlike previous discussions of the collage, which were scripted, this commentary by Martha Rosler was more "direct." See the script notes for *The Man Who Envied Women, Women and Performance* 3, no. 2 (1987–88), 144.

36. See Adrienne Rich, "Compulsory Heterosexuality and Lesbian Existence," *Signs* 5, no. 4 (Summer 1980), 631–60.

37. Witness, for instance, the controversy provoked by Barbara Smith's reading of the friendship between Nel and Sula in Toni Morrison's novel *Sula* in lesbian terms. See "Toward A Black Feminist Criticism," *Conditions,* no. 2 (1977), 25–44.

38. In her introduction to *Between Men,* Eve Kosofky Sedgwick distinguishes between women and men's different relationships to the continuum of homosexual and homosocial desire: "the diacritical opposition between the 'homosocial' and the 'homosexual' seems to be much less thorough and dichotomous for women, in our society, than for men." Sedgwick notes that for women, the "continuum is crisscrossed with deep discontinuities—with much homophobia, with conflicts of race and class—but its intelligibility seems now a matter of simple common sense." I find the "common sense" of this "intelligibility" much more problematic. The "continuum" model may have always been an *ideal* of feminism, but like most ideals it conceals conflicts and tensions. See *Between Men: English Literature and Male Homosocial Desire* (New York: Columbia University Press, 1985), p. 2.

39. Yvonne Rainer, filmscript to *The Man Who Envied Women,* p. 158.

40. See de Lauretis, *Technologies of Gender,* p. 126, n. 28; Fischer, *Shot/Countershot* pp. 317, 324.

41. Rachel Blau DuPlessis, *Writing beyond the Ending: Narrative Strategies of Twentieth-Century Women Writers* (Bloomington: Indiana University Press, 1985), p. 7.

3. FEMALE AUTHORSHIP RECONSIDERED

1. See Margaret Homans, *Bearing the Word: Language and Female Experience in Nineteenth-Century Women's Writing* (Chicago: University of Chicago Press, 1986); and Nancy K. Miller, *Subject to Change: Reading Feminist Writing* (New York: Columbia University Press, 1988).

2. Doris Lessing, *The Golden Notebook* (1962; rpt. New York: Simon and Schuster, 1973), p. 619.

3. Christa Wolf, *The Quest for Christa T.* (1968; English trans. Christopher Middleton, New York: Delta, 1970), p. 4.

4. In her essay on the relation between feminism and Christa Wolf's work, Myra Love analyzes the status of film as an image "used to evoke the connections among domination, manipulation and experiential impoverishment." See "Christa Wolf and Feminism," *New German Critique* 16 (Winter 1979), 36.

5. Wolf, *The Quest for Christa T.,* p. 170.

6. Mary Ann Doane, Patricia Mellencamp, and Linda Williams, "Feminist Film Criticism: An Introduction," in Doane, Mellencamp, and Williams, eds., *Revision: Essays in Feminist Film Criticism* (Frederick, Md.: The American Film Institute/University Publications of America, 1984), p. 7. The editors are responding to a definition of feminist literary criticism by Elizabeth Abel, as the exploration of "distinctive features of female texts" and "lines of influence connecting women in a fertile and partially autonomous tradition." Abel's comments are drawn from "Editor's Introduction," *Critical Inquiry* 8, no. 2 (Winter 1981), 173.

7. Maria LaPlace argues for Bette Davis's significance as a creative force in her own right. See "Producing and Consuming the Woman's Film: Discursive Struggle in *Now, Voyager,*" in Christine Gledhill, ed., *Home Is Where the Heart Is: Studies in Melodrama and the Woman's Film* (London: British Film Institute, 1987), pp. 138–66.

8. An excellent survey of the most significant texts on cinematic authorship is John Caughie, ed., *Theories of Authorship* (London: Routledge and Kegan Paul, 1981).

9. A useful survey and analysis of the different meanings that have been attached to

the term *auteurism* can be found in Peter Wollen, *Signs and Meaning in the Cinema* (Bloomington: Indiana University Press, 1969), chapter 2.

10. Roland Barthes, *The Pleasure of the Text* (New York: Hill and Wang, 1975), trans. Richard Miller, p. 27.

11. Alexandre Astruc, "The Birth of a New Avant-Garde: *La caméra-stylo*," in P. Graham, ed., *The New Wave* (London: Secker and Warburg, 1968), pp. 17–23. Susan Gubar and Sandra Gilbert begin their analysis of women writers with a query into the equivalence between pen and penis; see *The Madwoman in the Attic* (New Haven: Yale University Press, 1979), p. 3.

12. See Domna Stanton, "Language and Revolution: The Franco-American Disconnection," in Hester Eisenstein and Alice Jardine, eds., *The Future of Difference* (1980; rpt. New Brunswick, N.J.: Rutgers University Press, 1985), pp. 73–87.

13. For particularly lucid expositions of these two positions, as well as the problems involved in defining the positions as opposing in the first place, see Peggy Kamuf, "Replacing Feminist Criticism," and Nancy Miller, "The Text's Heroine: A Feminist Critic and Her Fictions," *Diacritics* 12, no. 2 (Summer 1982), 42–53.

14. Claire Johnston, "Women's Cinema as Counter-cinema," in Claire Johnston, ed., *Notes on Women's Cinema* (1973; rpt. London: British Film Institute, 1975), p. 26.

15. See Wollen, *Signs and Meaning in the Cinema*, chapter 2.

16. Johnston, "Women's Cinema as Counter-cinema," p. 27. A comparison between Hawks and Ford as *auteurs* is also central in Wollen's discussion of auteurism (*Signs and Meaning in the Cinema*, chapter 2).

17. One notable exception is Tania Modleski's study of women and female spectatorship in the films of Alfred Hitchcock, although it is in no way a conventional "auteurist" study. See *The Women Who Knew Too Much* (New York: Methuen, 1988).

18. See Raymond Bellour, "Hitchcock the Enunciator," *Camera Obscura*, no. 2 (Fall 1977), 66–91.

19. Nancy K. Miller, "Changing the Subject: Authorship, Writing, and the Reader," in Teresa de Lauretis, ed., *Feminist Studies/Critical Studies* (Bloomington: Indiana University Press, 1986), p. 104

20. Kaja Silverman, *The Acoustic Mirror: The Female Voice in Psychoanalysis and Cinema* (Bloomington: Indiana University Press, 1988), p. 209.

21. Ibid., pp. 212–17.

22. Ibid., p. 217.

23. This is suggested by de Lauretis herself: "the differences among women may be better understood as differences within women." See "Feminist Studies/Critical Studies: Issues, Terms, and Contexts," in de Lauretis, *Feminist Studies/Critical Studies*, p. 14.

24. Kaja Silverman refers to such a process as the "re-authoring" of a traditional text in feminist terms. See *The Acoustic Mirror*, p. 211.

25. For an insightful discussion of the ideology of auteurist critics in France, see John Hess, "La Politique des auteurs: Part One: World View as Aesthetic," *Jump Cut*, no. 1 (1974), 19–22; and "La Politique des auteurs: Part Two: Truffaut's Manifesto," *Jump Cut*, no. 2 (1974), 20–22.

26. Andrew Britton, *Katharine Hepburn: The Thirties and After* (Newcastle upon Tyne: Tyneside Cinema, 1984), p. 74.

27. Jacquelyn Suter, "Feminine Discourse in *Christopher Strong*," *Camera Obscura*, no. 3–4 (Summer 1979), 135–50.

28. Roland Barthes, *S/Z* (New York: Hill and Wang, 1974), trans. Richard Miller, p. 8.

29. See the editors of *Cahiers du cinéma*'s collective text, "John Ford's *Young Mr. Lincoln*," *Screen* 13 (Autumn 1972), 5–44; on *Mildred Pierce*, see Joyce Nelson,

"*Mildred Pierce* Reconsidered," *Film Reader,* no. 2 (1977), 65–70; Pam Cook, "Duplicity in *Mildred Pierce,*" in E. Ann Kaplan, ed., *Women in Film Noir* (London: British Film Institute, 1978), pp. 68–82; Janet Walker, "Feminist Critical Practice; Female Discourse in *Mildred Pierce,*" *Film Reader,* no. 5 (1982), 164–72; Judith Mayne, *Private Novels, Public Films* (Athens: University of Georgia Press, 1988), pp. 142–54; and Linda Williams, "Feminist Film Theory: *Mildred Pierce* and the Second World War," in Deidre Pribram, ed., *Female Spectators: Loking at Film and Television* (London and New York: Verso, 1988), pp. 12–30.

30. One of the best examples of this kind of analysis is Lea Jacobs, "*Now, Voyager:* Some Problems of Enunciation and Sexual Difference," *Camera Obscura,* no. 7 (1981), 89–109.

31. I am not arguing here, as Janet Bergstrom has done in her criticism of Johnston, that the problem is the ultimate recuperability of all forms of difference by the apparatus of the Hollywood cinema. Referring specifically to the work of Stephen Heath, and more generally to textual analyses by critics such as Raymond Bellour and Thierry Kuntzel, Bergstrom criticizes Johnston's proto-feminist claims for elements which, she says, fit quite readily into classical narrative cinema. Bergstrom speaks of the "seemingly unlimited capacity for classical narrative film to create gaps, fissures, ruptures, generated most of all by its difficulty in containing sexual difference, only to recover them ultimately and to efface the memory, or at least the paths, of this heterogeneity. It is just this rupturing activity that is said to be characteristic of the classical text, and which, moreover, is thought to be the condition of a large part of its pleasure." While I would agree with Bergstrom that Johnston makes somewhat extravagant claims for elements which may well be incorporated into the overall narrative and visual momentum of the individual film, the view of the Hollywood cinema put forth by those critics to whose work she points approvingly is no less monolithic in the articulation of oedipal scenarios and male heterosexual desire. And needless to say, if heterogeneity is effaced, then there is no room in which to speak of female authorship. See Janet Bergstrom, "Rereading the Work of Claire Johnston," *Camera Obscura,* no. 3–4 (1979), 27.

32. "Interview—1974: Julia Kristéva and Psychanalyse et politique," trans. Claire Pajaczkowska, *m/f,* no. 5–6 (1981), 166.

33. Claire Johnston, "Dorothy Arzner: Critical Strategies," in Claire Johnson, ed., *The Work of Dorothy Arzner: Towards a Feminist Cinema* (London: British Film Institute, 1975), p. 6.

34. Lucy Fischer reads *Dance, Girl, Dance* in terms of this "resistance to fetishism." See *Shot/Countershot* (Princeton: Princeton University Press, 1989), pp. 148–54.

35. Karyn Kay and Gerald Peary's reading of the film, however, focuses much more centrally on women's friendships and the rites of initiation. See "Dorothy Arzner's *Dance, Girl, Dance,*" in Karyn Kay and Gerald Peary, eds., *Women and the Cinema: A Critical Anthology* (New York: Dutton, 1977), pp. 9–25.

36. Barbara Koenig Quart stresses the relationship between Judy and the secretary in her reading of the scene. See *Women Directors: The Emergence of a New Cinema* (New York and Westport, Conn.: Praeger, 1988), p. 25.

37. Barbara Quart (ibid.) suggests a connection between Arzner's career and the show-business world depicted in *Dance, Girl, Dance:* "Arzner is clearly ambivalent about the vital, glamorous vulgarity of Bubbles, the Lucille Ball showgirl—but the scorn for Hollywood implicit in the film, and for the need to be a flesh peddler to survive there, is doubtless something Arzner herself felt in no small part, in this next to last of her films, close to her retirement."

38. Shoshana Felman, "To Open the Question," *Yale French Studies,* no. 55–56 (1980), 8.

39. Donna Haraway, "A Manifesto for Cyborgs: Science, Technology, and Socialist Feminism in the 1980s," *Socialist Review, no.* 80 (1985), 65.

40. Johnston, "Dorothy Arzner: Critical Strategies," p. 7.

41. The relationships of desire between women in Arzner's films are developed at length in my book-length study of Arzner (forthcoming, Indiana University Press). For an analysis of the secondary roles men play in Arzner's films, see Melissa Sue Kort, " 'Spectacular Spinelessness': The Men in Dorothy Arzner's Films," in Janet Todd, ed., *Men by Women, Women and Literature* (New Series), vol. 2 (1982), pp. 189–205.

42. Barbara Smith, "Toward a Black Feminist Criticism," *Conditions,* no. 2 (October 1977), 25–44; Interview with Toni Morrison in Claudia Tate, ed., *Black Women Writers at Work* (New York: Continuum, 1983), p. 118.

43. See, for example, Vito Russo, *The Celluloid Closet: Homosexuality in the Movies* (New York: Harper and Row, 1981), p. 50.

44. Sharon O'Brien addresses these questions in her study of Willa Cather. Noting that the definition of "lesbianism" and "lesbian writer" has been important in recent feminist criticism, O'Brien says, "For good reason, genital sexual experience with women has been the least-used criterion. As several critics have observed, to adopt such a definition requires the unearthing of 'proof' we do not think necessary in defining writers as heterosexual—proof, moreover, that is usually unavailable. . . ." See *Willa Cather: The Emerging Voice* (New York and Oxford: Oxford University Press, 1987), p. 127.

45. Bonnie Zimmerman, "What Has Never Been: An Overview of Lesbian Feminist Criticism," *Feminist Studies* 7, no. 3 (Fall 1981), 457.

46. Sarah Halprin, "Writing in the Margins (Review of E. Ann Kaplan, *Women and Film: Both Sides of the Camera)," Jump Cut,* no. 29 (1984), 32.

47. Russo, *The Celluloid Closet,* p. 50.

48. Karyn Kay and Gerald Peary, "Interview with Dorothy Arzner," in Johnston, *The Work of Dorothy Arzner,* pp. 25–26.

49. Jackie Stacey discusses female sexual attraction as a principle of identification in *All about Eve* and *Desperately Seeking Susan;* see "Desperately Seeking Difference," *Screen* 28, no. 1 (Winter 1987), 48–61.

50. Constance Penley, ed., *Feminism and Film Theory* (New York and London: Routledge, 1988). In Mary Ann Doane's essay *"Caught* and *Rebecca:* The Inscription of Femininity as Absence," Julia Kristéva is cited on "female homosexuality" (p. 199), but in order to demonstrate the radical difference between male and female spectatorship.

51. For an excellent discussion of the very possibility of a feminist fetishism, see Jane Marcus, "The Asylums of Antaeus. Women, War, and Madness: Is There a Feminist Fetishism?" in Elizabeth Meese and Alice Parker, eds., *The Difference Within: Feminism and Critical Theory* (Amsterdam and Philadelphia: John Benjamins Publishing Co., 1989), pp. 49–83. Marcus examines how feminists in the suffrage movement oscillated "between denial and recognition of *rape* as the common denominator of female experience" (p. 76). Naomi Schor has examined the possibility of female fetishism in the writings of George Sand; see "Female Fetishism: The Case of George Sand," in Susan Suleiman, ed., *The Female Body in Western Culture* (Cambridge: Harvard University Press, 1986), pp. 363–72.

52. See Christian Metz, *The Imaginary Signifier* (Bloomington: Indiana University Press, 1982), trans. Ben Brewster, pp. 69–80. A chapter of Octave Mannoni's *Clefs pour l'imaginaire ou l'autre scène* (Paris: Editions du Seuil, 1969) is entitled "Je sais bien, mais quand même . . ." ("I know very well, but all the same . . .").

53. Beverle Houston, "Missing in Action: Notes on Dorothy Arzner," *Wide Angle* 6, no. 3 (1984), 27.

54. See Suter, "Feminine Discourse in *Christopher Strong.*"

55. The phrase "lesbian continuum" comes from Adrienne Rich, "Compulsory Heterosexuality and Lesbian Existence," *Signs* 5, no. 4 (Summer 1980), 631–60.

56. Julia Lesage, "The Hegemonic Female Fantasy in *An Unmarried Woman* and *Craig's Wife,*" *Film Reader,* no. 5 (1982), 91. In Karyn Kay and Gerald Peary's interview, Arzner states that Kelley was angry at the changes in emphasis that were made.

57. Melissa Sue Kort also discusses Arzner's reading of the Kelley play, noting that the "shift from play to film changes Harriet from villain to victim." See her discussion of the film in " 'Spectacular Spinelessness,' " pp. 196–200.

58. See Esther Newton, "The Mythic Mannish Lesbian: Radclyffe Hall and the New Woman," *Signs* 9, no. 4 (Summer 1984), 557–75. See also Lillian Faderman, *Surpassing the Love of Men: Romantic Friendship and Love between Women from the Renaissance to the Present* (New York: William Morrow and Co., 1981), esp. parts II and III.

59. Nancy K. Miller makes this observation about irony: "To the extent that the ethos (charcter, disposition) of feminism historically has refused the doubleness of 'saying one thing while it tries to do another' (the mark of classical femininity, one might argue), it may be that an ironic feminist discourse finds itself at odds both with itself (its identity to itself) and with the expectations its audience has of its position. If that is true, then irony, in the final analysis, may be a figure of limited effectiveness. On the other hand, since nonironic, single, sincere, hortatory feminism is becoming ineffectual, it may be worth the risk of trying out this kind of duplicity on the road." See "Changing the Subject: Authorship, Writing, and the Reader," in de Lauretis, *Feminist Studies/Critical Studies,* p. 119, n. 18.

60. See the Camera Obscura Collective, "An Interrogation of the Cinematic Sign: Woman as Sexual Signifier in Jackie Raynal's *Deux fois,*" *Camera Obscura,* no. 1 (Fall 1976), 11–26.

61. See David Rodowick, "The Difficulty of Difference," *Wide Angle* 5, no. 1 (1982), 4–15; de Lauretis, *Alice Doesn't,* chapter 5; Miriam Hansen, "Pleasure, Ambivalence, Identification: Valentino and Female Spectatorship," *Cinema Journal* 25, no. 4 (Summer 1986), 6–32; Gaylyn Studlar, *In the Realm of Pleasure: Von Sternberg, Dietrich, and the Masochistic Aesthetic* (Urbana: University of Illinois Press, 1988). Mulvey herself has contributed to the discussion; see "Afterthoughts on 'Visual Pleasure and Narrative Cinema' Inspired by King Vidor's *Duel in the Sun* (1946)," in *Visual and Other Pleasures* (Bloomington: Indiana University Press, 1989), pp. 29–38.

62. David Bordwell, in David Bordwell, Janet Staiger, and Kristin Thompson, *The Classical Hollywood Cinema: Film Style and Mode of Production to 1960* (New York: Columbia University Press, 1985), p. 16.

63. Monique Wittig, "The Straight Mind," *Feminist Issues* 1, no. 1 (Summer 1980), 107.

64. Luce Irigaray, "Women on the Market," in *This Sex Which Is Not One,* trans. Catherine Porter (Ithaca: Cornell University Press, 1985), p. 172

65. Irigaray, "Commodities among Themselves," in *This Sex Which Is Not One,* p. 194.

66. Jacqueline Rose, "Dora: Fragment of an Analysis," in Charles Bernheimer and Claire Kahane, eds., *In Dora's Case* (New York: Columbia University Press, 1985), p. 135.

67. Sigmund Freud, "The Psychogenesis of a Case of Homosexuality in a Woman (1920)," in *Sexuality and the Psychology of Love,* ed. Philip Rieff (New York: Collier Books, 1963), p. 134. Subsequent page numbers will be indicated in parentheses in the text.

68. See Rose, "Dora: Fragment of an Analysis"; and Suzanne Gearhart, "The Scene of Psychoanalysis: The Unanswered Questions of Dora," in *In Dora's Case,* pp. 105–127.

69. Mandy Merck discusses the peculiar portrait of homosexuality in the case

history, and notes in particular that there is a sharp break between the young woman's homosexual and heterosexual pasts as described by Freud, suggesting that despite what Rose describes as a "nonneurotic" definition of homosexuality, there remains nonetheless the desire to read heterosexuality as the privileged source of all desire. See "The Train of Thought in Freud's 'Case of Homosexuality in a Woman,' " *m/f,* nos. 11–12 (1986), 37, 39.

70. I believe what I am describing as the desire for another representation of desire is quite close to Mandy Merck's discussion of the young woman's conflict about "masculine identification." See "The Train of Thought," p. 40.

71. Monique Wittig, "Paradigm," in George Stambolian and Elaine Marks, eds., *Homosexualities and French Literature: Cultural Contexts/Critical Texts* (Ithaca: Cornell University Press, 1979), p. 114.

72. Teresa de Lauretis, "Sexual Indifference and Lesbian Representation," *Theatre Journal* 40, no. 2 (May 1988), 159.

4. MISTRESSES OF DISCREPANCY

1. Joan Nestle, "The Fem Question," in Carole S. Vance, ed., *Pleasure and Danger: Exploring Female Sexuality* (Boston: Routledge and Kegan Paul, 1984), pp. 235, 236.

2. For differing views of Barbara Hammer's films, see Jacquelyn Zita, "The Films of Barbara Hammer: Counter-currencies of a Lesbian Iconography," *Jump Cut,* no. 24–25 (March 1981), 26–30; and Andrea Weiss, "*Women I Love* and *Double Strength:* Lesbian Cinema and Romantic Love," *Jump Cut,* no. 24–25 (March 1981), 30. For a brief but lucid discussion of *Desert Hearts* and its relationship to classical cinema, see Teresa de Lauretis, "Sexual Indifference and Lesbian Representation," *Theatre Journal* 40, no. 2 (May 1988), 173.

3. Whether *Entre nous* is appropriately described as a "lesbian film" has been a matter of some debate among lesbians. In a letter to the editors of *Gossip,* a British lesbian-feminist journal, Lynnette Mitchell criticizes two essays published in the journal which represent *Entre Nous* as "an unequivocally lesbian film." Mitchell notes that in the film, "the two women are shown admiring each other's bodies and at one point in the film they exchange a swift kiss, but this could just as easily be an expression of deep physical affection as erotic desire." The two essays to which Mitchell responds are Sibyl Grundberg, "Deserted Hearts: Lesbians Making It in the Movies," *Gossip,* no. 4 (n.d.), 27–39, and Lis Whitelaw, "Lesbians of the Mainscreen," *Gossip,* no. 5 (n.d.), 37–46. Mitchell's letter appears in *Gossip,* no. 6 (n.d.), 11–13.

4. "Mon père est parti au petit jour. Il n'a plus jamais revu ma mère. Madeleine est morte il y a maintenant deux ans. A eux trois, je dédie ce film."

5. Jean Narboni reads the third section of the film as being about "pornography and its *ruin,*" and notes the particular importance of the fact that one of the two women is played by Akerman herself, thus rupturing the male sexual fantasy of lesbianism. See "La quatrième personne du singulier *(Je tu il elle),*" *Cahiers du cinéma,* no. 276 (May 1977), 7.

6. Brenda Longfellow suggests that the "tu" of the film's title "remains unassigned, addressed, perhaps, to the space of the spectator." See "Love Letters to the Mother: The Work of Chantal Akerman," *Canadian Journal of Political and Social Theory* 13, no. 1–2 (1989), 86.

7. Françoise Audé discusses the relationship between food, narcissism, and the self-other relationship that structures *Je tu il elle,* as well as other films by Akerman. This

analysis is instructive for the overly "developmental" reading of *Je tu il elle* it provides, with more than a tinge of homophobia. The conclusion of the film "demonstrates," according to Audé, the necessity for separation and departure, and only in a later film, *Les Rendez-vous d'Anna,* is there evidence of a maturation process. See "Le Cinéma de Chantal Akerman, la nourriture, le narcissisme, l'exil," in Jacqueline Aubenas, ed., *Chantal Akerman* (Brussels: Ateliers des Arts, Cahier no. 1, 1982), pp. 151–65.

8. In an interesting discussion of the film, Fabienne Worth reads its third section as a deconstruction of voyeurism and a disruption of the Freudian oedipal narrative. See "*Je tu il elle:* Three Moments toward Feminist Erotics," paper presented at the Society for Cinema Studies/ Canadian Film Studies Association annual conference, Montréal, Canada, April 1987.

9. Jean Narboni describes the relationship between Akerman and the "strange mirror-door-windows" as simultaneously "narcissistic specular lure, psychotic passage through or beyond, and emancipatory accession to the realm of desire through departure and provocation of the look of the other." See "La Quatrième personne du singulier," p. 13.

10. Fabienne Worth, in "Three Moments toward Feminist Erotics," notes that in the second "moment" of the film, the man becomes the object of the female gaze, but without voyeurism or fetishism.

11. Jean Narboni remarks upon the cyclical structure of the film emphasized in particular by the opening words (in which one can hear, he says, the ellipses), and notes that the last shot of the film could easily precede the first. See "La Quatrième personne du singulier," p. 11.

12. Brenda Longfellow, noting that "it has long been an insight of feminism that lesbianism, the love of women, is profoundly connected to the archaic mother/daughter relation," stresses the importance of recognizing the "narcissistic phantasm" of the mother central to such a hypothesis. Following Irigaray and Kaja Silverman, Longfellow suggests that in Akerman's films, the "introduction of the third woman . . . re-negotiates the terms of the mother/daughter relation, provides both with a necessary mediating detour to the other which allows for the affirmation of self and other as sexal and desiring." See "Love Letters to the Mother," pp. 84, 85.

13. "Quand j'ai relevé la tête brusquement il y avait des gens qui marchaient dans la rue. J'ai encore attendu que ça passe ou qu'il arrive quelque chose. Que je croie en Dieu ou que tu m'envoies une paire de gants pour sortir dans le froid."

14. "Le huitième jour ou le neuvième, j'ai recommencé la deuxième lettre, et j'ai mangé beaucoup de sucre en poudre pendant huit pages. Et j'ai barré . . . raturé . . . il y restait quelques lignes. J'ai arrêté de manger et je me suis tu."

15. Hadelin Trinon, cited in Françoise Collin, "Cadres, cadrages et encadrement," in Aubenas, *Chantal Akerman,* p. 134.

16. Monique Wittig, *The Lesbian Body* (New York: Avon, 1975), trans. David Le Vay.

17. Elaine Marks, "Lesbian Intertextuality," in George Stambolian and Elaine Marks, eds., *Homosexualities and French Literature* (Ithaca: Cornell University Press, 1979), p. 376.

18. Noting the motif of constant movement (and Blumenschein's clicking heels) in the film, Renate Fischetti says that "the adventures are but variations on one theme, the theme of going somewhere, but ultimately to a dead end, to a barrier. These barriers are mostly windows, sometimes combinations of doors and windows, or combinations of mirrors and windows." Her analysis of the film focuses on the creation of *L'écriture féminine,* and the challenge to "woman as fetish." See "*Ecriture Féminine* in the New German Cinema: Ulrike Ottinger's *Portrait of a Woman Drinker,*" in Marianne Burkhard

and Jeanette Clausen, eds., *Women in German Yearbook, no. 4: Feminist Studies and German Culture* (Lanham, Md.: University Press of America, 1988), pp. 60, 64.

19. Peter Rosei, "Trinker," in *Reise ohne Ende* (Frankfurt am Main: Suhrkamp, 1983), p. 107. English translation by Andy Spencer. The version of Rosei's text quoted here is somewhat different from the obviously earlier version cited by Ottinger in the film, in that the individual identified as "a friend" in this version is referred to as "Lipsky" in the text read by Ottinger.

20. Ibid., pp. 108–109.

21. For two excellent readings of *Madame X,* see Patricia White, "Madame X of the China Seas," *Screen* 28, no. 4 (Autumn 1987), 80–95; and Sabine Hake, " 'Gold, Love, Adventure': The Postmodern Piracy of *Madame X,*" *Discourse* 17, no. 1 (Fall-Winter 1988–89), 88–110.

22. Hake, " 'Gold, Love, Adventure,' " p. 108, n. 8.

23. Karsten Witte discusses the strategy of citation in the film in *Im Kino: Texte vom Sehen & Hören* (Frankfurt: Fischer, 1985), pp. 63–65.

24. Miriam Hansen argues, "this collapse . . . is not the last word; it eludes narrative closure. Having taken an aesthetics of narcissism to the point of no return, the film offers an alternative in its final shot. The high heels are marching again, this time shattering the mirrors that reproduce the deceptive geometry of cinematic space." See "Visual Pleasure, Fetishism, and the Problem of Feminine/Feminist Discourse: Ulrike Ottinger's *Ticket of No Return,*" *New German Critique,* no. 31 (Winter 1984), 103.

25. In fact, Von Sternberg serves, in Laura Mulvey's "Visual Pleasure and Narrative Cinema," as exemplary of the way in which woman is fetishized in dominant cinema.

26. This discussion of *The Blue Angel* draws from my essay "Marlene Dietrich, *The Blue Angel,* and Female Performance," in Dianne Hunter, ed., *Seduction and Theory* (Urbana: University of Illinois Press, 1989), pp. 28–46.

27. In her analysis of female-to-female identification in *All about Eve* and *Desperately Seeking Susan,* Jackie Stacey, noting that "the pleasure of the woman spectator" has "hardly been addressed," observes that "the specifically homosexual pleasures of female spectatorship have been ignored completely." See "Desperately Seeking Difference," *Screen* 28, no. 1 (winter 1987), 48.

28. Jacqueline Rose, "Femininity and Its Discontents," in *Sexuality in the Field of Vision* (London: Verso, 1986), p. 90.

29. Nancy Chodorow, *The Reproduction of Mothering* (Berkeley: University of California Press, 1978), p. 200. A footnote is inserted in the middle of the second sentence (immediately after "Lesbian relationships do tend to recreate mother daughter emotions and connections"), enforcing a quite literal sense of the gap in Chodorow's analysis. The footnote refers the reader to three texts on lesbianism, one of which is extremely homophobic (Helene Deutsch) and one of which is lesbian-feminist (by Adrienne Rich). This curious "assortment" of the relationship between lesbianism and the mother-daughter bond stresses also the difficult position of difference within Chodorow's text.

30. Adrienne Rich, "Compulsory Heterosexuality and Lesbian Existence," *Signs* 5, no. 4 (Summer 1980), 636.

31. Julia Kristéva, "Stabat Mater," in *Histoires d'amour* (Paris: Denoël, 1983), p. 325. An abridged English translation of the essay appears in Susan Rubin Suleiman, ed., *The Female Body in Western Culture* (Cambridge: Harvard University Press, 1986), pp. 99–118. The passage cited appears in the English translation on p. 116. I have translated from the original in order to preserve the relation of self-other so central to the passage ("le rapport à l'autre femme") but translated as "the relationship of one woman to another."

32. Kaja Silverman reads Kristéva's "writing out of the maternal" as "a defensive mechanism, a way of safeguarding herself against the libidinal hold the mother exercises over much of her earlier writing." See *The Acoustic Mirror,* p. 119.

33. Judith Butler, "The Body Politics of Julia Kristéva," *Hypatia* 3, no. 3 (Winter 1989), 111, 112.

34. I cite from the English translation of "Stabat Mater," p. 113. This essay seems to juxtapose two radically different modes of exploring the maternal: the one, "analytical," in regular typeface occupying the bulk of the essay; the second, more "experimental" and attuned to the maternal as experience, in boldface type in separate columns. The passage cited previously is from the "analytical" mode; the passage cited here from the "experimental." By the conclusion of the essay, there is little difference between the two columns, suggesting quite literally the force of the symbolic/analytic mode in incorporating the semiotic.

35. Teresa de Lauretis, "The Female Body and Heterosexual Presumption," *Semiotica* 67, no. 3–4 (1987), 272.

36. Silverman, *The Acoustic Mirror,* p. 120.

37. Ibid., p. 123.

38. Ibid., p. 124.

39. See Rich, "Compulsory Heterosexuality and Lesbian Existence."

5. "PRIMITIVE" NARRATION

1. Noël Burch outlines these four traits of what he calls the "Primitive Mode of Representation" (in contrast to the Institutional Mode of Representation): the "*autarky* and *unicity* of each frame;" the "*noncentered quality*" of the image; the unchanging use of medium long-shot; and nonclosure. See "Primitivism and the Avant-Gardes," in Philip Rosen, ed., *Narrative, Apparatus, Ideology* (New York: Columbia University Press, 1986), pp. 486–88. For a more extensive discussion of nonclosure in the primitive cinema, see Burch, "Un mode de représentation primitif?" *Iris* 2, no. 1 (1984), 113–23.

2. That the reexamination of the early cinema involves of necessity a reevaluation of the status of D. W. Griffith is suggested by the title of a particularly influential anthology, edited by John Fell: *Film before Griffith* (Berkeley: University of California Press, 1983).

3. Noël Burch, pamphlet to accompany his film *Correction Please, or How We Got into Motion Pictures* (London: Arts Council of Great Britain, 1979), p. 14.

4. Tom Gunning, "An Unseen Energy Swallows Space: The Space in Early Film and Its Relation to American Avant-Garde Film," in Fell, *Film before Griffith,* p. 365.

5. Linda Williams, "Film Body: An Implantation of Perversions," *Ciné-tracts* 3, no. 4 (Winter 1981). 19–35; Lucy Fischer, "The Lady Vanishes: Women, Magic, and the Movies," *Film Quarterly* 33, no. 1 (Fall 1979), 30–40.

6. Lynne Kirby, "Male Hysteria and Early Cinema," *Camera Obscura,* no. 17 (1988), 128.

7. In addition to Gunning's "An Unseen Energy," see Rod Stoneman, "Perspective Correction: Early Film to the Avant-Garde," *Afterimage,* no. 8–9 (Spring 1981), 50–63; and Bart Testa with Charlie Keil, "The Avant-Garde and Primitive Cinema," in Catalogue to accompany *The Avant-Garde and the Primitive Cinema* (Toronto: The Funnel, 1985), pp. 2–9.

8. Noël Burch offers a peculiarly ambivalent reading of the significance of the divided body in early film. On the one hand, he notes that the theme "derives no doubt in large part from the popular stage (where women were sawed in half by the villains of

Grand Guignol and melodrama as gleefully as by the conjurors of the variety stage)." But given the remarkable prevalence of the theme, Burch suggests, on the other hand, that the transition from "infantile rippings and tearings" to "the mature Institutional dialectic between the part and the whole (through editing)" is "isomorphic" with the "stage in human psychic development," theorized by Melanie Klein, whereby the child moves from a perception of the mother as a series of fragments to be possessed, to a perception of her as a whole object. What seems to get lost in the transition from devices of the popular stage to "human psychic development," is any specificity insofar as sexual difference is concerned. This is not to say that the transition of which Klein speaks is male-specific, but rather that such fantasies of the mother's body are fully consonant with a theory of psychosexual development that takes the development of the male as norm. See *Correction Please*, p. 18.

9. John Hagan, "Erotic Tendencies in Film, 1900–1906," in Roger Holman, comp., *Cinema, 1900/1906: An Analytic Study* (Brussels: International Federation of Film Archives, 1982), pp. 234–35.

10. In Burch's 1979 film *Correction Please, A Subject for the Rogue's Gallery* is cited as just such an acting out of the function of the close-up.

11. See André Gaudreault, *Du Littéraire au filmique: Système du récit* (Paris: Méridiens-Klincksieck, 1988), esp. chapters 6–11. See also "Narration and Monstration in the Cinema," *Journal of Film and Video* 39, no. 2 (Spring 1987), 29–36.

12. Tom Gunning, "The Cinema of Attraction: Early Film, Its Spectator, and the Avant-Garde," *Wide Angle* 8, no. 3–4 (1986), 64, 66.

13. Ibid., p. 64.

14. Christian Metz, *The Imaginary Signifier*, trans. Celia Britton, Annwyl Williams, Ben Brewster, and Alfred Guzzetti (Bloomington: Indiana University Press, 1982), p. 95.

15. Laura Mulvey, "Visual Pleasure and Narrative Cinema," *Screen* 16 (1975), 6–18.

16. Gunning, "The Cinema of Attraction," p. 65.

17. Edward Branigan retains the term *narrator,* but only after qualifying its use. Noting that the term tends to conflate narration with the real-life author of a text, Branigan says: "If the narrator is not a real-life author, then who is he or she? To state the question in this manner betrays the fact that we have not yet left traditional notions of persons, personalities, day-to-day reality. We cannot ask for a biological person; instead, we must seek a symbolic activity—the activity of narration. This activity of narrating (or, of reading) is a role or function—a particular relationship with respect to the symbolic process of the text. For convenience, however, I shall continue to use the terms 'narrator' and 'activity of narration' interchangeably, provided that it is understood that 'narrator' is a metaphor, an anthropomorphism." See *Point of View in the Cinema: A Theory of Narration and Subjectivity in Classical Film* (Berlin, New York, Amsterdam: Mouton, 1984), p. 40.

18. André Gaudreault, "Temporality and Narrativity in Early Cinema (1895–1908)," in Holman, comp., *Cinema, 1900/1906: An Analytical Study,* p. 205.

19. Tom Gunning, "Weaving a Narrative: Style and Economic Background in Griffith's Biograph Films," *Quarterly Review of Film Studies* 6, no. 1 (Winter 1981), 24.

20. See Gaudreault, *Du Littéraire au filmique,* chapter 12.

21. In a survey on the status of film narrative in 1907, John Fell notes that "[a] very few films continue altogether to construct themselves in dream format, although the framing narrative varies. Fuzzing over the dream 'entry' serves to becloud the main story body in useful ambiguity, better to enlist spectator interest." See "Motive, Mischief, and Melodrama: The State of Film Narrative in 1907," in Fell, *Film before Griffith,* p. 275.

22. Both Gunning and Burch note that the difference between single- and multiple-shot voyeur films speaks to the difference between primitive cinema in what Gunning calls its "exhibitionist tendency" and "the creation of a fictional diegesis." Burch says that in the multiple-shot, point-of-view voyeur film, "we are already dealing with a step towards the system of découpage which was indeed ultimately to make of the spectator an invisible, ubiquitous voyeur. . . ." See Gunning, "The Cinema of Attraction, p. 65; and Burch, *Correction Please,* p. 14.

23. In his analysis of *A Search for Evidence,* Tom Gunning assigns the film a transitional status, arguing that it is much closer to classical narrative than are other early voyeur films: "Rather than mischievous embodiments of the joy of forbidden curiosity, the detective and wife are embedded in an already initiated drama of deceit and transgression." Noting that the series of views through the keyhole "follows a narrative trajectory," Gunning sees in this film the attempt to "solve the narrative enigma. . . ." I am suggesting that the transitional status of *A Search for Evidence* needs to be seen not only in the structure of question-and-answer, but also within a narrative framework that establishes a difference in the gazes the man and the woman bring to bear upon the "evidence." For Gunning's analysis of the film, see "What I Saw from the Rear Window of the Hôtel des Folies-Dramatiques, or The Story Point of View Films Told," in André Gaudreault, ed., *Ce que je vois de mon ciné: La représentation du regard dans le cinéma des premiers temps* (Paris: Méridiens Klincksieck, 1988), pp. 39–40.

24. John Fell cites *Terrible Ted* as an example of how "fuzzing over the dream 'entry' serves to becloud the main story in useful ambiguity. . . ." See "Motive, Mischief, and Melodrama," p. 275.

25. Fischer, "The Lady Vanishes," p. 34.

26. Tom Gunning quotes Frank Woods, film reviewer for the *New York Dramatic Mirror,* who in 1910 wrote, "Facial remarks directed at the camera destroy the illusion of reality." See Frank Woods, "The Spectator, in the *New York Dramatic Mirror,* April 10, 1910, cited in Gunning, "An Unseen Energy Swallows Space," p. 361.

27. Gunning notes that the individual "scenes" glimpsed in *Scenes on Every Floor* were sold as autonomous films. See "What I Saw from the Rear Window," p. 37.

28. Janet Bergstrom, "Alternation, Segmentation, Hypnosis: Interview with Raymond Bellour," *Camera Obscura,* no. 3–4 (1979), 89.

29. I have explored the subject at length in my *Private Novels, Public Films* (Athens: University of Georgia Press, 1988).

30. Gunning, "What I Saw From the Rear Window," pp. 37, 38.

31. Tania Modleski, *The Women Who Knew Too Much* (New York: Methuen, 1988), pp. 73–85.

32. Susan Stewart, *On Longing: Narratives of the Miniature, the Gigantic, the Souvenir, the Collection* (Baltimore: Johns Hopkins University Press, 1984), p. 63; cited in Modleski, *The Women Who Knew Too Much,* p. 79.

33. See E. Ann Kaplan, *Women and Film: Both Sides of the Camera* (New York: Methuen, 1983), pp. 49–59; Bill Nichols, *Ideology and the Image* (Bloomington: Indiana University Press, 1981), chapter 4; and Robin Wood, "Venus de Marlene," *Film Comment* 14 (1978), 58–63.

34. I am grateful to Mária Minich Brewer, whose response to an earlier version of some of the ideas presented here was most helpful in my reading of *Blonde Venus.*

35. In his study of narrative in literature and film, for instance, André Gaudreault criticizes in passing the use of the word *primitive* to describe early cinema. See *Du Littéraire au filmique,* p. 17, n. 1.

36. Tom Gunning, " 'Primitive' Cinema—A Frame-up? or The Trick's on Us," *Cinema Journal* 28, no. 2 (Winter 1989), 4.

37. Ibid. p. 10.

38. Kristin Thompson, in David Bordwell, Janet Staiger, and Kristin Thompson, *The Classical Hollywood Cinema: Film Style and Mode of Production to 1960* (New York: Columbia University Press, 1985), p. 158.

39. The relationship between the "primitive" cinema and "primitivism" in modernism has been noted by other historians of the period as well. Tom Gunning compares the relationship between avant-garde and "primitive" cinemas to the relationship between modernist painting and "primitive" art; and Noël Burch, in claiming *The Cabinet of Dr. Caligari* as the "first" avant-garde film to revive what he calls the "Primitive Mode of Representation," says that it was "no accident" that it should be a film of expressionist inspiration to make this connection, since expressionism "had for nearly two decades been keenly attentive to 'primitive' art of all kinds: the sculptures of Africa and the folk woodcuts of Germany, as well as the creations of mental patients and children." See Gunning, "An Unseen Energy Swallows Space," p. 356; and Burch, "Primitivism and the Avant-Gardes," p. 495.

40. Lynne Kirby's reading of *Uncle Josh at the Moving Picture Show* is extremely interesting in this regard. She discusses Uncle Josh in relationship to both a "primitive" spectator and a "modern, train-trained subject suffering traumatic neurosis à la railway brain. . . . In the confusion of the two in Uncle Josh, we can identify confusion or conflation of shocks that find a common center in the early film spectator, the hysterical, traumatized subject of both the railroad and film." See "Male Hysteria and Early Cinema," 122.

41. Michel Marie, "La Scène des fantasmes originaires," in Gaudreault, ed., *Ce que je vois de mon ciné: La représentation du regard dans le cinéma des premiers temps* (Paris: Méridiens Klincksieck, 1988), p. 62.

42. See, for example, Mary Ann Doane, "Misrecognition and Identity," *Ciné-tracts* 3, no. 3 (Fall 1980), 25–32.

43. Gunning, "The Cinema of Attraction," p. 66. While it is beyond the scope of the present chapter, it would be intersting to read the claims for "exhibitionism" in the avant-garde cinema in relationship to Constance Penley's interrogation of many of the assumptions that inform avant-garde filmmaking. See "The Avant-Garde and Its Imaginary," *Camera Obscura,* no. 2 (Fall 1977), 3–33.

6. REVISING THE "PRIMITIVE"

1. Tom Gunning, "An Unseen Energy Swallows Space: The Space in Early Film and Its Relation to American Avant-Garde Film," in John Fell, ed., *Film before Griffith* (Berkeley: University of California Press, 1983), pp. 357–58.

2. Maya Deren, "From the Notebook of 1947," *October,* no. 14 (Fall 1980), 29, 30.

3. Ibid., p. 37.

4. The notable exception is VèVè A. Clark, Millicent Hodson, and Catrina Neiman, *The Legend of Maya Deren: A Documentary Biography and Collected Works,* vol. 1, pt. 1 (*Signatures* [1917–1942]) (New York: Anthology Film Archives, 1985); vol. 1, pt. 2 (*Chambers* [1942–1947]) (New York: Anthology Film Archives, 1988). The approach taken by the authors is distinctly different, however, from most of the work that has characterized feminist approaches to women's cinema. See, for example, Lauren Rabinowitz's review of the first volume in *Wide Angle* 8, no. 3–4 (1986), 131–33.

5. Maya Deren, *An Anagram of Ideas on Art, Form, and Film* (Yonkers: The Alicat Book Shop Press, 1946); reprinted in Clark, Hodson, and Neiman, *The Legend of Maya Deren,* vol. 1, pt. 2, p. 565.

6. P. Adams Sitney analyzes the category of the "trance film" as it applies both to Deren's and Hammid's work, and to their influence on the subsequent history of the avant-garde film. See *Visionary Film: The American Avant-Garde, 1943–1978* (1974; 2nd ed. Oxford and New York: Oxford University Press, 1979) chapters 1 and 2.

7. Eleanora Deren, "Religious Possession in Dancing," pt. 4 (previously unpublished), in Clark, Hodson, and Neiman, *The Legend of Maya Deren*, vol. 1, pt. 1, pp. 489–91. Parts 1–3 of the essay were published originally in *Educational Dance*, March-April, August-September 1942. The journal ceased publication before the last section was to appear.

8. P. Adams Sitney compares *Ritual in Transfigured Time* with Jean Cocteau's *Le Sang d'un poète* (1930), which is—in ways more explicit than Deren's film—a meditation on the primitive cinema, especially insofar as keyholes and hotel corridors are concerned. See *Visionary Film*, pp. 33–37.

9. Sigmund Freud and Josef Breuer, *Studies on Hysteria* (1893–95; New York: Pelican, 1974), p. 64.

10. Sigmund Freud, "Revision of the Theory of Dreams," in *New Introductory Lectures on Psychoanalysis* (1933; New York: Norton, 1964), trans. James Strachey, p. 18.

11. For a detailed examination of the stylistic components of cinematic impressionism, see David Bordwell, "French Impressionist Cinema: Film Culture, Film Theory, and Film Style," Dissertation, University of Iowa, 1974, chapter 4 ("A Paradigm of Impressionist Film Style").

12. For a remarkably detailed study of French film production in the 1920s, see Richard Abel, *French Cinema: The First Wave, 1915–1929* (Princeton: Princeton University Press, 1984).

13. Richard Abel notes that the most significant difference between Dulac's film and the play by André Obey and Denys Amiel upon which it was based is precisely the representation of Madame Beudet's inner life. See *French Cinema*, p. 341.

14. Sandy Flitterman's analysis of *The Smiling Madame Beudet* focuses on how Dulac creates a textual system that works against the system of classical representation; see "Montage/Discourse: Germaine Dulac's *The Smiling Madame Beudet*," *Wide Angle* 4, no. 3 (1980), 54–59; and Sandy Flitterman-Lewis, *To Desire Differently: Feminism and the French Cinema* (Urbana: University of Illinois Press, 1990), chapter 4.

15. For an extended analysis of the scenes leading up to Madame Beudet's loading of the gun, see Flitterman-Lewis, *To Desire Differently*, pp. 102–112.

16. Sandy Flitterman discusses the disjunction between the two kinds of images in "Montage/Discourse: Germaine Dulac's *The Smiling Madame Beudet*."

17. For an analysis of Dulac's identification with Madame Beudet, see Wendy Dozoretz, "Madame Beudet's Smile: Feminine or Feminist?" *Film Reader*, no. 5 (1982), 41–46.

18. That Dulac's film functions as a critique of the institution of marriage has been pointed out by Abel, Flitterman-Lewis, and Dozoretz. See also William Van Wert, "Germaine Dulac: First Feminist Filmmaker," *Women and Film* 1, nos. 5–6 (1974), 55-57, 103; and Sandy Flitterman, "Heart of the Avant-Garde: Some Biographical Notes on Germaine Dulac," *Women and Film* 1, nos. 5–6 (1974), 58–61, 103.

19. See James Monaco, *The New Wave* (New York: Oxford University Press, 1976).

20. See Natasa Durovicova, "Biograph as Biography: François Truffaut's *The Wild Child*," *Wide Angle* 7, nos. 1–2 (1985), 126–35.

21. Flitterman-Lewis, *To Desire Differently*, p. 283.

22. André Gaudreault, "Temporality and Narrativity in Early Cinema, 1895–1908," in Fell, *Film before Griffith*, p. 317.

23. Claudia Gorbman, "*Cleo from 5 to 7:* Music as Mirror," *Wide Angle* 4, no. 4 (1981), 40. See also Roy Jay Nelson, "Reflections in a Broken Mirror: Varda's *Cléo de 5 à 7*," *French Review* 56, no. 5 (April 1983), 740: "The little film-within-the film, in which a man commits a grotesque error because he is wearing dark glasses, provides a first lesson: the costumes we don to protect ourselves from exterior harm change our own perception of the outside world."

24. I believe this is quite close to Roy Jay Nelson's observation that "superstition and medical science are two contexts from which to view reality, and the film gives them equal validity. Whether or not the fortune teller's predictions 'come true' in the film depends upon the individual viewer's interpretation of them, and that interpretation is a function of his or her own mind set, of the context in which the film is viewed." See "Reflections in a Broken Mirror," p. 738.

25. Danièle Dubroux, Thérèse Giraud, and Louis Skorecki, "Entretien avec Chantal Akerman," *Cahiers du cinéma*, no. 278 (July 1977), 35.

26. It has always seemed "obvious" to me that Jeanne's response is unexpected orgasm. But Brenda Longfellow raises a question concerning Jeanne's response: "How do we read her contorted expression: one of pleasure or of pain, orgasmic or disgusted?" Longfellow reports these interesting results of a "random survey" of women who had seen the film: "the readings seem to divide, interestingly enough, according to the sexual preference of the spectator. For the lesbian spectator, Jeanne's response represents a flash of consciousness and a frightening recognition of her own alienation, her own status as sexual object. For the heterosexual female spectator, the movement of the head and arm connote sexual pleasure, an eruption of the disordering possibility of desire against which Jeanne reacts with a gesture of violent negation." See "Love Letters to the Mother: The Work of Chantal Akerman," *Canadian Journal of Political and Social Theory* 13, nos. 1–2 (1989), 84.

27. B. Ruby Rich, "Chantal Akerman's Meta-cinema," *The Village Voice*, March 29, 1983, p. 51; Marsha Kinder, "Reflections on *Jeanne Dielman*," in Patricia Erens, ed., *Sexual Stratagems* (New York; Horizon Press, 1979), pp. 253, 255.

28. Ruth Perlmutter, "Feminine Absence: A Political Aesthetic in Chantal Akerman's *Jeanne Dielman, 23 Quai du Commerce, 1080 Bruxelles*," *Quarterly Review of Film Studies* 4, no. 2 (Spring 1979). On the self-reflexivity of *Jeanne Dielman* and other films by Akerman, see Rich, "Akerman's Meta-cinema."

29. Claire Johnston, "Towards a Feminist Film Practice: Some Theses," *Edinburgh Magazine: Psychoanalysis/Cinema/Avant-Garde* (1976), p. 58.

30. Jayne Loader, "*Jeanne Dielman:* Death in Installments," *Jump Cut*, no. 16 (1977), 10–12.

31. Brenda Longfellow, "Love Letters to the Mother: The Works of Chantal Akerman," 84.

32. Laleen Jayamanne, "Modes of Performance in Chantal Akerman's *Jeanne Dielman, 23 Quai du Commerce, 1080 Bruxelles*," *Australian Journal of Screen Theory*, no. 8 (1981), 107.

33. Janet Bergstrom, "*Jeanne Dielman, 23 Quai du Commerce, 1080 Bruxelles* by Chantal Akerman," *Camera Obscura*, no. 2 (Fall 1977), 117.

34. Danièle Dubroux, "Le familier inquiétant *(Jeanne Dielman),*" *Cahiers du cinéma*, no. 265 (March-April 1976), 17–20.

35. I confess that the first time I saw the film, I did not notice the "game" of the missing chair; and the second time I saw *Jeanne Dielman*, I "noticed" it but thought it to be my misperception. Having had the opportunity to see the film numerous times since, I am astounded that I did not notice it on first viewing. Is it possible that the creation of "order," of such precise and seemingly controlled framing and mise-en-scéne, is not only so strong but so seductive that blatantly disruptive details such as this pass unnoticed?

In any case, in all of the writings that have appeared on *Jeanne Dielman*, I have seen only one reference to the missing chair. Laleen Jayamanne, in "Modes of Performance" (p. 110, n. 26), calls this a "visual joke," and notes, "The pleasure of noticing this reflexive joke (or bad continuity according to the codes of Hollywood) took my attention away from Jeanne/Delphine's actions and also served to denaturalise the naturalistic mise-en-scène." Noting that Babette Mangolte was the cinematographer for *Jeanne Dielman* as well as for Yvonne Rainer's *Lives of Performers*, Jayamanne suggests that "the way in which objects like chairs and tables are photographed in both films, within the overall structure, makes one attentive to these mundane objects which are usually devoured by the realist text."

36. Silvia Bovenschen, "Is There a Feminine Aesthetic?" *New German Critique*, no. 10 (Winter 1977), trans. Beth Weckmueller, 111–37.

37. Noël Burch, "Primitivism and the Avant-Gardes: A Dialectical Approach," in Philip Rosen, ed., *Narrative/Apparatus/Ideology* (New York: Columbia University Press, 1986), p. 503. The essay by Peter Wollen referred to by Burch is "Godard and Counter-cinema: *Vent d'est*," *Afterimage*, no. 4 (1972).

38. Burch, "Primitivism and the Avant-Gardes," p. 501. Burch's specific point of reference for this definition of the "primitive stare" is Andy Warhol's *Chelsea Girls*.

39. Ibid., p. 504.

40. For a discussion of how the style and structure of the film replicate the primal scene, see Perlmutter, "Feminine Absence," p. 132.

41. See, for example, Perlmutter, "Feminine Absence," and Longfellow, "Love Letters to the Mother."

42. Trinh T. Minh-ha, "*Reassemblage*—Sketch of a Sound Track," *Camera Obscura*, no. 13–14 (1985), 105.

43. Trinh T. Minh-ha, "Mechanical Eye, Electronic Ear, and the Lure of Authenticity," *Wide Angle* 6, no. 2 (1984), 63.

44. Constance Penley and Andrew Ross, "Interview with Trinh T. Minh-ha," *Camera Obscura*, no. 13–14 (1985), 90.

45. The most influential formulation of the opposition can be found in Siegfried Kracauer, *Theory of Film: The Redemption of Physical Reality* (New York and Oxford: Oxford University Press, 1960), pp. 30–36. See also Roy Armes, *Film and Reality: A Historical Survey* (Baltimore and Middlesex: Penguin, 1974), pp. 22–29.

46. Trinh T. Minh-ha, "*Reassemblage*—Sketch of a Sound Track," p. 105.

47. Ibid., pp. 107–108.

48. Trinh T. Minh-ha, *Woman, Native, Other* (Bloomington: Indiana University Press, 1989), p. 148.

49. Laleen Jayamanne, "Do You Think I Am a Woman, Ha! Do You?" *Discourse* 11, no. 2 (Spring-Summer 1989), 49.

50. Ibid., p. 50.

51. Gananath Obeyesekere, "Psychocultural Exegesis of a Case of Spirit Possession in Sri Lanka," in Vincent Crapanzano and Vivian Garrison, eds., *Case Studies in Spirit Possession* (New York: John Wiley and Sons, 1977), p. 249.

52. Ibid., p. 268.

53. Jayamanne, "Do You Think I Am a Woman?" p. 51.

54. "The visual dissonance is not only in the variety of clothes from different cultures worn by the actors but also in the juxtaposition of faces and bodies as they participate in a Western musical ritual. The ethnography here is one of cultural hybridization which if viewed negatively may be seen as one of dispossession of pristine cultural identities." Ibid., pp. 51–52.

55. Ibid.

56. See Sigmund Freud, *Dora: An Analysis of a Case of Hysteria* (1905; New York:

Macmillan, 1963). Describing Herr K.'s advances to Dora, Freud writes (p. 43): "This was surely just the situation to call up a distinct feeling of sexual excitement in a girl of fourteen who had never before been approached."

57. Jayamanne, "Do You Think I Am a Woman?" p. 52.

58. Freud and Breuer, *Studies on Hysteria*, p. 74.

59. Catherine Clément, in Catherine Clément and Hélène Cixous, *The Newly Born Woman*, trans. Betsy Wing (Minneapolis: University of Minnesota Press, 1986), p. 13.

60. Obeyesekere, "Psychocultural Exegesis," pp. 276, 280.

INDEX

254

JUDITH MAYNE, Professor of French and Women's Studies at Ohio State University, is the author of *Kino and the Woman Question: Feminism and Soviet Silent Film* and *Private Novels, Public Films*.